IT HAPPENED TO ME

Series Editor: Arlene Hirschfelder

Books in the It Happened to Me series are designed for inquisitive teens digging for answers about certain illnesses, social issues, or lifestyle interests. Whether you are deep into your teen years or just entering them, these books are gold mines of up-to-date information, riveting teen views, and great visuals to help you figure out stuff. Besides special boxes highlighting singular facts, each book is enhanced with the latest reading lists, websites, and an index. Perfect for browsing, there are loads of expert information by acclaimed writers to help parents, guardians, and librarians understand teen illness, tough situations, and lifestyle choices.

CHRONIC ILLNESSES, SYNDROMES, AND RARE DISORDERS

THE ULTIMATE TEEN GUIDE

MARLENE TARG BRILL

IT HAPPENED TO ME, NO. 49

ROWMAN & LITTLEFIELD
Lanham • Boulder • New York • London

Published by Rowman & Littlefield
A wholly owned subsidiary of The Rowman & Littlefield Publishing Group, Inc.
4501 Forbes Boulevard, Suite 200, Lanham, Maryland 20706
www.rowman.com

Unit A, Whitacre Mews, 26-34 Stannary Street, London SE11 4AB

British Library Cataloguing in Publication Information Available

Library of Congress Cataloging-in-Publication Data

Names: Brill, Marlene Targ, author.
Title: Chronic illnesses, syndromes, and rare disorders : the ultimate teen guide / Marlene Targ Brill.
Description: Lanham : Rowman & Littlefield, [2016] | Series: It happened to me ; no. 49 | Includes bibliographical references and index.
Identifiers: LCCN 2015049693 (print) | LCCN 2016001463 (ebook) | ISBN 9781442251618 (hardback : alk. paper) | ISBN 9781442251625 (electronic)
Subjects: LCSH: Chronic diseases—Popular works. | Teenagers—Life skills guides.
Classification: LCC RA644.6 .B75 2016 (print) | LCC RA644.6 (ebook) | DDC 616/.0440835—dc23
LC record available at http://lccn.loc.gov/2015049693

∞™ The paper used in this publication meets the minimum requirements of American National Standard for Information Sciences—Permanence of Paper for Printed Library Materials, ANSI/NISO Z39.48-1992.

Printed in the United States of America

To all the teens and their families
who are thriving with—or in spite of—their chronic illness,
syndromes, or rare disorders,
and to the memory of Madeline Horwitz Boccuzzi and Kody Beach,
two vibrant and talented young people whose lives were cut short by melanoma

Contents

Acknowledgments

Every book takes a community to produce. Sure authors do the organizing and writing. But what about help with research, editing, proofreading, and production? And a book with a different topic for each chapter takes even more investigating and leads from a host of experts in their fields. This is the case with *Chronic Illnesses, Syndromes, and Rare Disorders: The Ultimate Teen Guide.*

I am indebted to the following people for their professional expertise and assistance finding teens to interview: Jennifer Glicoes, JPA Health Communications for the Melanoma Research Foundation; Mary Buhring, National Foundation for Celiac Awareness; Michelle Pernsteiner, National PKU Alliance; Barry Siegel, DS, Center for Independent Futures, HEARTwords program; Janie Baskin, author and HEARTwords volunteer; Julie Rowe and Josh Radinsky, Sam's educators and parents; Dr. Robert Magrisso; Shonda King, Sickle Cell Center, University of Illinois Hospitals; Ann Garcia, National Association for Down Syndrome, Family Support Coordinator; Laura Drower, Down syndrome advocate and Adrian's mother; and Sharon Brill, Crohn's expert.

Without question, this book would never have the heart it has without the kindness and bravery of the teens and young adults who agreed to share their stories about living with a syndrome, chronic illness, or rare disease. My gratitude goes to Kristi and Sydni Rotunno; Rachel Brill; Billy Buhring; Olivia Cummings; Leah Kanihan; Matthew and Robin Roberts; Sean Giblin, also of the Multiple Sclerosis Foundation; Sam Radinsky; Adrian Drower; Suzi Shulman; Michael Goodman; Dan Weber; Carly Festenstein; Kody Beach; Michelle and Bo Laraia; Michelle R.; and Molly Lamick.

To all these people who guided my vision of this book and anyone I may have forgotten, I say a hearty thank-you.

DEFINING SYNDROME, CHRONIC ILLNESS, AND WHAT'S RARE

Why a book about syndromes, chronic illness, and rare disease, you might ask? The reason is simple—because too many misconceptions, falsehoods, and lack of understanding exist about many of these conditions and the teens who experience them. In fact, you could fill an encyclopedia with conditions that most of you probably have never heard of, yet they affect many teens, some you might know.

Many conditions are invisible to classmates. Others provoke teasing or anxiety because they may appear odd or cause behavior that is different. With this book, I hope to alert the public about what living with a chronic illness, syndrome, or rare disorder is like.

Cole

My name is Cole. I am 15 and I have Tourette syndrome. I was diagnosed last year. I have always had tics [uncontrollable body movements]. My mom says that I have had them my whole life. I have been to doctor after doctor, and they have all told my mom that I have ADHD [attention-deficit/hyperactivity disorder], but she knew better. I was put on medication in elementary school because my teacher couldn't deal with my tics and told my mom my ADHD was getting out of hand. My mom took me off the meds after school was out, and I never had a problem with ADHD. After a few years of no one wanting to help me or my mom, we finally found a doctor who would. My new doctor sent me to Childrens Hospital, where a specialist diagnosed me with Tourette syndrome.[a]

What Is a Syndrome?

The word *syndrome* evolved from the Greek word *sundrom*. In ancient times, the term referred to symptoms that ran together, *drome* meaning to run. Modern usage of syndrome defines the word as a set of signs that appear in a single person. These signs taken together point to a particular condition that can be a physical disease, psychological disability, or different abnormal condition. Therefore, a syndrome becomes a collection of observed traits that have been given a name. Because no single symptom defines a syndrome, the main way to pinpoint one is to rule out other health concerns.

In this book, you will read about Down syndrome and Tourette syndrome, which Cole discussed. Each syndrome presents a different set of symptoms. But teens who receive a diagnosis of either syndrome share certain underlying characteristics, although they develop differently. Some syndromes, such as Down syndrome, appear at birth. Others can develop later in life, such as Tourette syndrome. More often, but not always, teens live with symptoms from their syndrome throughout their life.

What Is Chronic Illness?

Getting sick is part of life. So are occasional aches and pains. Flu. Colds. Accidents. Infections that invade various parts of the body. Each can cause all sorts of havoc. None of these physical problems are any fun. Usually, the disturbances last a short time. Then they disappear. Not so with chronic illness.

Webster's dictionary defines *chronic* as a condition "marked by long duration or frequent recurrence."[1] To the medical community, chronic illness is "long-lasting; long-term; always present, . . . one lasting three months or more."[2] In other words, chronic illnesses refuse to go away. Even when they do, there is always the threat they will return. And if you are born with a chronic condition, you never know what life is like without it.

When Chronic Means Rare

Many chronic conditions are rare, sometimes affecting only a handful of people. Others appear more often in the general population. But since they lack a cure or treatment, researchers consider them rare.

In some cases, mutations of a known condition alter its classification. Even the slightest deviation from a general disease category defines a condition as rare. For example, many cases of skin cancer known as melanoma appear in the general

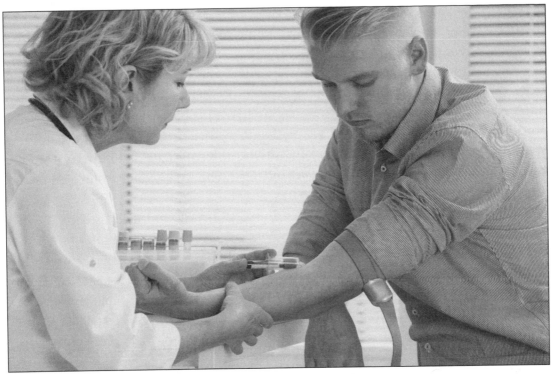

Many teens endure numerous tests to discover what they have.

population each year. But thankfully, way fewer teens are diagnosed with the lesser-known pediatric melanoma, which the medical community considers rare.

The National Organization of Rare Disorders (NORD) is a government-sponsored group dedicated to providing services to anyone affected by long-term health issues, especially those considered rare. The organization was established after Congress passed the Orphan Drug Act of 1983. According to the act, NORD defines a rare disease as one that strikes fewer than two hundred thousand people in the United States. But almost 30 million Americans struggle with versions of the 6,800 uncommon conditions NORD identifies on its website. That's about one in ten people who live with a disease or genetic disorder that is so complicated, or rare, that medical science knows no cause, cure, or treatment.

Sadly, more rare illnesses are emerging all the time. Researchers often call these very rare conditions orphan diseases. The term indicates how few people have these illnesses. Families dealing with orphan diseases struggle to find diagnoses, causes, and treatments to heal their teens. The Orphan Drug Act has been helpful in encouraging drug companies to work toward finding medications to ease complications of chronic conditions.

What does this mean for you or anyone you know with a chronic condition? Chronic conditions have direct impact on teens and their families and friends, depending upon what they are and how severely they affect the body. Dealing with chronic illness means always being on your toes. You constantly work toward living a regular and full life while managing possible discomfort that either comes and goes or remains constant.

Yet, communities touched by these disorders find little information or support from the general public. By featuring several of these conditions in this book, I hope readers discover ways to better deal with symptoms, whatever the condition. Another reason for this book is for readers to gain information. To me, understanding helps reduce prejudice against others who may have one or another of these conditions. So this book is for readers without a syndrome or disease, too.

Chronic Illnesses, Syndromes, and Rare Disorders covers nine conditions. Brave teens tell their stories and offer suggestions for living with their syndrome or rare or chronic disease. Many of these stories are difficult to read. They are sad. All are triumphs of how teens and their families handle the journey with health differences.

In some cases, you will identify ways to help prevent acquiring the disease. For others, you may gain direction for finding a correct diagnosis and for increasing skills to better deal with your condition. For readers who know someone with a syndrome or chronic illness, you can discover information about how to help your friend or family member. Knowledge is power.

Why Do These Conditions Occur?

A syndrome or chronic illness usually comes about in one of two primary ways. You may be born with a condition, for example, Down syndrome, sickle cell anemia, or hemophilia. A combination of genes that you receive from both your parents increases the likelihood that certain conditions such as these will develop. Or you may be exposed to something in the environment that triggers symptoms, for example, as with celiac or multiple sclerosis.

Sometimes, your illness derives from a combination of heredity and the environment. Your family makeup contributes to your being more prone to a condition that lies dormant for years. One day you encounter a disease trigger, whether an infection, allergy, or chemicals in the environment. Your body overreacts to the trigger, often by attacking the invading substance. After each attack, you find yourself on a roller coaster of chronic illness.

Autoimmune Causes

A major reason for chronic illness involves the immune system. Your body continually produces a random assortment of immune cells. These come from a

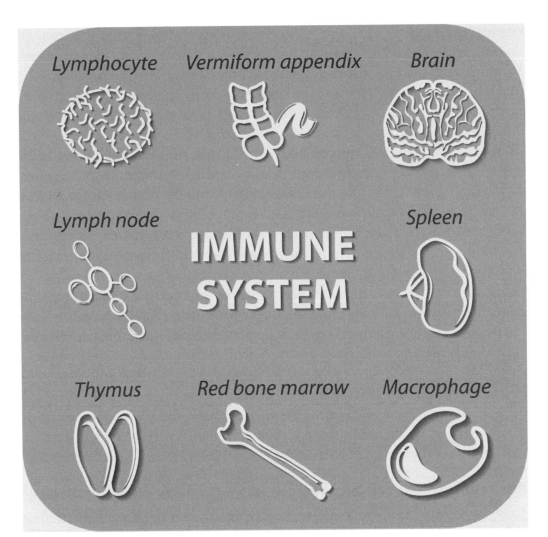

Lymphocyte   Vermiform appendix   Brain

Lymph node   **IMMUNE SYSTEM**   Spleen

Thymus   Red bone marrow   Macrophage

These body parts are involved in the complicated immune system response.

network of glands, tissues, and circulating cells that provide the body's frontline defense against infection.

The cells multiply to create an army of cells called antibodies. When antibodies work properly, the army identifies new cells that might invade the body as infection and attacks the invaders. Sometimes, the immune cells change shape or make mistakes. Instead of recognizing healthy cells, wayward immune cells attack healthy cells, causing a different set of symptoms.

Even in these situations, sometimes triggers come from the environment or genetics or some other mix. This may be the case in Crohn's disease, when antibodies attack the lining of the intestines, and multiple sclerosis, which involves nerve cell destruction. Conditions that result from errors in how antibodies work are called autoimmune diseases.

Genetic Causes

Many of you studied basic human genetics in elementary or junior high school. That's a good beginning. But by high school and college, you may have to relearn what you've been taught. Even adults need to review what they know about genetics every couple years. The field changes that fast.

Genetics provides clues to your body's basic makeup. All people have millions of cells in their bodies. Each cell carries an individual set of traits that determine growth, development, and physical characteristics such as eye color, facial shape, and voice quality. These traits are regulated by message centers in cells called genes.

You receive a set of genes from each parent before you are born. Genes contain all the biological information your body needs to develop. Besides physical traits, cells control whether your body will display or develop certain chronic conditions.

Genes are microscopic rods located in parts of body cells called chromosomes. Usually, there are forty-six chromosomes in every human cell. These chromosomes are arranged in twenty-three pairs. Scientists number each pair from one to twenty-three to study them more easily. They have mapped each gene's job and are trying to understand how these jobs—and the genes that regulate these jobs—contribute to illness and treatment.

The National Human Genome Project discovered that humans have at least twenty thousand genes. Genes prescribe how proteins in your cells react as they control body functions. As reporter Dan Vergano wrote in *USA Today*, "Genes themselves are written in DNA. DNA is made of four chemicals that pair off to create . . . structure of interwoven base pairs. Human DNA is built on three billion of these base pairs" that are being mapped to learn more about health and illness.[3]

In the past twenty years, the field of human genetics has exploded with possibilities. Investigators began finding links between genetic makeup and causes of little understood diseases. Then research expanded into preventing diseases that have confirmed genetic links. Now study continues to define treatments that can change genetic makeup either before birth or afterward. The hope is to alter the course of a condition, hopefully, to eliminate it.

Environmental Causes

Research shows that the environment plays a serious role in illness. The air we breathe. Infections and medications that cure them. Chemicals and processing techniques for foods. Household chemicals in your clothing, building products, cleaning agents, and furniture.

Most people are not exposed to high enough levels of these irritants to cause disease. Some chemicals, however, stay in the body after exposure and can build to

New Test with Exciting Possibilities

Genetics professor Stephen Elledge of Harvard discovered an inexpensive blood test that reveals almost every virus someone has ever had. For twenty-five dollars, researchers can track patterns of disease in different populations. They can identify whether viruses or the body's immune system response to the invaders lead to chronic conditions and cancers. This could be a huge leap forward for many reasons:

- Testing large populations could discover which ages kids and teens tend to get certain illnesses. This information might help determine the best times to vaccinate and prevent disease.
- Storing these tests would allow research laboratories to study historical patterns of disease.
- Discovering certain viruses that trigger specific autoimmune diseases, such as multiple sclerosis, may lead to a cure or prevention.
- Identifying viruses that contribute to cancers, such as melanoma, might help explain differences in how the disease progresses and which chemotherapy works better in some patients than others.

The test is not perfect—yet. Sometimes tests miss small viruses. But study continues to improve the test to make it more sensitive.[b]

dangerous levels over time. Too many teens live in environments that can promote illness, such as areas with bad air. If heredity makes some teens sensitive to any of these agents, chronic diseases, such as asthma, can occur.

When You Can't Discover What You Have

Imagine feeling awful and not knowing what the problem is. You're sure you are sick. Some of your symptoms are specific. You find a spot or bruise on your body. Or you feel pain or discover unexplained swelling, or you become dizzy several

Sometimes, teens find discovering a lifelong condition troubling.

times a day. In other instances, your symptoms seem vaguer. You lack energy. Or you experience pains, but they come and go and in different areas. At times, you just feel crummy but cannot explain why.

You try doctor after doctor. But no doctor can pinpoint why you feel so poorly. Without constant exposure to certain conditions, the number of doctors who see many disorders enough to diagnose them is limited. Families dealing with rare and nongenetic chronic conditions often find it difficult to even get an accurate diagnosis, let alone effective treatment. Teens even experience these frustrations with diseases that should be caught but aren't.

Michelle L.

I remember having a little mole on my leg for about a year at age six. It was fine for a while. Then it started itching and became annoying. I wanted it off by age seven.

My parents took me to a dermatologist to have it removed. She didn't think anything of it. Neither did my uncle, who is a doctor. None of us expected this [melanoma] to happen. They had to send the mole sample to multiple labs to get it checked because this diagnosis was so uncommon for kids.[c]

A major annoyance is that each doctor sends you for more blood work or other intrusive tests. Depending upon symptoms, you undergo different forms of body imaging. One or two investigations might indicate a direction to check. But most come up empty for a sure diagnosis.

All these tests and visiting different doctors takes time, sometimes years. Some doctors may tell you "it's all in your head." Others may fake knowing the reason for your illness and come up with a broad diagnosis that really tells you nothing about how to proceed or which specialist can help you. The lack of evidence only brings you down more, and you question whether your symptoms might be in your mind.

Locating the Right Doctor

At times, the problem with finding a diagnosis lies in the type of doctor you see. Health-care knowledge has expanded over the past few decades. Who knows what the expanding medical landscape holds?

Historically, families sought medical advice from the nearest doctor's office or hospital. Nowadays, many neighborhoods house wellness and urgent care centers; free-standing emergency rooms detached from a hospital; chain pharmacies with occasional doctors; and nurse practitioners working with doctors, inside pharmacies, or on their own. Families face a dizzying array of choices to start their journey for answers. Not all medical staffs are equal in their knowledge and exposure to various syndromes or chronic and rare conditions.

Molly

My journey was six months long. Those six months or so were filled with doctor's appointments and every test imaginable. I was originally diagnosed with GERD and put on antacids, which only made my symptoms worse. Antacids made my stomach hurt more since I did not even have excess stomach acid.

I had an endoscopy where they tried to verify my GERD and did not think to check for celiac disease. If the doctor had performed this test at the time of my endoscopy, I would have been diagnosed only a month into my illness.

I was finally "diagnosed" by my uncle, not even a doctor. He suggested I ask my doctor to test me for celiac disease since some of my cousins have it. The thought had never crossed my parents or my minds because I had grown up eating gluten. Surprisingly enough, my uncle was right.[d]

Going to a specialist isn't always the answer either. Specialists tend to know about one body system. While physicians gain general knowledge in medical school, once they specialize, they tend to focus on that system to the exclusion of the rest of the body. Based on your symptoms, specialists might exhaust all testing in one area and pronounce you fine. They never figure the same symptoms might be a sign of problems in another system.

That said, start your diagnostic search with your primary/general physician. If that doctor cannot identify a diagnosis or sends you to someone who is also stumped, review your symptoms on an online symptom checker. This might give you some alternatives to suggest to your doctor.

Make sure the symptom checker is from a reliable medical source, such as the Mayo Clinic or MedicineNet.com or another reputable university or other teaching hospital. Take the list of possibilities to your trusted physician. *Be forewarned: the list of alternatives can be scary to read. You probably won't have these conditions.* But offering the range of possible diagnoses to your primary doctor may jog the professional brain enough to send you to someone with a different focus, someone who can help you.

Before Your Doctor Visit

Bring as much information as you can to an appointment with a new doctor. The best idea is not to rely on your memory. Keep a daily log of symptoms for at least a week or two. Be sure to include what the symptoms are, when they occur and for how long, and what happened before and after you noticed them. In some cases,

---

Computer Alert

Online is the wild west for health information. Don't be surprised if after using a symptom checker you think you have every disease offered to you. That's natural, though usually inaccurate. The best choice for answers about your situation is your local physician or another trusted health-care provider. If you must check symptoms—or changing symptoms—online, consider the following guidelines:

- Many question-and-answer sites are written by regular consumers like you. Opinions from other people may be interesting and give you some ideas to suggest to your doctor. But these are opinions, something that happened to one person. The information often lacks authority—and accuracy.

- Several health information sites are sponsored by companies or medical groups that are trying to sell their products or services. The information has a certain bias because the company wants to promote what it sells. Before taking the information you find too seriously, check the bottom of the site page to see who is writing and sponsoring the information.

- The best online information comes from respected medical centers, such as the Mayo Clinic, or university-related hospital centers, such as Johns Hopkins Medical Center. Other resources for solid information come from government agencies sponsored by the National Institutes of Health (NIH). NIH is the most up-to-date resource about specific disorders. The agency funds research, which includes some studies that teens can join. Study results offer reports about the latest developments. These studies can be about diagnosing a given disease or participating in drug and other treatment tests.

- Another excellent source of information and support is the specific association related to your suspected condition. You can find the national organization by either keying in the type of condition, once you have a diagnosis, or by going to the NIH website and locating the disease name. Resources are usually listed after explanation of the condition. See the resource list at the end of this chapter.

you and the doctor might discover a pattern that points to a particular avenue to investigate, such as an allergic reaction.

Never let a doctor shake your confidence. You have a right to have your questions answered. Prepare a list of questions for the doctor before the appointment or as you think of them. Speak up if you cannot get a diagnosis that seems reasonable. If your treatment isn't working, tell the doctor. Be prepared to try something else or to see yet another doctor. You know best how your body works. Be an empowered patient.

Waiting for Diagnosis

The unknowns—and constant waiting for a diagnosis—can drive you crazy. You may need to arrange one or more doctor's appointments. Some specialists take months to see. Once you finally snare an appointment, you may wait what seems like forever to actually see the doctor. If different doctors call for tests, they may take days or weeks to produce results, as some are sent to faraway labs. Identifying a diagnosis can take months; for some, years. When nothing pans out, you're telling the same story to yet another doctor. If you hand the doctor your written story, you have to wait some more while the doctor reads your particulars.

You and your family naturally become impatient. Why not? The world is fast paced. Instant messages require instant responses. You may wonder why all these processes take so long. Waiting time causes anxiety about what results will be and what the future holds for you.

Stress and frustration build. Some teens show stress by having trouble sleeping or eating. Others become unusually nervous. You may snap at family and friends for the littlest things. You just want to feel better.

Some of you may get angry. You feel like a pin cushion with so many tests. You may get sad or depressed. The medical system is failing you. Why can't they identify a diagnosis? All you want are answers that refuse to materialize.

These are all normal reactions to waiting for a difficult diagnosis. Even a condition you were born with may cause other medical problems that trigger similar responses to frequent medical interventions. Anger, frustration, and anxiety are all normal responses to a stressful, sometimes painful, situation.

Stephanie's Story

Stephanie Foster, age twenty-three, struggled for ten years with a rare neurological disease. But she never received a diagnosis.

"This last year I have been getting progressively worse. My doctors are still testing to find out which rare disease I have. Each rare disease they test for takes months to diagnose or rule out," she told a crowd at a fund-raiser she organized.

But she added advice to others experiencing the same tough diagnostic journey: "Ask yourself, what do you want—and what do you want to do to help others? Then do it!"[e]

Why Me?

Hearing you have a condition, and one that never leaves, can be a blow. For some teens, there is initial relief at finally knowing what you have. Then shock settles in. You are confused by the label and wonder what it means. You might have heard of your condition and have misconceived notions about what it is.

If your condition is life threatening, you might go through periods of grief and sadness. You have so many plans for your future—college, work, family. Now your future is a mystery. You might ask yourself, "Why me?"

Your family may be experiencing similar feelings. These—and more—are normal. They may come and go, as you embark on treatments or have symptoms that wax and wane. Whatever your situation, symptoms may interfere with your life.

When times get difficult, try to find some way to reward yourself. You may find solace in music, keeping a journal, or drawing. Think about talking with someone. You can also try one or more of the following:

- Check out an organization that focuses on your condition to find someone going through what you're experiencing.
- Share your feelings with family and friends.
- Talk with your doctor.
- Discuss feelings with your clergy.
- See a counselor.
- Join a support group with others going through similar situations.
- Find an online chat group of teens with the same illness.
- Take advantage of the appropriate resources in this book.

Resources

Organizations

GARD (Genetic and Rare Diseases) Information Center
Office of Rare Diseases Research
PO Box 8126
Gaithersburg, MD 20898-8126
888-205-2311
www.rarediseases.info.nih.gov/gard
National Institutes of Health information center that provides information and referrals about genetic and rare diseases.

Maternal and Child Health Bureau
Division of Health Resources and Services Administration
Parklawn Building, Room 1805
5600 Fishers Lance
Rockville, MD 20857
301-443-2170
www.mchb.hrsa.gov
Government program to ensure equal access to quality health care in your community.

Mayo Foundation for Medical Education and Research
Symptom Checker—Mayo Clinic
www.mayoclinic.org/symptom-checker/select-symptom/itt-20009075
A reliable site to check symptoms. The Mayo Clinic is a network of respected diagnostic and treatment medical centers. The symptom checker tends to be on the conservative side, which means it won't automatically take you to the scariest conditions, as with other sites.

National Organization for Rare Disorders
www.raredisease.org
Nonprofit organization that provides information for patients and families about a range of conditions. The site includes descriptions, resources to contact, and the latest research and information about clinical trials in addition to a Patient Assistance Program that helps families with financial assistance for insurance and medical expenses.

Undiagnosed Diseases Network
National Institutes of Health
rarediseases.info.nih.gov/undiagnosed
Under the National Institutes of Health, this network of seven university and government institutions works to evaluate data to help diagnose hard-to-discover diseases.

Law

Orphan Drug Act of 1983
www.ncbi.nlm.nih.gov/books/NBK56187
The law provides incentives for pharmaceutical companies to create treatments for rare diseases.

CELIAC: SILENT SYMPTOMS, ROARING REPERCUSSIONS

Gluten, the protein found in wheat, rye, and barley, has gotten tons of media attention lately. But not enough correct information reaches regular audiences. For many teens, eating gluten-free is not a choice. It's not a weight-loss plan. Teens living with celiac disease (CD) need to eat foods without gluten to protect their internal organs. In other words, they must eat gluten-free foods to stay healthy. Otherwise, serious symptoms that are painful and life alerting can occur.

Defining Celiac

CD is an autoimmune condition that causes the small intestine to inflame. If inflammation continues unchecked, the lining of the intestine becomes damaged. The damage prevents absorption of key food nutrients. Without proper nutrition, pain and discomfort can extend from the intestine throughout the digestive system and beyond.

Michelle R.

People don't know what celiac is. They can't pronounce the word. I say it means I can't eat gluten. But gluten-free has become such a fad that people don't know there's a disease behind it.

In fact, a substitute teacher came to my class when we were studying human geography and had no idea I had celiac. She said she lost weight eating gluten-free. I had to put her in her place talking about something she's not knowledgeable about. It's kind of frustrating.[a]

Molly

I first noticed symptoms when I was driving home from college two days before Thanksgiving. I had shooting pains in my lower stomach. I immediately called my parents, who assumed it was gas or cramping of some type. I knew it was more: I had never felt pain like this before. My stomach pain did not subside and was accompanied by a lot of other symptoms. I had horrible heartburn, constant nausea, diarrhea, gas, and lethargy.

Because my stomach hurt so much, I lived off pretzels and saltines for about four months, not knowing this was the type of food that was actually making me sick. I quickly lost twenty-five pounds—and most of my hair.

In retrospect, I had symptoms long before I was twenty years old. Growing up, I constantly had bright red cheeks after eating. When I was little, it was cute. By the time I was a teen, it was just embarrassing. Since going gluten-free, I have never had that symptom again. I also used to get hives on my chest and face when I ate. These also subsided once I was diagnosed.[b]

The heart of the disease lies in villi, small projections lining the small intestine. Villi provide the vehicle to absorb vitamins, minerals, and calories. But when the immune system recognizes gluten as a problem, the body reacts by destroying the villi. Without proper absorption through the villi, teens suffer malnutrition no matter how much food they eat.

According to the National Institutes of Health, the exact cause of CD is unknown. Scientists do know that these intestinal problems stem from eating foods containing the protein gluten. Teens with severe celiac cannot eat anything made from oats in addition to glutinous wheat, rye, and barley. That's because some oats grow near other grains containing gluten.

Cross contamination, where a food merely touches or is grown or prepared on the same surface with gluten, can be a serious problem. Even ingesting the tiniest bit of gluten can destroy villi. Celiac makes someone that sensitive. Removing gluten from the diet goes beyond the obvious breads and other grain products. Soups with gluten thickener, beer, and soy and other sauces remain off-limits— forever—to someone with celiac.

People can develop celiac at any age, from early childhood to adulthood and every age in between. Once you receive a diagnosis of celiac, however, the condition stays with you a lifetime.

Symptoms of celiac vary from teen to teen. According to the Celiac Disease Center, "There are more than two hundred signs and symptoms of celiac disease."[1] But many people experience no symptoms at all. The wide range of possible symptoms sometimes creates problems finding an accurate diagnosis. More common problems include

- pain or bloating in the abdomen;
- diarrhea, constantly or irregularly;
- appetite changes, more commonly decreased but also increased;
- constipation;
- difficulty digesting lactose in milk products;
- nausea and vomiting;
- stools that smell awful and are oily or mushy; and
- weight loss that is unexplained.[2]

Other symptoms result from the lack of nutrients being absorbed in the intestines. These can include sudden depression or anxiety, bruising, tiredness, hair loss, skin rash, muscle cramps and joint pain, tingling or numbness in hands or feet, mouth ulcers, or lack of growth and delayed puberty.[3]

Expanding History of Celiac

Thousands of years ago, hunters and gatherers survived mainly on fruits, nuts, and meats. As they evolved, tribes migrated from Southeast Asia into Europe. Here they settled and farmed wheat as a major food source. This activity led to the dawn of agriculture.

Not everyone digested the new food easily. In 2008, archeologists uncovered a skeleton in Tuscany, Italy, of a young female from the first century AD. Scientists believe she was between eighteen and twenty years old. Remarkably, the scientists determined that her signs of malnutrition looked typical of those resulting from unchecked celiac damage.

The first known description of CD occurred elsewhere during the first century AD. The Greek doctor Aretaeus of Cappadocia wrote about a condition with several symptoms, including intestinal distress and stomach pains. Back then, he never equated the symptoms with gluten and grains. Aretaeus named the condition *koiliakos* after the Greek word for abdomen. The current spelling appeared some time later when researchers translated his writings into English.

The first person to connect food with symptoms was a nineteenth-century English physician, Dr. Samuel Gee (1839–1911). After several trials with children and adults, he determined that only diet altered symptoms of celiac. He noticed

Billy

I was a swimmer before this whole celiac issue started. A few weeks after my fifteenth birthday, I did some weight training to get in shape to swim better. I went to the YMCA and did exercises that had to do with shoulders. About a week after starting exercises once every three days, I noticed bad shoulder pain. The pain persisted, so I stopped exercises. After two months, I went to physical therapy, and they said I had muscle spasms. I did physical therapy for three months without improvement. I had to forgo swimming season because I couldn't do any strokes. Here I am an accomplished swimmer and wasn't able to do anything.

I eventually stopped therapy and had two MRIs done, one for each shoulder. They showed no apparent issue. But I still had unexplained shoulder pain.

The next summer I went to another physical therapist who handles athletes. After two months, shoulder pain continued whenever I tried to do something. So I stopped that. After a few weeks, I went to a chiropractor who specialized is soft tissue massage. I felt better for a couple days after each visit but still couldn't engage in activity because it eventually caused pain.

The chiropractor asked if I had celiac. I said no but my mom has it. He suggested I get tested for celiac with a blood test. When that showed high numbers for gluten, I had a biopsy. Sure enough, they confirmed that I had celiac. Once I switched to a gluten-free diet, my pain started to decrease after about two weeks. After another two weeks, my pain went away, and I could get into more activities.

The whole reason celiac wasn't considered was because it is thought to be a digestive issue. It's rare that someone gets joint and muscle pain. I was told one in one hundred people experience the symptoms I did. The assumption was something went wrong with weight training that triggered pain that wouldn't go away.[c]

how children thrived during mussel season but regressed once they returned to their regular diets. Because of his discoveries, the Celiac Support Association celebrates National Celiac Disease Awareness Day on September 13, Gee's birthday.

Other physicians around the world tried different diets to heal symptoms of CD. During the 1920s, Dr. Sidney Hass claimed success with a banana diet. He observed how children with celiac improved from eating only bananas. He never figured out that the real success resulted from eliminating all grain products from the diet.

In 1953, Dutch doctor Willem Dicke wrote a thesis of his study that confirmed how wheat proteins in particular caused celiac disease. He based his findings on observing how children with celiac improved during bread shortages caused by World War II. He further documented how symptoms reversed after helpful allied troops dropped care packages of bread for starving children to eat. From then on, doctors realized that wheat protein was the true culprit causing CD.

Celiac by the Numbers

At one time, doctors considered celiac a rare disease. With improved testing and awareness, celiac disease has become one of the more common chronic diseases.

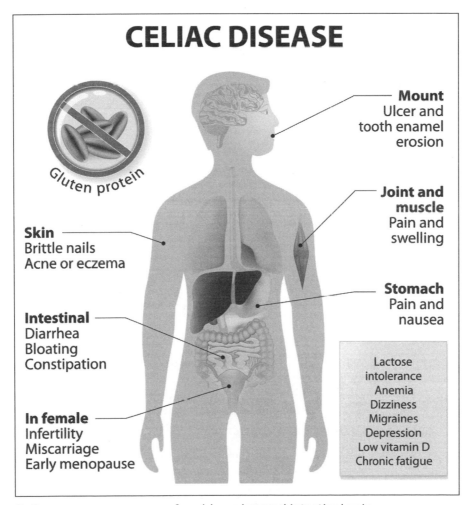

CELIAC DISEASE

Gluten protein

Mount
Ulcer and tooth enamel erosion

Joint and muscle
Pain and swelling

Skin
Brittle nails
Acne or eczema

Stomach
Pain and nausea

Intestinal
Diarrhea
Bloating
Constipation

Lactose intolerance
Anemia
Dizziness
Migraines
Depression
Low vitamin D
Chronic fatigue

In female
Infertility
Miscarriage
Early menopause

Celiac can cause a range of problems beyond intestinal pain.

About three million Americans live with celiac. That's 1 in 133 otherwise healthy individuals who suffer from celiac disease. According to the Celiac Disease Center, the number of people with celiac disease in the United States roughly equals the number of passengers in 114,400 Boeing 747 jet airplanes.[4]

About 17 percent of kids between ages four and twelve may develop celiac. And numbers increase with age. Between ages twelve and twenty, 27 percent of teens have a chance of acquiring celiac. For those more than twenty years of age, the percentage increases to 34 percent. So screening for the disease becomes important at any age.[5]

Many teens never know they have celiac disease. One study showed that 21 percent of patients whose blood tested positive for celiac were unable to confirm their disease. Doctors refused to test further. Insurance companies turned down payments.[6] These reactions left patients unsure what they had. Worse yet, teens could have done something about their symptoms, if they had only known what triggered them.

Disease versus Intolerance

You may find that your body reacts to wheat and related grains. But that doesn't necessarily mean you have CD. You may have a sensitivity to these foods. Or you may be allergic to them.

Wheat allergies list as one of the top eight food allergies in the United States. Reactions from eating wheat range from rashes, swelling, and wheezing to abdominal pain and gas related to CD. Similarly, teens often react to the lactose sugar in dairy products with abdominal pain, bloating, and intestinal distress.

What's the difference between CD and these allergies and sensitivities? The main difference is allergies rarely cause permanent damage, although an allergic reaction can cause low blood pressure and throat closing from swelling. Once the offending wheat or lactose passes through your system (or you get an antidote to the allergen), you feel better. With celiac, damage can be lifelong—and lead to other serious problems. When you experience symptoms you don't understand, be sure to get checked out to determine a definite diagnosis.

Causes of Celiac

The exact cause of celiac remains a mystery for now. But researchers point to three main factors that contribute to developing celiac. These boil down to what's inside and outside your body. And their interaction may be what triggers CD, rather than one specific cause.

Blame Your Family

Statistics show that celiac runs in families. Around the world, more teens with celiac inherited the condition from a parent. Other first-degree relatives, including siblings and any offspring you may have, also have a greater chance of inheriting the condition. By the numbers, being from a family with celiac or related gastrointestinal conditions accounts for one in twenty-two cases of celiac. So heredity plays a significant role in this and related conditions.

Different studies report your chances of acquiring celiac from a relative between 4 and 16 percent. The University of Chicago Celiac Center, which tests first-degree relatives whether or not they show signs of celiac, puts the increase in finding celiac around 5 percent, or one in twenty family members tested. For second-degree relatives, there is still a chance to inherit the condition. But risk drops to 2.6 percent, or one in thirty-nine people.[7]

Rachel

Basically, I was in so much pain I couldn't eat or drink anything I was so dehydrated. My mom has a history of Crohn's disease, so she pushed for me to go to the gastrointestinal doctor. Previous to that, I went to a regular internist, who recommended an upper and lower GI test and CAT scan. Nothing had showed up. That doctor put me on antacids.

Because my pain was intermittent, we couldn't figure out what was working. Then my mother said enough and pushed me to go to the GI doctor. He looked at all the testing and said, "You haven't been tested for celiac." He gave me a blood test that shows whether gluten has ignited antibodies that attack the body. Then he did an upper endoscopy and found I had the beginning of damage to my small intestine. That's why I was getting symptoms that felt like stomach flu.[d]

Another factor is race. For unknown reasons, celiac disease now claims one in one hundred Caucasians. Other races receive the diagnosis, but at much lower rates.[8]

Remember to consider other autoimmune conditions family members may have. If your family has a history of rheumatoid arthritis, lupus, Type I diabetes, and Crohn's, you might benefit from being tested for CD.

Other Factors in Your Life

Researchers recorded that one twin may develop celiac disease without the other. If exact genes do not produce CD for sure, then what does? Recent thinking points to something in the environment that may trigger a response to gluten. Some physicians report the onset of celiac symptoms after pregnancy, a round of antibiotics, another intestinal illness, or other reasons not yet uncovered.

Another issue talked about as a possible cause for increase in celiac is excessive hygiene. Being too careful about cleanliness can be just as disruptive to the body as the other extreme. Researchers link overcleaning to autoimmune diseases in general, including CD.

A different reason for a rise in celiac involves how grains are bred nowadays. Genetically modified grains, fertilizers, and other changes in farming that came since the 1970s all possibly contribute to the rise of CD. *Whatever the trigger, you did nothing to cause your celiac.*

Look under the Microscope

Investigations are under way to determine the role of microbes in the body and whether they can be changed to cure celiac. You were born with a unique set of trillions of microbes. These are organisms so small they can only be viewed under a microscope. Diverse communities of microbes live in different parts of the body, including the intestines. That's a healthy sign.

What's not healthy is when microbes overgrow as bacteria, viruses, protozoa, and fungi and cause trouble. The National Institutes of Health conducts a Human Microbiome Project to identify the role microbes play as disease-causing agents. Once researchers pinpoint links between microbes and celiac, they can work to alter the balance that may cure the disease.

Diagnosis

Early diagnosis of CD is important to prevent complications. But diagnosis can be difficult with the changing and wide range of symptoms, many that mimic other

Molly

I had mixed emotions when I was diagnosed. Initially, I was beyond relieved. I was finally able to put a name on what was making me so sick. After just a week or so of being gluten-free, I finally had energy and was not controlled by my symptoms. A week before I was diagnosed, I had gotten so sick my parents and professors had suggested I take the semester off to focus on my health. This was devastating to me, and I did not view it as an option. My diagnosis allowed me to get back to living my life.

However, when the reality of being a celiac set in, I grew resentful of the new constraints put on me. I could no longer eat whatever I wanted. I now had to worry about accessing food I can eat, accidentally consuming gluten, and educating my friends and family on my new dietary needs. Luckily, my loved ones were supportive. But three years later, and I'm still adjusting to my celiac lifestyle.[e]

disorders. The most effective diagnostic tool is a simple blood test. This blood test measures the level of specific antibodies to gluten in the body.

If levels are high, doctors recommend a biopsy. A biopsy involves clipping a small piece of tissue from the small intestine. Usually, the patient is given medication to induce sleep. At that point, you don't have to worry about feeling anything. Since the sample is small, reactions to the procedure are minimal. But make sure your doctor takes six or more samples from different areas along the intestinal wall to confirm a diagnosis. If too few samples are tested, lab technicians can easily miss severe damage in the small intestine.[9]

The biopsy tissue goes to a lab for analysis. Technicians look for any damage to the villi that might indicate celiac is the problem.

Treatment

Without treatment, celiac may contribute to several other health issues, such as difficulty getting or maintaining pregnancy, the bone disease osteoporosis, or disease of the nervous system. Celiac can also morph into other autoimmune disorders, if left untreated. Sticking to treatment is important with any condition. But with celiac, it's the only way to feel better and live symptom-free.

Michelle R.

After I was diagnosed, I don't think it was too big a deal. I just had to learn the diet and to cook and advocate for myself. For a while my mom was doing a lot of the [advocating] for me. I know I did slip up a ton because I didn't really grasp the magnitude of the disease. At first, I had no idea what gluten was. It looked weird to me. As I've gotten older, I can handle things pretty well on my own. Now my friends can't tell the difference between my food and theirs.

Problems developed when I got older and went on trips. I'm in color guard at school. We do a ton of traveling. During marching season we travel to places out of state for three- or four-day trips. I have to figure out where to eat and locate different foods for myself. We call ahead. Sometimes, there's a mess up with the kitchen. Life happens: you have to be prepared to handle it.

In school the only real thing is to pack a lunch, which others do anyway. I can buy things at school, like fruit or a drink. I was aware I could talk with the school dietician, but it became too much trouble. Lunch ladies would forget. If they made something it was after they prepared the regular lunch. I would have to eat late and gobble it up. It was just easier for me to bring my own food.[f]

The sole proven treatment for CD requires a change in diet. By eliminating gluten from your diet, you can heal your small intestine and feel better, often within days. All you need to do is avoid any foods that contain gluten. Sounds simple, but it can be more difficult than you think. Eliminating gluten might mean giving up your favorite pasta, cereal, pizza, or sandwiches. And your family should try to skip favorites when you're around to avoid cross contamination. The worst part involves the fact that you need to follow a gluten-free diet for the rest of your life to stay healthy.

Another problem is avoiding not only wheat, rye, and barley but also the grains that derive from them. You and whoever cooks for you need to become familiar with names like triticale, durum, kamut, semolina, and spelt. These grains must be avoided. They may sound like healthy, more exotic options. But they cause the same symptoms as their more traditional relatives.

Luckily, most grocery chains now offer gluten-free lines of products. You can practice replacing healthy food choices by learning to cook and bake yourself. A teen named Lauren did just that. She created a website to highlight recipes and

You can buy or make a variety of gluten-free products that use allowed grains.

tips that she learned during her celiac journey. Check out her battles and successes in staying healthy at www.celiacteen.com.

Restaurants, too, have gotten on the gluten-free bandwagon and usually include gluten-free items on their menus. Eateries that do not advertise gluten-free options often have chefs who might prepare similar menu choices with gluten-free ingredients. But you need to speak up, which often isn't easy.

One way to bolster your confidence with eating gluten-free is to arm yourself with information. Then consult with a knowledgeable dietician. Get a recommendation from your doctor or a local celiac center, if one is near you. Major centers investigating celiac include University of Chicago, University of Utah (Salt Lake City), Columbia University (New York City), University of Tennessee (Knoxville), and University of Maryland (Baltimore). But local hospitals and universities may have their own centers that aren't running government studies. Be sure to call ahead before arranging a dietician appointment to ensure the professional has experience with a celiac diet.

A dietician who understands celiac can educate you on which food products are okay to eat. This person may have information about manufacturers of food products, such as flours, breads, and pastas, and the best, inexpensive way to access them. Dieticians can show you how to read ingredients on food labels, so you can navigate food aisles by yourself. In addition, search resources online.

Rachel

When I first learned I had celiac I said this is not what I have. It didn't align with my symptoms. And I thought, "What the hell was gluten?"

I was sent to a dietician to learn what to eat. Insurance wouldn't pay for the dietician, but I went head-to-head with them. I told them they had two choices. Either pay for the dietician or pay for my deficiencies later.

The dietician gave me a basket of gluten-free products as a starter kit. Now gluten-free products are everywhere. Not so earlier. In the beginning, I found it hard to get products. You could only get them mail order. My mother spent a lot of time finding recipes to make me cookies and other foods. She experimented with different combinations of foods.

I couldn't go to restaurants. Lots of sauces and salad dressings had flour in it. I couldn't go out for pizza. Now every place will make gluten-free dough. I had to go to special stores, so the diet wasn't cheap or convenient. When the Atkins diet came out advocating no carbohydrates, things got easier. I'm not that picky an eater otherwise, so I could always find something to eat. Now it's hard because restaurant French fries put coating on them, and cross contamination can make someone sick. But food products have changed one thousand percent.[9]

KidsHealth (see the Resources section at the end of the chapter) shows a list of foods and ingredients to avoid along with tips to take better care of yourself.

Equally important, a trained professional, whether doctor or dietician, can dispel myths surrounding gluten. You'll learn that gluten cannot make you fat, nor can it make you skinny. The usual weight-loss rule applies—amount of food in versus the amount of calories burned—whether or not you have celiac disease.

Recently, new Food and Drug Administration guidelines made life with celiac easier. Rules now demand that any food labeled gluten-free must contain less than twenty parts per million of gluten, a number considered safe for most teens with celiac. That's the amount in eighteen slices of gluten-free bread. Labels can claim all uncoated, unprocessed meats, nuts, beans, fruits, vegetables, poultry, and fish naturally gluten-free. But you still need to check labels, especially for any foods containing processed ingredients. Danger lurks in such additives as hydrolyzed vegetable protein. Even reused water that boiled wheat pasta can be hazardous.

A good dietician understands the fine points of navigating food situations in school and at home. That person can help you plan a diet that works for your particular lifestyle, give you food alternatives, and provide recipes for you or someone in your family to prepare.

Fun Food Preparation

Unable to access a dietician? Then prepare your own plan. In fact, start cooking for yourself, if you enjoy that type of activity.

Begin with foods you know are healthy for you. All plain meats, fish, chicken, legumes, nuts, seeds, oils, milk products, fruits, and vegetables provide enough variety to get you safely started. Investigate other sources of flour. You can eat flour from corn, rice, buckwheat, sorghum, arrowroot, chickpeas (garbanzo beans), quinoa, tapioca, teff, and potatoes. Just make sure they are prepared without added gluten and away from other meals containing gluten.

Be alert to cross contamination. Never work in a bakery if you have CD because inhaling flour is enough to cause bad reactions. In grocery stores, check that gluten-free products are baked in an environment separate from the company's other gluten goods. Be forewarned that many natural goods and health foods come in large bins, so customers can scoop the size portion you prefer. These products can easily be cross contaminated, so avoid them.

Preparing desserts that fit your diet can be a family affair.

At home, make sure to thoroughly clean work surfaces, appliances, and utensils before using them for gluten-free preparation. For example, find a separate toaster for your gluten-free breads. Suggest that your family give you squeezable bottles for your condiments, jams, and spread. That way, crumbs will not contaminate your foods.

When Diet Isn't Everything

If you still experience symptoms—and you've followed a gluten-free diet religiously—you may require additional treatment. Keep a log of foods you've eaten, their reactions, and any other symptoms you still experience. That way, your celiac physician can better evaluate whether you need added vitamins and iron supplements.

Common vitamin deficiencies linked to celiac include vitamin D, iron, calcium, B12, copper, folate, magnesium, niacin, riboflavin, or zinc.[10] Some doctors regularly suggest that anyone on a gluten-free diet take a general multivitamin to prevent problems from eating foods without vitamins and minerals added to gluten products.

In addition to supplements, some doctors recommend specific drugs to suppress action of the immune system.[11] This may mean you have a form of celiac

Billy

On a normal day, having celiac isn't that big a deal. I can pretty much find a good gluten-free version of anything I want. But going out to eat can be tricky. I know some people with celiac are very sensitive from cross contamination. That's not a problem for me. But options are limited at some places.

The only problem I've ever had in school is when people bring in unhealthy food for parties. Usually, there's something available, or I bring food for myself. Going out with friends, we try to pick a restaurant where I can eat, but it can be difficult in that area.

For me, I don't eat in the high school cafeteria, so I don't run into any issues. I know college will be difficult with that. Last summer I did a summer program away, and I let people know there I can't eat gluten. They brought out a different meal. I'll definitely have to explore gluten-free options in college and let people know I can't eat anything with gluten.[h]

called sprue (or refractory sprue), which used to be the other name for celiac disease. With sprue, symptoms mimic CD. But the body refuses to respond to a gluten-free diet. This is serious because you cannot absorb nutrients, which leads other serious disabilities. The situation mimics when someone with celiac never follows the gluten-free diet. With sprue, treatment requires medication, such as steroids, to suppress the immune system.[12]

If one of your symptoms includes extreme fatigue, your doctor may recommend that you eat a diet rich in meats and other iron-containing foods. In addition, you may benefit from visits to a physical therapist for strength training. Both are necessary if celiac has been robbing you of normal growth and stamina.

Taking Celiac to School and Other Places

Eating out is possible with a celiac diet. Order an individual pizza that is gluten-free. Suggest a Mexican restaurant that uses corn flour in most dishes. Bring snacks with you so you always have something you can eat. It just takes a little planning and creativity. If you ever feel unsure about a food, don't eat it. Trust your judgment. It's your body.

The American with Disabilities Act requires that schools provide safe, nutritional options to students with celiac disease and food allergies. For students

Michelle R.

Sometimes, friends don't know about cross contamination. Some bring snacks for others and feel really badly if I don't take them. Dinner at friends and relatives can be a minefield. But I went to one friend's house where her mom was a dietician, and I felt normal. I want to feel normal and handle things myself.

My parents are divorced. My father didn't take my diagnosis of celiac very well. After I got diagnosed, we'd go to restaurants, and he'd get upset because he didn't know what to feed me. One time my grandmother on my father's side got me a cake that wasn't gluten-free. I told them I couldn't eat it, and they made me eat it.

You can't go to the hospital and get treatment after you eat gluten. You have to wait it out. It's the long-term effects of celiac disease that are the problem. It's scary when you don't know when something is happening. Even if I don't feel it, I might have gotten a celiac attack, and my intestines won't heal for months.[i]

who have a formal plan for documented disability, the school must provide lunch, if other students receive a lunch program. The caveat is gluten-free meals need not be the same as for other students. So you may not get enough or the same quality meals as students who eat gluten.

To make sure you receive the correct diet, talk with the school or dorm dietician. Even then, you may still choose to bring or prepare your own food. Colleges have been slower to act on behalf of gluten-free students. According to a recent poll by the National Foundation for Celiac, 60 percent of dining services directors said they were unaware of what a gluten-free diet entailed. Similarly, 61 percent of students with celiac reported being uneasy eating in the dining hall. That's because 60 percent said they experienced symptoms after unintentionally eating meals containing gluten or prepared near gluten foods. Consequently, 38 percent told investigators they never eat in school and dorm dining halls. [13]

Dealing with Friends and Relatives

It's bad enough explaining what you need in restaurants and school dining halls. But life can get much more complicated when dealing with people close to you. Feelings get hurt if you don't eat what others prepare. Friends don't understand when you can't eat what they eat.

Molly

I would say celiac disease has the greatest impact on my social life. I was diagnosed a month before my twenty-first birthday. Celiac disease limits the types of alcohol you can drink. I was suddenly unable to drink beer and different types of hard liquor along with most readily available foods. I have had to take it into my own hands to be prepared for social situations. I bring my own food and alcohol to parties. I check ahead at bars and restaurants to make sure there are options for me.

Dating is also hard. Many people do not know a lot about celiac disease, so explaining it to guys I am dating is hard. Many of them have accused me of being dramatic, dared me to eat something with gluten, or talked about how it's a burden on them to worry about me being able to eat at a restaurant or to cook for me. However, the people in my life who understand are really the only people I want to keep around anyways![j]

Most teens with celiac who were interviewed for this book tell others about their celiac on a need-to-know basis. For some the journey is more personal—and more difficult—than others. One young woman tells friends and coworkers but few others. She feels her journey is private.

"I will tell staff at a restaurant to be careful with food," Billy says. "I don't think all restaurants have formal knowledge about celiac. Occasionally, people will ask, 'Can you have this or that foods?' Overall I don't have any real issues with it."[14]

Choosing a restaurant only complicates an evening out. Big cities have many choices of menus and restaurants that will cater to gluten-free. Not so in more rural areas.

Then there's the matter of calling attention to yourself. No one, especially a teen, enjoys being put under a spotlight. Billy talks about feeling weird at first. He hated the attention, like when ordering in a restaurant. But after reading about celiac and learning how to navigate sticky food situations, he now says, "It's not a big deal."[15]

Molly discussed other feelings after learning her diagnosis.

When I was first diagnosed, I viewed my disease as my defining characteristic. Sometimes, people still try to define me as Molly the celiac. However, this is not me. This is just my diet. For teens, I think it is easy for them to be overwhelmed by this diagnosis and focus on how this will build walls between them and their peers. I felt the same way when I was diagnosed. But soon they will realize being a teen with celiac disease may present a few more challenges. But every teen and every person struggles in some way.[16]

But Michelle R. discovered a different way to cope with celiac. "Make yourself really knowledgeable about your disease because you're the only one taking care of you. When you're out, don't worry about taking time and holding up lines. It's not about those folks in line: it's about your being healthy for the next sixty to seventy years."[17]

Resources

Organizations

Celiac.com
www.celiac.com
One of the first websites dedicated to offering information and recipes about celiac. One caveat: the site is loaded with advertising and access to information, like

the *Journal of G-F Sensitivity* and other publications, written by the site founder, and these are for fees only. So check the information with another source before jumping onto the recommendations.

Celiac Disease Foundation
20350 Ventura Boulevard, Suite 240
Woodland Hills, CA 91364
818-715-1513
www.celiac.org
Twenty-five-year-old nonprofit founded to support the celiac community by providing advocacy, education, and research. The organization includes a medical board that verifies patient information, holds a national conference of experts, and supports a variety of local group programs and studies.

Celiac Teen
www.celiacteen.com
Site started in 2011 by a teen with celiac who loves to cook. It is packed with novel recipes and blog entries about tested gluten-free products.

Kids Health
Nemours Foundation Center for Children's Health Medicine
kidshealth.org/teen/diseases_conditions/allergies_immune/celiac.html
Physician-reviewed website with information and advice for kids and teens, with special sections for parents and teachers.

Beyond Celiac: National Foundation for Celiac Awareness
124 South Maple Street
Ambler, PA 19002
844-856-6692
www.beyondceliac.org
National nonprofit organization that promotes understanding of celiac through its websites, webinars, training for dieticians and pharmacists, and special sections for teens, including negotiating college eating.

PubMed Health
"Celiac Disease"
www.ncbi.nlm.nih.gov/pubmedhealth/PMHT0024528
Government-sponsored source for the latest information and research.

Teens Living with Celiac Foundation
www.teenslivingwithceliac.org

Organization that provides online support and resources and information for kids and teens with celiac disease.

University of Chicago Celiac Disease Center
5839 South Maryland Avenue, MC4069
Chicago, IL 60637
773-702-7593
www.celiacdisease.net
University-based medical program with information, support, and national celiac testing capabilities.

Books

Sure, you can find tons of information and recipes online. But sometimes a book gives a more complete understanding of all aspects of dealing with celiac disease. Check out these choices that focus on specific issues.

Carlyn Berghoff, Sarah Berghoff McClure, Susan P. Nelson, and Nancy Ross Ryan. *Cooking for Your Gluten-Free Teen: Everyday Foods the Whole Family Will Like.* Kansas City, MO: Andrews McMeel Publishing, 2013. Solid, simple recipes that show how you can eat gluten-free without giving up favorite dishes.

David Burns. *100 Question and Answers about Celiac Disease and Sprue.* Sudbury, MA: Jones and Bartlette Publishing, Inc., 2008. Answers to common questions people ask about celiac disease written in an accessible style.

Jennifer Esposito. *My Journey with Celiac Disease.* Boston: Da Capo Press International, 2014. The author's personal story of reactions to learning and dealing with celiac disease.

Alessio Fasano, MD. *Gluten Freedom: The Nation's Leading Expert Offers the Essential Guide to a Healthy Gluten-Free Lifestyle.* New York: Wiley, 2014. Informative, easy-to-read overview of life with celiac.

CROHN'S: MORE THAN INDIGESTION

Crohn's disease infects the digestive tract. Different parts anywhere along the tract can become inflamed and irritated. You may feel pain, bloated, gassy, or any number of uncomfortable symptoms. The disease can come and go, but it always returns, interfering with your life. When symptoms occur, what you ingest and how you eliminate digested food become more important than normal teen activities, at least until you find treatments that reduce or block the discomfort.

Carly

I was in seventh grade and noticed symptoms six-to-eight months beforehand. I had rapid loss of weight, like forty pounds in two months. I was super fatigued. I couldn't walk because it was so painful to move. I was dry heaving a lot. I remember having symptoms on vacation. I was in a hot tub in Florida, and I was shivering. My grandma said something was wrong.

I had a bumpy journey to diagnosis. I was sent to the hospital a couple times. I was told it was the flu. Or it was a fever. My symptoms got worse. Finally, after my colonoscopy, I was diagnosed with Crohn's. When they told me I was so tired and sick it didn't register to me.

I had anxiety. I was depressed at the time because when you have something like this and do not know what you have, it's depressing. Inflammatory bowel disease didn't have much exposure ten years ago. I felt alone and confused, and that it was happening to me personally. I was in the middle of puberty. One of the darkest times in my life.[a]

> ### Dan
>
> I was twelve and in sixth grade and started to notice blood in my stool. My mom had been treated for colon cancer, so we had a heightened awareness of intestines. My symptoms didn't invade my life until about age seventeen. Until then, I had occasional pain, blood in my stool, and urgency, needing to go to the bathroom really quickly. Not easy going to a party or going to a concert. By age eighteen, I was in and out of the hospital. It was hard dealing with the uncertainty of how to lead a normal life and go to college and have to account for my health on top of these other things.[b]

The Long and Short of Healthy Digestion

Digestion is how your body converts food into usable materials. When you eat something, different chemicals in a series of organs break down food into simpler components. These chemicals extract nutrients that energize body cells. From there, nutrients in blood travel throughout the bloodstream as nourishment or leave the body as waste.

The digestive system, sometimes called the gastrointestinal (GI) tract, comprises the chain of joined and twisted tubes that extend from your mouth down and out the anus. The entire system consists of about half your internal organs. These include the mouth, esophagus, stomach, small and large intestines, rectum, and anus.

Stretched out, your intestines unravel to become longer than you are tall. The human small intestine extends twenty feet (six meters). The large intestine is actually shorter, a mere five feet (1.5 meters) long. The large in its name comes from a wider diameter compared with the thinner small intestine.

Rhythmic contractions of muscles that surround each organ push food and liquid you ingest through the digestive tract. This wavelike movement is called peristalsis. Some scientists liken peristalsis to the movement of an ocean wave on its way to shore.

Digestion with Crohn's Disease

Crohn's is a chronic disease of the digestive tract. Your doctor may refer to the illness as one form of inflammatory bowel disease or as enteritis, ileitis, or regional ileitis, depending upon the location of your particular symptoms. Crohn's shares

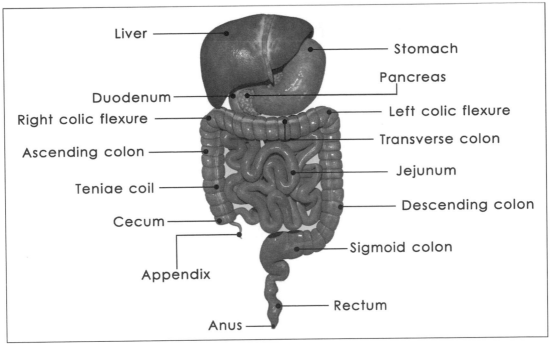

Ingested food goes through the digestive system's many organs to be broken down to enter the bloodstream as nutrients or leave the body as waste.

many characteristics with ulcerated colitis, also a serious inflammatory bowel disease. The main similarity between the two is inflammation. But with Crohn's, inflammation can occur anywhere along the digestive tract, whereas colitis is limited to the colon, or large intestine. Neither condition feels pleasant.

"I first had it in 1986 at 21 years old," Mike McCready, Pearl Jam lead guitarist, told a FOX interviewer. "I was down in Los Angeles trying to make it. I had to go to the bathroom really quickly; had amazing pain in my gut; also there was blood. I felt I needed to look at it. I was afraid. I was in unbearable abdominal pain: I barely got off the stage in time."[1]

An inflamed or irritated lining of the GI tract can lead to difficulties anywhere from the mouth to anus. More common areas for Crohn's to develop are the last segment of the small intestine, or ileum, and the colon. In some teens, inflammation skips over healthy areas only to form irritating patches somewhere else along the digestive tract.

This skipping around accounts for the varied symptoms from teen to teen. Symptoms can be mild or severe, and they can appear gradually or suddenly. Some teens experience periods between bouts without symptoms, which is welcome remission. But these periods may or may not last long.

You may feel pain or irritation or diarrhea or constipation, depending on how swelling or blockage interferes with regular routines. Sometimes, pain can be debilitating. When complications occur, Crohn's can threaten your life.

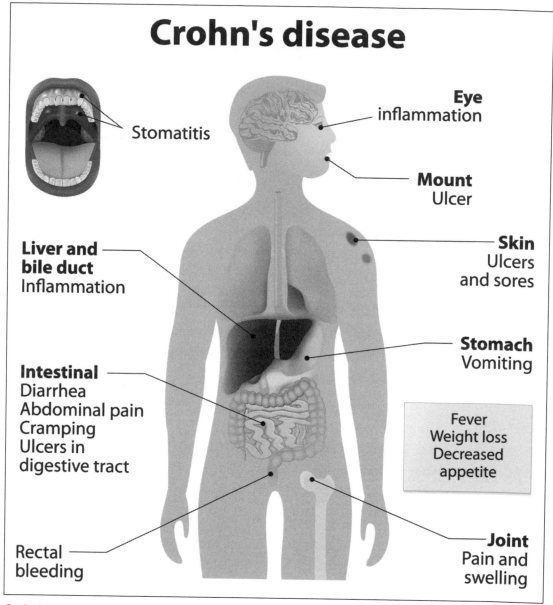

Crohn's disease

Stomatitis

Eye
inflammation

Mount
Ulcer

**Liver and
bile duct**
Inflammation

Skin
Ulcers
and sores

Stomach
Vomiting

Intestinal
Diarrhea
Abdominal pain
Cramping
Ulcers in
digestive tract

Fever
Weight loss
Decreased
appetite

Rectal
bleeding

Joint
Pain and
swelling

Crohn's causes a variety of symptoms throughout the digestive system.

"In high school, I had everyday concerns about going to the bathroom. I was a frequent visitor," Dan said. "To hide Crohn's in class, I just didn't go to the bathroom. I didn't fill my belly with stuff that made me go to the bathroom. I was constantly concerned with how I eat, so I don't have to go to the bathroom."[2]

Who Is More Prone to Crohn's?

According to the Crohn's and Colitis Foundation of America,[3] Crohn's affects about seven hundred thousand people in the United States. Teens and young

> ### Signs of Crohn's Disease
>
> ● Symptoms of Crohn's are usually not pretty. In fact, more often than not they are embarrassing. Butt jokes, tooting, talk of bowel movements. Not usual teen talk, except when fooling around.
>
> Here are the more common and not-so-common signs of Crohn's disease according to the Crohn's and Colitis Foundation of America:
>
> Main symptoms
> - continual diarrhea
> - immediate need to reach the bathroom
> - abdominal cramps and pain
> - bloody stools
> - feelings of not eliminating completely
> - constipation
> - fever
>
> Secondary symptoms
> - loss of appetite
> - fatigue
> - weight loss
> - irregular periods
> - night sweats
> - joint pain
> - inflamed skin, eyes, or liver
> - delayed sexual development[c]

adults between the ages of fifteen and thirty-five are more likely to develop the disease, although it can strike at any age. Most people who receive this diagnosis know they have Crohn's disease by the time they are thirty.

Crohn's is one condition that affects males and females equally, and the condition develops in any ethnic group. But people of Eastern European (Ashkenazi) Jewish descent face the highest risk.[4]

Early News about Crohn's Disease

Possibly the first recorded signs of Crohn's appeared in 1769. Italian doctor Giovanni Morgagni wrote about a man with chronic painful disease that included diarrhea. Over the next two centuries, physicians in different countries described patients, especially teens and young adults, with cramps, fever, diarrhea, and weight loss. They began to focus on bowel inflammation as the source of disease.

Mostly, Crohn's disease is thought of as a twentieth-century disease. That's when the medical community first teased out the range of symptoms and gave them a single name. American gastroenterologist Dr. Burrill Crohn observed

Know Your Poop

Usually, teens don't sit around looking at or discussing what they defecate. But you or someone you know has intestinal disease. It's important to understand that what passes out of you counts. Every so often you need to check for signs of disease and its worsening. So here's the poop on poop.

Color

Color of your stool varies with what you ingest. Foods, medications, supplements: these can all alter bowel movements. Color can also signal disease.

For example, most stools are shades of brown. When you see green, this suggests that food may be speeding through the large intestine. Bile from liver has too little time to break down foods enough. This signals possible diarrhea.

Yellow, foul-smelling stool contains too much fat, signaling a problem with absorption, such as with celiac disease (see chapter 2). Black or really dark red indicates bleeding in the upper GI tract, whereas bright red suggests bleeding in the lower GI tract.

Shape

Stool shape is another indicator of health. Hard balls or lumpy sausages may mean you need to drink more water because you're constipated—or heading in that direction. Smooth snakes are the perfect poop. But liquidy blobs or fluffy chunks may indicate diarrhea that needs attention if it continues for too long.

Frequency

Every teen has a different pattern of pooping. Don't freak out if you usually miss a day or two or you visit the bathroom several times a day. If that's your normal, go with your body's rhythms. The average schedule is once or twice a day, but the range is wide. The main point is how you feel. "There is no normal when it comes to frequency of bowel movements, only averages," Barnard Aserkoff, GI doctor at Boston's Massachusetts General Hospital says.[d]

Remember: If you experience a sudden and lasting change in color, shape, or frequency, you may want to consult the doctor.

the condition in 1932. He presented the first article about symptoms that was published in a professional journal. This publication gave Crohn's widespread attention among professionals. Scientists have been researching causes and remedies of Crohn's since then.

"Sometimes, when I get sick my bun hurts," Ashley wrote. "Don't be stupid and not tell anyone. Let your parents know what's wrong. Then they could take you to the doctors. That just happened to me, and it made me lose eight pounds. Now I have to drink Boost [a nutrition shake] to gain the weight back."[5]

Understanding Causes of Crohn's Disease

Investigations continue into the exact causes of Crohn's. So far, they add up to a complicated mix of origins that includes the immune system, genes, and environmental conditions.

Off-Kilter Immune System—Again

Your GI tract is loaded with bacteria. Mostly, these organisms stay in balance and are either helpful or harmless. Your immune system protects this balance against any invaders by sending out chemicals that fight off anything that threatens to cause you harm.

With Crohn's disease, however, something triggers a different reaction in your intestines. Your body attacks its own healthy bacteria. Perhaps a virus or bacteria sparks the attack, which causes inflammation in the intestines instead. This response refuses to subside. Inflammation can lead to scarring and thickening of the intestinal wall. Wherever irritation occurs, you feel symptoms.

Genetic Link

For now, a direct link to specific genes is unknown. But the thinking is that a defective gene may leave teens more prone to Crohn's, if conditions are right. You inherit this gene, or a combination of genes, from a biological parent. If a parent, sibling, or offspring has intestinal bowel disease, chances are higher that you will develop Crohn's. In fact, family history can raise your chances of developing Crohn's by 20 percent, although most cases of Crohn's develop without a family history of the disease. Still, up to one in five teens with Crohn's has at least one family member with the condition. Studies also link a family history of other autoimmune diseases to an increased risk of Crohn's.

"My grandmother on my dad's side died of colon cancer, my aunt has Crohn's, and my cousin has celiac," Carly remembered. "My mother worried I had cancer."[6]

Controllable Risks

Genes and an autoimmune response—these risk factors usually happen out of your control. But there are other risks you can control to ease or prevent development of Crohn's. The Mayo Clinic[7] suggests areas that can affect Crohn's disease:

1. Smoking: Teens who smoke wind up with more serious Crohn's. Even worse, smokers are more likely to relapse after remission and require surgery for their Crohn's. So many diseases, especially of the digestive tract, become worse after smoking; why risk them?
2. Fats and refined foods in your diet: Generally, the more processed prepared foods are, the more fats and damaging chemicals they contain. Fats are difficult for the small intestine to digest. Avoiding them can lessen diarrhea from Crohn's.
3. Nonsteroidal and over-the-counter anti-inflammatory medications: Such medications, like Advil, Aleve, and Motrin, do not cause Crohn's. But teens who regularly consume these and other pain- and inflammation-reducing medications find their Crohn's symptoms worsen.
4. Environment: Teens who live in urban regions and industrialized nations develop Crohn's in larger numbers than teens who live in small towns or on farms. Maybe it's the greater access to foods that are more processed and loaded with fat and sugars that cause reactions in some teens. Or the research that links colder, northern climates with added risk of Crohn's. While your family probably cannot or will not move, the idea of environment affecting Crohn's is thought provoking.

Discovering Crohn's

Like many other illnesses, diagnosing Crohn's is another process of elimination, as Erik can confirm. "I was diagnosed with Crohn's after having sharp pains in

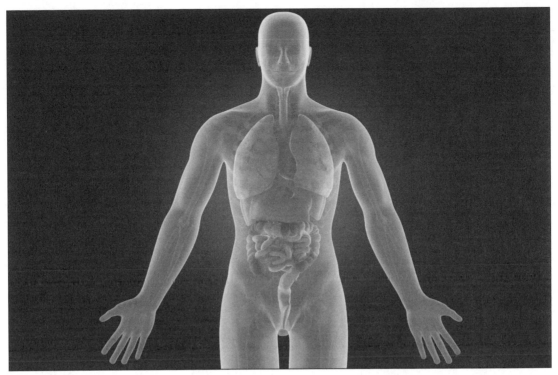

This 3D images of the body shows how Crohn's can invade several parts of the colon at once.

my lower right side and began experiencing weight loss," Erik remembers. "As a weightlifter and a very active person, this began to seriously affect me. After going to several doctors, I finally found one who found out what I had, but that was after several uncomfortable tests."[8]

Doctors may order a combination of tests before confirming your Crohn's. The least intrusive tests are blood tests. These examine whether you have enough red blood cells to carry oxygen to your tissues. If your red blood cell count is low, you may be treated for anemia, a sign of possible bowel problems. Blood tests also help identify whether you have infection.

Another blood test is called the fecal occult blood test. This can be the more embarrassing test, as you may need to provide your doctor with a sample of your precious output. Sometimes, the doctor merely swipes somewhere in your rectum. Once the deed is done, checking for hidden blood in your stool is the easy part.

Other tests, such as the following, look into your GI tract to assess condition of the lining and possibly take a sample for laboratory analysis.

Colonoscopy: This test, usually done while you sleep, allows the doctor to put a thin, flexible tube into your colon. The tube has a camera that projects onto a monitor and shows whether you have clusters of inflamed cells that may signify Crohn's. The test rarely causes pain, as you are sedated. But extensive preparation before for the test can be grueling because you need to clean out your colon.

Jocelyn

I had Crohn's disease for over two years, but my doctor was too stupid to figure it out. She insisted that I had an ulcer, and the pain couldn't possibly be as bad as I said. My grandparents were convinced I was anorexic and would beg me to eat every time I saw them. My mother said they would never find what was wrong with me, so I should just learn to deal with it. I was beginning to think I was crazy, even though I had all these symptoms.

Finally, after having a routine physical, I got help. My hemoglobin [red blood cells that transport oxygen] levels were so low that my doctor thought I had been in a serious car accident. I was referred to a specialist who in turn referred me to another specialist. If my blood levels had not been so low, the Crohn's probably never would have been found.[e]

The scouring involves lots of laxatives and eating only clear foods and liquids the day before.

Flexible sigmoidoscopy: This procedure involves winding a lighted tube into your body and into the last section of your colon, the sigmoid.

Imaging tests: Computerized tomography (CT) scans use X-ray machinery to look into and outside the entire bowel. Similarly, magnetic resonance imaging (MRI) employs magnetic fields and radio waves to produce cross-section images of organs and tissues. Both methods produce visuals for doctors to evaluate.

Another way to see inside your body is for you to swallow a capsule with a camera. The tiny camera transmits pictures to a computer worn on your belt. These images are downloaded and examined for signs of Crohn's. The camera leaves the body painlessly through your stool. This imaging offers clues about Crohn's, but doctors may still need the other imaging tests to confirm a diagnosis.

A word about testing: You may think that once you receive a diagnosis, your testing days are over. Not so with a chronic disease like Crohn's. You may be asked to occasionally take tests to monitor your condition, especially if you feel worse.

Treatments

As with other conditions in this book, Crohn's has no cure. You might find relief from disease for long stretches of time, only to suffer a surprise explosion of symptoms. That said, there are options to lessen and ease Crohn's attacks.

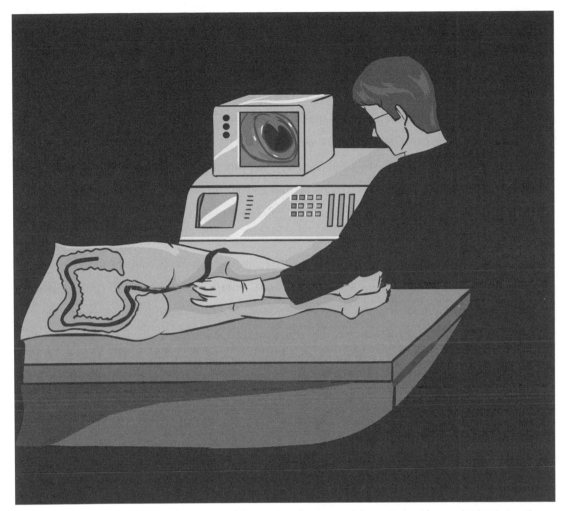

During a colonoscopy, you lie on a table as the doctor guides a tube through the intestines.

The goal of treatment is to help you control your disease enough to live a symptom-free life. Your doctor may suggest a combination of medications, diet, probiotics (supplements with natural bacteria to balance those in your intestines), and stress-reduction therapies. This combination may vary, depending upon your specific symptoms.

Medicines

Doctors usually begin treatment with anti-inflammatory drugs. These can either be prescription or over-the-counter medications that you can purchase without a prescription. The idea behind these medications is to suppress your immune system's painful attack on your intestines. Doctors may also prescribe targeted

Alan

As my own case of Crohn's disease has taught me, there is a certain difference between disease management and pain management. After resigning myself to the diagnosis, I felt there wasn't much to be done about it, so I tried always to ignore my symptoms, which was a costly mistake.

Treatment was available, but by not treating my disease, I allowed myself to be damaged to the point that surgery was an emergency. I would never recommend to anyone to ignore their disease—be alert to changes in your condition, usually measured by pain.

Pain is hard to ignore, but if it is all that you ever think about, your life will be pain. Whatever is on your mind the most—that's your life. . . . I understand there are times when you can't shift your focus away from the pain; but when you can, try to make pain like the radio you listen to while you do something else. Background noise. Pain won't be your friend, but with practice it won't be the enemy either. Pay enough attention to it, so that you can manage your disease without damaging your body. And don't get your nose pierced either.[f]

medications to relieve diarrhea, pain, fever, and associated discomfort, and to reduce bloating and gas.

But as with any medications, especially powerful ones you may need for your symptoms, you can experience side effects. Even over-the-counter pain relievers, like acetaminophen, can cause GI problems that worsen the disease they are supposed to help. So take medications sparingly, and tell your doctor whenever you experience any changes.

Some treatment focuses on specific symptoms, such as drugs to reduce painful muscle spasms in your intestines, diarrhea, and fever from inflammation. Many teens require a combination of medications to control and suppress flare-ups. So many drugs are available—and appearing regularly—that you may need to try several individual or combinations of medications to find the right balance for you.

More recently, doctors began recommending probiotic supplements. Some teens find they help lessen Crohn's symptoms. Probiotics are tiny living organisms, such as bacteria, that reside in your GI tract. They work to balance imbalances caused by intestinal inflammation. You can buy probiotics without a prescription in capsules, tablets, and powder supplements and certain foods, such as

Carly

I think the hardest part of having Crohn's is having to limit what I eat. It's even harder knowing I can't eat something at all. I would eat it anyway, thinking it wouldn't matter. I've had one or two flare-ups after that.

I was in remission for a long time. This past summer, I didn't take my medicine, and I had a flare-up. I had another test, and the doctor discovered eighteen centimeters of my intestines were sick. It was scary to me that I had put myself in that position. I couldn't even go to school.

Now I'm taking my medicine. It's been a rough couple of first weeks [at college]. I've gained coping mechanisms. I know as an adult I have to cope by myself.[g]

specific yogurts. Check with your doctor and read labels to make sure you find probiotic supplements that provide enough live bacteria to make a difference.

Caring for Yourself: Diet

A well-balanced, healthy diet helps prevent and reduce Crohn's symptoms. This is a no-brainer for any condition mentioned in this book. Diet involves the foods you eat to maintain good nutrition that gives you enough energy, especially when Crohn's symptoms can reduce energy levels and get you down mentally. Treating other conditions involves following a specific diet for targeted symptoms. With Crohn's, however, symptoms can vary with the individual and which foods you find escalate attacks.

"Foods that affect Crohn's changes for me," Carly said. "Lately it's been red sauces or pasta or pizza. Skin on fruits are hard to digest. Having Crohn's is an everyday thing, and you can eat something one day and have a reaction and never eat it again. Mostly I watch something that can get stuck in the intestinal tract. Corn, seeds, blueberries. It varies with every patient."[9]

One myth about Crohn's is that following a diet can cure your symptoms, which has never been proven. Many teens with Crohn's are left to trial and error to decide what sort of diet works best for them. The main focus should be on eating a healthy and varied diet that replaces lost nutrients and encourages healing after an attack. Foods may trigger a flare-up, but they do not cause the disease. Some foods can make you feel worse while a flare-up is occurring. For example,

Balancing What You Eat

The National Institutes of Health and Crohn's and Colitis Foundation offer suggestions to ease uncomfortable diarrhea, gas, and other effects of Crohn's:

- Drink plenty of water (eight to ten glasses a day) in small amounts throughout the day to keep your digestive system working smoothly and ensure you never get dehydrated from diarrhea.
- Eat small meals throughout the day, rather than loading up at three meals a day; smaller meals are easier to digest.
- Avoid high-fiber foods, such as bran, beans, seeds, nuts, popcorn. Fiber is not easily digested; teens with bowel disease may find it makes symptoms worse. Instead eat carbs with soluble fiber, such as oat bran, legumes, and barley.
- Stay away from fatty, greasy, or fried foods and sauces, especially those made from butter, margarine, or cream. Instead eat healthy fats, such as olive oil and canola oil that provide omega-3 fatty acids.
- Stop ingesting caffeine products, such as tea, soda, coffee, and other caffeinated beverages. Caffeine stimulates the bowel, triggering diarrhea.
- Limit dairy products, if they cause digestive problems. Buy low-lactose cheeses, such as Swiss or cheddar, or lactose-free dairy products, such as Lactaid.
- Eat proteins, such as lean meats, poultry, fish, eggs, and soy.
- Add deep-colored skinless and seedless fruits and cooked vegetables to your meals and snacks. Remember that cooked veggies and fruits are easier to digest.
- Keep a food diary of what you eat and how your body reacts to these foods. This helps you figure out what foods cause your symptoms and should be limited and what you can safely eat.
- Experiment to figure out which foods cause your gas; then stop eating them—another no-brainer.[h, i]

you may find that soft, bland foods go down easier than spicy or high-fiber foods when you're having a flare-up.[10]

Caring for Yourself: Vitamins and Supplements

Bowel disease often inhibits the body's ability to absorb nutrients. Poor digestion contributes to your body's being unable to use proteins, fats, carbohydrates, and water properly. Yet proteins, vitamins, minerals, and other nutrients from foods are essential to helping you stay healthy and heal better. Besides feeling better all-around, a well-nourished body increases the likelihood of medications working more effectively.

The reality of Crohn's symptoms is they can cause loss of appetite. Nausea, pain, and fear of setting off symptoms contributes to either not eating or eating a steady diet of foods that lack the balance needed to fight disease. Other conditions result when your diet is off balance.

Your doctor should check to make sure you are getting enough food and nutrients. If there is any doubt, ask about taking vitamin and mineral supplements. Bleeding stools can contribute to anemia, or reduced levels of iron in the bloodstream. Anemia causes low energy levels. A simple blood test examines iron levels to check if iron supplements and vitamin B12 are warranted to help prevent anemia.

Calcium and vitamin D supplements help you maintain strong bones. Bone loss is one side effect of certain medications. And a general vitamin can balance the loss of nutrients when you feel like eating less than usual. If you still believe you are not getting the right diet balance, ask your doctor to refer you to a dietician or nutritionist who can help you establish a workable diet plan.

Caring for Yourself: Managing Stress

You get stressed about something that happened at home or school or with a friend. That is part of life. But stress is never easy on the body. With Crohn's, stress can trigger symptoms or a full-blown flare-up. If the stress lasts long enough, your muscles tighten, including those in your GI tract. Pretty soon, discomfort occurs. Be sure to check out methods for reducing stress in chapter 11, "Taking Care of Everyday Business."

Surgery

You can do everything correctly and still find your Crohn's disease worsens. When drug therapy, diet, and other options don't lessen symptoms, some form

> ## Carly
>
> It's hard knowing that you go through every day with anxiety. I'm tired all the time—from being anemic, from wanting to sleep all the time. Sometimes, I don't sleep and don't want to do homework. You can be healthy one day and the next day be over the moon with pains—joint pains, stomach pains.
>
> My teachers are very understanding. Some of them know what it is, so they understand. Other teachers who may not know what it is but support me through it as well. I have disability accommodations. Teachers send tests, so I can get extra time. They let me go to the bathroom. They let me drink water or eat in class. These accommodations are needed.[j]

of surgery may be your best option. You're not alone. The Crohn's and Colitis Foundation estimates that "about 70 percent of people with CD eventually requires surgery."[11]

Different forms of surgery apply to different types of Crohn's. Some surgery removes the damaged portion of the GI tract. Once removed, healthy sections of bowel are joined to keep a pathway open for stool. Other procedures may close tears or drain patches of infection that can form. Still other surgery may widen areas of the intestine that have grown too narrow due to inflammation and scarring.

According to the Crohn's and Colitis Foundation of America, the problem with surgery is it rarely solves the problem completely. Disease often reoccurs. Scar tissue can form over incision areas, which further complicates Crohn's. But surgery gives you time to try and control further return of symptoms and lengthen time between attacks.[12]

In extreme cases, when the intestine is too damaged, doctors perform surgery to allow feces to move out of the body without going through all or part of the intestine. They cut a hole in the abdomen wall through which stool exits into a bag outside the body. When the surgeon connects the large intestine, or colon, to the abdomen opening, the surgery is called a colostomy. If the procedure is done in the small intestine, or ileum, it's called an ileostomy. Colostomies and ileostomies can be temporary, to allow the GI tract to heal, or they can be permanent.

Understanding Life with Crohn's Disease

Yes, Crohn's means medication for the rest of your life. Yes, you are going to experience symptoms, usually ones that are unpredictable, many painful. Even

Dan

I fought the surgery [colostomy]. It's rough. I was feeling like my life would fall apart. It did. My first year after surgery, I had to learn everything, from how to shower to how to exercise. And how do you tell a date that you look different when you take off your shirt?

There is a movement by people who want to take the seriousness away from the ostomy bag. They decorate their bags. They put action figures on them.

Over time you learn to adjust, and you learn about people. Your family and friends don't care how you look. Today, it's not an issue. I work with lots of people who don't know I have Crohn's.

I'm able to go to the beach, play golf, ride my bicycle—all the things I thought I could never do. And I don't have to worry about side effects of Crohn's. No medication. Now I eat everything in my way. So much of life is consumed with what is going to touch off symptoms and where is the bathroom. I'm no longer focusing on my body. I survived and can get through.[k]

when Crohn's goes away, there will always be the chance remission will end, unless you've had surgery. That's life with Crohn's disease.

The important thing to remember is you are still you, whether you have Crohn's or not. You can get good grades. You can hold a job. You can play sports and date. You can take part in the same range of activities as any other teen. You just need to plan for times when you're not feeling so hot.

That said, the pain, discomfort, and embarrassment with symptoms of Crohn's disease can be depressing. Make sure you build a support system to help you through rough times. A good friend. Family. A support group, possibly one recommended by the Colitis and Crohn's Foundation of America. If life gets you down for too long, consider seeing a therapist. You don't have to go it alone.

Many teens find that planning ahead lessens some of the stresses from having Crohn's. One way to reduce stress is to keep emergency supplies handy. Carry these basic supplies with you, either in your backpack or purse:

- medication
- toilet paper
- wipes that might irritate less than toilet paper
- powder
- hand sanitizer

- air freshener, if gas is your problem
- clean underwear and pants or a skirt
- plastic bag to carry soiled clothes
- disposable gloves to handle cleanup and clothes[13]

At home, make sure you practice good anal hygiene. That means showering and using cleaning products that won't irritate your butt more. Afterward, apply a skin cream that may relieve irritation around the anus. If soreness from bowel movements becomes too painful, soak in warm salt water. Mouthwash or hydrogen peroxide in water can ease mouth sores, called canker sores.

Generally, take care of yourself, which can get boring. But it's important with Crohn's. Keep to a diet of foods that agree with you. Exercise to relieve muscle stresses. Practice stress relieving activities you feel comfortable performing (see chapter 11). Take your medications as directed, and tell your doctor when anything changes or the drugs stop working. Check with your doctor for more effective pain management—and trust yourself to know what's best for your body.

"With positive attitude and personal dedication, Crohn's can be controlled and someday be beaten," Erik wrote on Angelfire.com. "Crohn's can control your life, or you can control it. See your doctor and experiment with different foods and drugs. Be positive and reassure yourself that you can beat it. Good luck."[14]

Resources

Organizations

Crohn's Disease Web Site
www.angelfire.com/ga/crohns/
Website coordinated by a Crohn's patient, sandee@freestamp.com, who has gathered general information and national and international connections. The site offers personal stories and a place where teens and young adults connect and share stories about life with Crohn's disease.

Crohn's and Colitis Foundation of America
733 Third Avenue, Suite 510
New York, NY 10017
800-932-2423
www.ccfa.org
Largest organization devoted to inflammatory bowel disease that posts general information about Crohn's and hosts local chapters, support group access, and a teen website, www.justlikemeibd.org. The group also prepared the helpful *A Guide for*

Teens with IBD that you can download at www.ccfa.org/assets/pdfs/teenguide
.pdf and runs a help center (888-694-8872) and live chat at www.ccfa.org.

National Institute of Diabetes and Digestive and Kidney Diseases
Bethesda, MD 20892-2560
301-496-3583
www.niddk.nih.gov/search/pages/Results.aspx?k=crohn%27s
Site for government-sponsored research and information about CD.

Books

John Bradley, *The Foul Bowel: 101 Ways to Survive and Thrive with Crohn's
Disease*, Dexter, MI: YKnot Publishing, 2010. Offers tips about dealing
with symptoms, doctors, diagnostic tests, relationships, and more and is
recommended by Teens with Crohn's.

Andrew Warner and Amy Barto, *100 Questions and Answers about Crohn's
Disease and Ulcerated Colitis*, Burlington, MA: Jones & Bartlett, 2009. A
comprehensive guide published with the Lahey Clinic.

4

DOWN SYNDROME: CHANGING ATTITUDES

∙∙

One teen fashion model landed projects with three different national campaigns in Australia and the United States. Her name is Madeline Stuart,[1] and she happens to have Down syndrome (DS) along with a twinkling smile. In fact, you probably have seen other teens with DS over the years. Some are young adults who have acted on popular television shows, such as when Laura Potter appeared regularly on *Glee* from 2009 to 2015. Many may go to school or work with you.

These are only a few of the many teens with varied interests and skills who have the Down syndrome. At one time, doctors told parents whose newborns received this diagnosis not to expect them to do very much. Now the sky is the limit!

"I work in a tile showroom," Adrian said. "I do a lot of writing—poetry, lyrics, stories. I actually have two poems published in *A Room of Golden Shelves*, a poetry book."[2]

"I'm in a drama group," Sam said. "We made movies [videos] about *Alice in Wonderland*, *Taming of the Shrew*, *The Tempest*, and *Romeo and Juliet*. One movie teens [who also have DS] in this group wrote."[3]

What Exactly Is Down Syndrome?

Down syndrome is a genetic condition that can change every aspect of someone's development. The extent of change depends upon a child's individual makeup. As a baby matures, a wide variety of mental abilities, behavior, and physical growth appears.

Often, teens with DS are noticeable by their characteristic features. Some of these traits remain constant throughout someone's life. Yet, teens with DS display the same range of differences and capabilities as in the typical population.

That said, there are a host of common signs of Down syndrome. All or most of these traits rarely occur in the same person. Those that are present appear in a mix and range of combinations. Some traits only a doctor can identify. Here are the most common characteristics that indicate DS.[4]

Muscles, Joints, and Tissues

Babies with DS exhibit poor muscle tone for longer than the usual month or two after birth. Muscles stay so relaxed that head and body parts flop. Arms and legs move too easily and show little strength. The infants lack certain reflexes that require muscle tension. Poor muscle tone affects movement, strength, and general development. These traits make it difficult for babies to roll over, sit unassisted, and hold their heads up. With early exercises, however, muscle strength improves with age, and babies—including those with DS—usually gain these skills.

Tissues encircling bone joints can be weak, also. Weak joints, especially at the top two backbones of the neck, risk greater stress on the head or neck. This condition can be corrected through surgery. But teens who have had this surgery must avoid most sports and strenuous physical activity to prevent further stress on the spine, joints, and muscle tissues.

Head Differences

Down syndrome often shows a distinct physical appearance. Sometimes, the head looks somewhat smaller than usual, and the neck appears shortened. You might notice loose folds of skin at the back of the neck after a baby with DS is born.

All babies have soft head spots at birth. Soft spots help ease the trip down the birth canal. The spots also allow some flexibility as the baby's brain grows, which happens really quickly during the first year of life. These spots usually begin to close at about six months and complete the process at about eighteen months. But babies with DS may have larger soft spots that take longer to close. Skin folds and soft spots do eventually disappear with age.

Facial Features

Most babies with DS have eye openings that slant upwards. Folds of skin called epicanthal folds cover inner corners of both eyes. The iris, the colored portion of each eye, may have white specks on the outer rim called Brushfield spots. You barely notice these spots, and they never impair vision, but doctors can tell they are there.

This baby with Down syndrome displays the characteristic protruding tongue through her smile.

Other facial features tend to be slightly smaller than those of typical kids. Smaller noses with a flat bridge mean smaller nasal passages. Smaller nose size contributes to more runny, congested noses.

Children with DS also have smaller mouths. That might be why you see some kids display what appear to be larger tongues. Poor muscle tone plus a smaller mouth cavity may cause the tongue to protrude. By teenage years, many people with DS—but not all—have had years of speech therapy to strengthen mouth muscles and control the tongue thrust.

Outer ears can be smaller, misshapen, or set lower on the head. Smaller ear canals contribute to fluid collecting, which increases the risk of ear infections. Sometimes, pathways become blocked and cause hearing loss.

Babies with DS follow their own patterns of growing teeth. Some teeth refuse to erupt, are missing, or arrive in different sizes, shapes, or colors of enamel. Usually, these differences can be corrected by the teenage years.

Hands and Feet

As children with DS mature, they tend to have hands and feet that remain on the small and thick side. The fifth finger may curve inward. A space between the first and second toes may form. Fingerprints and footprints may show characteristic DS creases across the soles and palms. These features are rarely noticeable and never affect development.

Overall Development

Most babies with DS behave much like other infants, as long as there are no other health problems. But some babies with DS cry less and sleep more. They take longer to learn basic baby skills, such as sucking from a nipple, rolling over, or crawling. They develop at a slower rate.

At one time doctors identified all children with DS as severely retarded or extremely slow at developing. More recently, studies confirmed that most of these children functioned within the mild to moderate range of slower learning rate. Now, people who know someone with DS understand that their potential is limitless—rather most people know this, but not everyone.

"Down syndrome is more of an inconvenience in a way," Adrian said. "In science class freshman year, they were showing *The Magic School Bus* [a children's picture book]. We were supposed to be like baking a cake for a science activity. And we're freshmen, not two years old! I was the only one who complained. My parents got me switched out of the class, fortunately."[5]

Sleep Problems

Teens with DS may have sleep apnea. This is a sleep disorder that involves repeated episodes when a person stops breathing while asleep. The disorder may be caused by temporary throat or upper airway blockage. Or it may come from a problem in the area of the brain that controls breathing. With DS, doctors believe that soft tissue and bone changes in DS that narrow airways lead to obstructed airways, contributing to sleep apnea.[6]

Other Health Issues

Down syndrome, and whichever features it brings, may create other health problems. Some appear at birth, while others develop later in life.

Vision Problems

About three out of one hundred teens with DS develop cataracts. This is a cloudy film that grows over the front of the eye, blurring vision. More often, cataracts occur in typical older adults. Whatever someone's age, cataracts can be surgically removed and vision restored.

Teens with DS are more apt to have the usual vision problems, such as difficulty seeing close up or far away. They are also more likely to be cross-eyed, where both eyes turn inward toward the nose. These problems are easily corrected with glasses.

Hearing Loss

About 50 percent of babies born with DS are born with or develop hearing loss. As mentioned earlier, hearing loss can stem from fluid buildup in the ears or abnormal development of bones in the outer, middle, or inner ear. When the problem becomes more severe and cannot be corrected, language development suffers. Without speech and language, social, thinking, and self-help skills suffer as well.

Heart Defects

About one in every two babies born with DS suffers from some form of heart irregularity. Defects can be found in one of the four heart chambers or in the walls separating these chambers. Sometimes, a hole in the wall between two chambers appears. Or chamber walls and valves pumping blood to and from the heart are malformed.

If heart problems are not corrected quickly, blood flow slows. This can cause heart failure, as body functions become sluggish from a lack of oxygen that the blood carries to all parts of the body. At one time, doctors rarely suggested surgery, preferring instead to let babies with DS die. But thankfully times have changed. In some cases, heart problems continue to affect activities. More often, routine but delicate surgery corrects most heart problems, if caught early.[7]

Seizures

About 5 to 10 percent of teens with DS experience seizures. These are abnormal electric discharges from an injured or scarred part of the brain. What you see can be as small as a blink or as serious as a total loss of body control. With severe seizures, the body stiffens and falls and jerks. Sometimes, the loss of control causes drooling, urinating, or a bowel movement.

Seizures can last a few seconds or several minutes. The number of seizures someone has may increase with age. Doctors prescribe medicine to control them, but these medications are strong and require constant monitoring. A greater chance of brain damage exists with uncontrolled seizures.[8]

Seizures look scary and painful. But teens who experience them usually feel no pain. In fact, they rarely remember what occurred, although they may feel sleepy and need to rest afterward. If you ever see anyone go through a seizure, be sure to remove dangerous objects from the area, so the person doesn't get hurt falling or thrashing around. Then leave the individual alone.

Aging Concerns

Teens with DS tend to get age-related conditions besides cataracts earlier than the general population. Gray hair and wrinkled skin may appear in the twenties or thirties, long before the time when other teens worry about these problems.

About this time, young adults with DS are at greater risk for dementia and Alzheimer's disease. Dementia winds up causing memory loss. Alzheimer's disease affects memory and brain function as well. Reduced brain function results in disorientation and sluggishness. Alzheimer's disease also affects the ability to perform daily activities, such as eating and dressing. Both dementia and Alzheimer's disease ultimately decrease average life span and quality of life for adults with DS, the same as with adults without DS.[9]

Research into treatments and cures promises to reduce the trauma of these diseases. Studies indicate that changes shared by DS and Alzheimer's disease are helping scientists understand both disorders better.

Weight Control

This is a big issue for some teens. Down syndrome can affect the thyroid, the gland that controls metabolism. A slower metabolism slows growth in height. Teens with DS may lack energy to be more active. Then there is inactivity due to low muscle tone that makes it more difficult to move, or a lingering heart problem that requires avoidance of too much exercise. Weight can creep up when you're younger and less active. Even worse, weight becomes more difficult to shed as you age. That occurs for teens with and without DS.

"The main thing about DS for me is the weight," Adrian said. "I have a younger but taller brother. He's about six-foot something. I'm about five foot six. If I can get that under control, the rest shouldn't be a problem."[10]

Life Span

As late as the 1960s, children with DS were lucky to live until their first birthdays. Now life spans of sixty years and beyond are common for anyone with DS.

Myths and Facts about Down Syndrome

Most people have a positive image of what someone with DS can accomplish. But many myths still linger from the time when people had limited knowledge about the condition. Here are some of the more common myths that need to be eliminated:

Myth: Children with DS progress better in a sheltered living residence than living at home with their family.

Fact: Doctors used to tell new parents to send their baby with DS to an institution. But the general emphasis has changed. Now most students with disabilities live and go to school in their family's community. Since the days of wholesale institutionalization, researchers have documented that children who live with their families—and attend school with students who do not have DS—thrive beyond previous expectations.

Myth: Babies with few DS features at birth will outgrow the condition.

Fact: Down syndrome is a chromosome error. As such, it is part of someone's genetic makeup and cannot be outgrown. Someone either has the condition as determined by a blood test, or not. As with typical kids, each child with DS displays a unique number of characteristics. Some become less prominent, but they cannot be outgrown.

Myth: Babies with fewer DS features reach a higher intellectual level as teens.

Fact: Teens with DS vary in the number and type of characteristic DS features they display. Someone may have any number of possible DS traits. Each trait is independent and individual. The number of DS traits bears no relation to mental ability.

Myth: Teens with DS are always happy.

Fact: This is one of the strangest myths to come down through the decades. In truth, teens with DS possess the same range of feelings as someone without the syndrome. They want to be happy, make friends, and feel they belong. Similarly, they are hurt, angry, or upset by unkind or thoughtless behavior—just like you or anyone else would be.

Myth: Teens with DS are always fat and sluggish.

Fact: Although the tendency is there, research shows that only about 25 percent of teens with DS become overweight. Some teens, however, struggle to reach a healthy weight. Many teens with DS maintain a good weight, exercise, and are proud of their body image.

Myth: Teens with DS are significantly slower.

Fact: Most people with DS test within the mild to moderately slow range. But differences and broader ranges are common as more opportunities for teens with DS become available. Some teens achieve nearly normal intelligence; others are severely disabled.

Previously, society had low expectations for anyone with DS. Communities provided little opportunity for kids with DS to show how capable they are. Now expectations are higher. Better educational programs start earlier. Unless someone has severe medical complications that interfere with learning, teens with DS are making greater educational gains than ever thought possible.

Forms of Down Syndrome

Not all teens with Down syndrome display the same genetic makeup. Doctors identify three types of DS. Each has a slightly different chromosome makeup, but each involves chromosome 21. You cannot see a difference among the types of DS, as characteristic features appear similar. Because differentiating types can be difficult, exact percentages of each form differ with reporting groups. The following information comes from the Centers for Disease Control.[a]

Trisomy 21

About 95 percent of teens with DS have an extra chromosome in pair 21. The extra matter creates three separate copies of the chromosome in each cell, rather than the usual two. This distinction is reflected in the name: *tri* means three, and *somy* refers to chromosomes.

Translocation

This form of DS accounts for about 3 percent of teens with DS. With translocation, newborns possess the usual number of chromosomes, forty-six. But chromosome 21 contains an extra part. The abnormal part attaches, or translocates, to another chromosome, instead of forming a separate chromosome 21. DS develops as a result.

The Mayo Clinic claims "translocation DS is the only form of the disorder that can be passed from parent to child."[b] Either the mother or father can carry the rearranged gene. An affected father raises the risk about 3 percent. Moms as carriers raise chances to 10 or 15 percent. Still, only about one-third of teens with translocation find their DS is inherited.

Mosaicism

This type of DS occurs in about 2 percent, or two in one hundred, of teens with DS. With mosaicism, cells contain mixed numbers of chromosomes. Some contain forty-six chromosomes, and some show forty-seven. The different numbers result in either two or three copies of chromosome 21. The term *mosaic* refers to the mixture or combination of chromosomes. Teens with mosaicism may or may not appear with the same features. The difference depends upon whether cells contain the usual number of chromosomes. In that case, fewer features of DS develop.[c]

The challenge is to find ways for these young adults to live free of diseases that interfere with daily living, and to maintain a healthy lifestyle—just like the rest of the population.

DS by the Numbers

According to the National Down Syndrome Society, Down syndrome is the most common chromosome condition. More than four hundred thousand people in the United States live with DS. That means 1 in every 691 babies are born with DS.[11]

Like many conditions in this book, DS does not discriminate. All races and economic levels see the same ratio of babies born with DS. What may be different is the type of Down syndrome someone has. Read "Forms of Down Syndrome" to learn about the three different types of DS: trisomy 21, translocation, or mosaicism.

Genetic Accident

Babies with DS do not generally inherit the condition from their parents. That's because DS results from a mistake in how the cell divides during development of the egg, sperm, or resulting embryo. Even when there is an inherited component, as in some translocation DS, it is the tendency toward an irregularity that contributes to the gene differences.

Doctors usually describe DS as a genetic accident. They emphasize that parents did nothing before or during pregnancy to cause the condition. Nothing anyone felt, drank, or ate at the time altered their baby's genetic makeup. The same is true with any genetic condition.

A Little History

The condition currently known as DS first appeared centuries ago. Writings, pictures, and research reports depicted the condition as far back as the 1500s. Yet no one identified a specific syndrome with particular characteristics. Most often, teens with any disability were thrown into institutions, sometimes with robbers, murderers, orphans, or families too poor to pay their bills. They received care in unclean or dangerous settings.

Through the centuries, scientists have suggested many theories about the collective traits now known as DS. British doctor J. Langdon Down first isolated and described characteristics of DS in 1866. He wrote about certain children with common features beyond slowness, or mental retardation. He used the term *Mongoloid* to describe them.[12] The term referred to people from Mongolia in Central Asia who have similar eye structure and round faces. Mongolians found this term insulting because of slower DS intelligence. But for some unknown reason, Mongoloid stuck in medical lingo anyway. In the 1960s, doctors in the United States and Europe finally dropped Mongoloid as a scientific term. They decided to name the syndrome Down after the man who described it earlier, thereafter eliminating the racist term.

The *R* Word

Ever call someone a retard? Think it's okay to throw out meaningless descriptions of others, even to friends? Think again. Calling someone the *r* word is the same as any minority insult, so think before you shoot off your mouth.

After a bully television news commentator used the term, Global Messenger for Special Olympics John Franklin Stephens wrote her an open letter about how he felt as a person with Down hearing that term. In an excerpt:

I realized you just wanted to belittle the President [Barack Obama] by linking him to people like me. You assumed that people would understand and accept that being linked to someone like me is an insult, and you assumed you could get away with it and still appear on TV. I have to wonder if you considered other hateful words. . . . Well, you and society need to learn that being compared to people like me should be considered a badge of honor. No one overcomes more than we do and still loves life so much. Come join us someday at Special Olympics. See if you can walk away with your heart unchanged.[d]

Down might also have contributed to the myth that teens with DS are always happy. He believed that educating women caused them to have these retarded, but funny, children. "They have considerable power of imitation, even bordering on being mimics," Down wrote. "They are humorous, and have a lively sense of the ridiculous that often colors their mimicry."[13]

Since then, researchers have linked DS to hormone imbalances, poor fetal development, virus, alcohol-drinking parents, vitamin deficiencies, powerful drugs, lack of oxygen at birth, or X-rays. None of these theories confirmed the origins of DS.

Educators persisted in thinking that teens who seemed slow could never progress. Doctors still cautioned parents to put their child with DS into an institution. By 1900, however, administrators began devoting a few special classes in public schools to students who were slower. Mostly, these classes cropped up in institutions where more students with DS lived.

In 1959 French Drs. Jerome Lejeune, Marthae Gauthier, and Raymond Turpin reported the first serious breakthrough in finding a cause for DS. The same year Patricia Jacobs made the same discovery in England. Both research teams confirmed that DS resulted from an extra chromosome in every cell of the body. This discovery freed parents from the guilt of causing their child's DS. Genetic makeup was beyond anyone's control.

Discovering a Cause

Since genetic makeup was discovered as key, few findings have definitively explained why certain cells divide improperly and result in DS. Modern genetic research is trying to understand the way genes work. But the exact cause of DS remains a mystery. New investigations focus on different genes that might trigger cataracts, bone problems, and heart defects, or other signs of early aging that often accompany DS. And studies continue to examine risk factors for having a baby with DS.

"I am a Brooklyn diva. I am homosexual and I feel fabulous about it. One of my favorite hobbies is karaoke. If you want to come out, express yourself. It felt great. I feel powerful."—Paul, a young man with DS[e]

So far, the age of parents is the only factor known to increase the chance of having a child with DS. Women under thirty-five bear more babies, so more are born with DS. But as women age, risk of DS increases. A thirty-five-year-old mom has a 1 in 350 chance of conceiving a baby with DS. That ratio rises to 1 in 100 by age forty. After forty years, the risk for a woman increases to 1 in 30 births. Doctors reason that older eggs are more prone to irregular cell division. Studies continue to factor the role older fathers have in their partners bearing a baby with DS.

There's another risk factor for moms of any age: having one child with DS increases the risk of bearing a second child with the condition. No matter what their age, moms with one DS child have a one in one hundred chance of having a second baby with DS. With translocation DS, however, older men and women both share the risk of increasing the odds of having a child with DS.

Screening for DS

Screening tests alert the woman and her doctor about the likelihood of giving birth to a baby with DS. Knowing helps parents both adjust and plan. Initial screenings can tell whether there is a risk of DS, which helps parents decide to pursue a diagnostic test or not (see "Diagnostic Tests for Down Syndrome").

Usually, a combination of screening tests helps evaluate risk. Some screening tests are not very intrusive. One is a blood test that measures a sample of the mother's blood. A small sample is enough to detect any of three substances that may indicate the possible presence of DS.

Another painless screening involves ultrasound, which shows a picture of the developing fetus. From an ultrasound, a doctor examines whether fluid exists behind the fetus's neck, one sign of possible DS. If ultrasound indicates the potential for DS, the doctor will recommend further diagnostic tests.

Diagnostic Tests for Down Syndrome

After doctors screen for genetic problems, they may recommend that mom undergo more intrusive diagnostic testing to confirm a DS diagnosis. This involves one of three main types of tests:

Chorionic villus sampling: At-risk mothers receive this test between nine and eleven weeks into pregnancy. Technicians take a tissue sample from inside the mother. The doctor inserts a needle into the sac that holds the fetus, the developing unborn human. The mother's abdomen is numbed, but the test is still stressful.

Amniocentesis: This diagnostic test studies the amniotic fluid, the fluid from the sac around the fetus, to determine whether cells contain an extra chromosome in the twenty-first pair. Usually, doctors administer the test when women are between fourteen and eighteen weeks pregnant.

Percutaneous umbilical blood sampling: This test examines blood from the umbilical cord connecting the fetus to the sac that surrounds it inside the mother. The blood sample is then tested for the presence of an extra chromosome. More often, doctors recommend this test to confirm one of the others.

All three tests cause some risk to the baby and mother. So doctors recommend them only when chances are high that results will show DS.

Occasionally, screening results produce errors. On occasion tests indicate an abnormal result when none exists. Conversely, test results can come back normal when a problem actually exists. That's why doctors recommend them when chances are high that results will show DS. Once clues become known, scientists hope to learn how to change genes in the womb, so specific defects never occur. One day this study should improve the lives of teens with DS.

What Do You Think?

Two issues in particular have become hot-button topics in the DS community: diagnostic testing and genetic research to prevent DS. Each topic has its promoters and detractors. Both sides are understandable.

The case for diagnostic testing suggests that knowing whether a baby will be born with DS is helpful. The knowledge allows the woman to adjust to having a child with a condition she never expected. The news is not necessarily bad: it's just different. Moms can find support groups, learn about DS, and prepare for their children better. Similarly, doctors can make plans to ensure safe delivery and follow-up in case other health issues become evident.

"Research knows how DS works," said Ann Garcia, National Association for Down Syndrome family support coordinator. "We want to improve gene therapy to lessen effects of DS to allow better cognitive abilities. This is controversial. But parents want to alleviate problems their children have."[14]

Those opposed to diagnostic testing worry that more parents will choose to end their pregnancies. These tests may become another way to select preferred characteristics and eliminate an infant who may be less than perfect. Governments ban gender selection, choosing to keep or abort a fetus on the basis of being male or female. Should abortion be encouraged when DS is involved? Those who advocate ending all abortions worry that the earlier DS is identified, the more a woman might decide to end her pregnancy.

The other side of this argument is some families cannot handle the news. Chances are greater—but not for sure—that this baby will bring challenges beyond those of raising a typical child. There may be extra health issues, time, and money for extra therapies (speech, physical, occupational), and the emotional stress of raising a child who is potentially disabled. Some organizations host baby foster programs to give parents time to adjust to the news before they agree to give up their baby for adoption. More recently, the availability of abortion has lowered the number of parents who consider adoption.

Another issue is genetic research to prevent DS. Scientists are looking for a way to eliminate DS by altering the genetic code in the womb. If that happens DS will disappear. That may be fine, but what about the kids and adults with DS who still live everyday lives? What does that make them? Will they suffer more discrimination for being less than perfect?

"I heard the word 'Down syndrome,' and my world collapsed," Renate Lindeman wrote in the *Washington Post*. "It didn't take me a long time to figure out that my ideas were based on negative, outdated information that had nothing to do with the reality of life with Down syndrome today. My daughter is an active, outgoing girl. She's my nature child, wildly passionate about anything with four legs. . . . Through her, I've learned that Down syndrome is not the scary, terrible condition it's made out to be."[15]

Living with Down Syndrome

"When I was born, the doctor who delivered me didn't think I would ever amount to anything. He didn't think people with disabilities could accomplish things and have a full life. He told my parents to put me in an institution and tell people I had died. But look, here I am, a published author at 20 years of age, giving a speech to parents and teachers and professionals about the success I have in my life," said Jason Kingsley, a teen with DS who wrote in his book *Count Us In: Growing Up with Down Syndrome*.[16]

Today, some uninformed doctors still offer this advice to new parents of a baby with DS. The reality is parents no longer must raise their child with DS alone. A number of educational and community programs exist for children and teens with DS. You probably know about some of these in your community.

School and DS

Some teens with DS never need special support beyond what the school offers any student. Others may require special classes, transition planning for work and living, and adult services. You already read in the first chapter that Section 504 of the Rehabilitation Act addressed equal opportunity for school, job training, and employment for anyone with a disability.

Another law—IDEA, or Individuals with Disabilities Education Act of 2004, revised Public Law 94-142 of 1975—grants every student the right to free public schooling. Under IDEA, schools must prepare guidelines for educating each teen with disabilities according to his or her needs. Teachers, parents, therapists, and sometimes the teen student meet to review progress and ensure guidelines are followed and updated regularly, whenever fitting.

These guidelines are called an individualized education plan. They apply to any student up to age twenty-two. Individualized plans state whether a student needs

Some teens with Down syndrome like to cook, just like typical teens.

speech therapy or physical therapy. Plans cover whether a student works best in a class with nondisabled students or can benefit from separate classes with a specially trained teacher and smaller class size. Some teens may be included in a regular class and receive extra assistance with homework or extra time to take tests and complete homework. The setup depends upon a teen's ability and behavior.

For older students with disabilities, the law states that local schools must help families plan for future schooling or jobs, housing, recreation, and general adjustment to adulthood. This planning starts by the time a teen is sixteen years old. Planning may include access to transportation and state and local government services. The main objective is to figure out how teens can learn and achieve the greatest independence in programs that are most integrated within the typical community.

This teen enjoys working on his laptop outdoors.

"We're doing culinary arts in my school, and we make ice cream and breads," Sam explains. "I'm learning about cooking. Pasta and pizza. Kids work at a café. We bring snacks and cookies from the culinary arts program. Maybe I'll serve next year."[17]

Developing Interests

Most teens, including those with DS, know what they prefer to do. They may enjoy playing sports, listening to music, and creating crafts, activities other teens enjoy. But some teens with DS may need an extra push to find and become involved in activities outside of school and work.

This talented teen twirls a basketball on his finger, something not everyone can do, before shooting baskets.

"I hang out with my brothers. I read a book and watch television. I like Harry Potter. I like comics. School. Summer camp. At camp, we go bowling, exercise, yoga, swimming, tennis, weight lifting. Must best buddy and I go on field trips," Sam says.[18]

Communities vary in the types of activities open to teens with DS—or general activities that work for teens with and without DS. Be creative and investigate in your area. Park districts offer a range of classes, lessons, and team sports. Some special education districts pool their funds for recreational activities for teens with developmental delays. Districts may offer after-school activities or programs on weekends and during summers. Boy Scouts and Girl Scouts organize troops with disabled and nondisabled. People with delays can participate in programs through the YMCA, YWCA, and religious organizations.

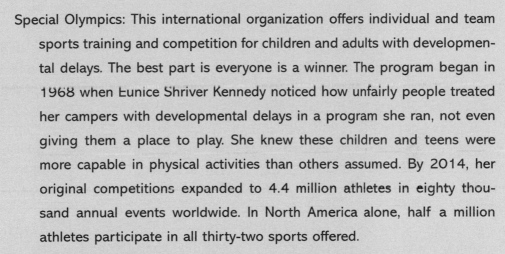

Special Olympics

Special Olympics is an umbrella group for several different programs. Each focuses on helping teenagers and adults with DS make friends and enjoy fun activities.

Special Olympics: This international organization offers individual and team sports training and competition for children and adults with developmental delays. The best part is everyone is a winner. The program began in 1968 when Eunice Shriver Kennedy noticed how unfairly people treated her campers with developmental delays in a program she ran, not even giving them a place to play. She knew these children and teens were more capable in physical activities than others assumed. By 2014, her original competitions expanded to 4.4 million athletes in eighty thousand annual events worldwide. In North America alone, half a million athletes participate in all thirty-two sports offered.

Unified Sports: This project grew from the success of the original Special Olympics program. The goal of Unified Sports is to include teens with disabilities in activities with nondisabled partners. They play on the same teams and share the same fun of participation.

Best Buddies: This program matches nondisabled college students with teenagers and young adults who have disabilities. Pairs meet on a regular basis to talk, play sports, or watch movies, whatever they choose to do together. The main emphasis is on friendship.

Becoming Social

Every teen experiences the same physical and emotional changes. Having DS does not change that. But teens with DS may be less skilled at understanding what is happening to their bodies. They may need specific instruction about what they can expect and how boys' and girls' bodies mature differently. Teens with DS may require special guidance as to what is private and what is public. This specific instruction limits embarrassing situations or times when other teens might take advantage of them as a joke.

Role playing, when people act out situations, is one way to help teens with DS learn how to deal with new situations. Role playing helps teens practice how to act and what to say with friends, dates, and strangers, and during job interviews. Acting out situations is one way to help teens with DS fit in, something all teens want to do.

After High School

Teens with DS display a range of interests, skills, and talents—just like teens without DS. Some go to college, a few at places that offer programs for students who need extra assistance. Most teens find jobs. For someone who is limited by physical skills, ability to pay attention, difficulties working safely, and skills to travel independently to and from work, finding employment can be tricky. High schools are supposed to offer training in areas geared toward future employment. But many cash-strapped school districts cannot. That means families often have to fight to find the best after-school setting for their teen with DS. Federal, state, and local agencies try to work with schools to offer a variety of employment settings.

The same situation exists in other Western countries. Interestingly, one woman with DS was elected to office in Spain. She champions laws that improve conditions for all people with disabilities.

"I want to be an honest politician," said Angela Covadonga Bachiller, Spain's first councillor with DS. "I don't like dishonest politicians and those who don't work for the people. I've always voted since I was eighteen years old, but other people [with DS] have never been able to. We [people with disabilities] want the laws relating to the right to vote changed."[19]

Types of Work Settings

Competitive employment is a full-time or part-time job in a regular work setting. Often, teens with DS begin working in high school to prepare them for employment after graduation. As with any worker, the teen receives wages and performs job tasks alongside others without DS.

Supported employment involves a regular work setting. But a job coach teaches job tasks and monitors the person with DS until independence is achieved. With some programs, the worker belongs to a crew of other teens who need monitoring. They travel to various work sites to perform simple tasks together, such a groundskeeping or housecleaning services.

Helping Someone Who Has DS

Ever get frustrated with a sibling or friend who has DS? Or do you find others get frustrated with your lack of understanding? Here are some tips to help learning—on both sides:

- Make sure someone gives instructions in simple language. Family and school rules need to be easy to understand.
- Request that directions remain fair and consistent. Rules need to apply over and over in the same way for all family members or classmates, no matter if DS is involved or not.
- Break down activities into smaller steps. If you are learning a new work task, ask someone to show one part of the job at a time, starting from the beginning. Once this step is practiced and mastered, perform the next step until all steps lead to a complete job.
- Repeat activities often. Teens with DS may need more practice to learn new information. Repetition provides that practice and helps them feel comfortable with learning something new. The same goes for anyone in a new situation.
- Give and receive praise. Everyone likes to feel that what he or she does is valued. If you receive praise—a pat on the back, kind words, whatever—for a job well done, you feel better about yourself and want to repeat what you have done. That goes for teens with or without DS.

With sheltered employment, the young adult with DS works with others who have DS in a sheltered workshop, adult day-care program, or work activity center. Staff members train these workers to complete jobs from community industries, such as bagging headsets or stuffing pillows for airlines. The work may include packaging, assembling, or sewing. Or workers might stuff envelopes or packages for mailing. Everyone on the job performs the same task that is supervised by staff trained to work with adults who have limited skills. Workers receive a small amount of pay for each completed item.

Adults who exhibit fewer skills remain in sheltered programs, too. But these programs concentrate on social, daily living, and recreation skills. Workers receive no pay.

Living Arrangements

The goal for every older teen should be to eventually achieve independent living; it's no different for teens with DS. But the type of residence depends upon how skilled someone is in managing food preparation, paying bills, and keeping house. Housing also depends on what your community offers.

Planning for independent living starts in high school, just as it does for college and employment. For some teens, learning how to manage on their own takes a little longer to master. Finding housing also may take longer, as many communities have limited choices for young adults who have a disability.

Twenty-four-hour programs care for adults who cannot manage for themselves. Staff members supervise every activity, from morning routines of dressing and eating to leisure activities and household chores. Some housing may be in group homes or apartment buildings. These residences house several young adults with live-in support staff who coordinate activities. Residents may work outside the home or go to adult day care or other community programs.

Semi-independent apartments offer similar supervision but allow residents to live alone or with a small group of friends. Residents usually hold daytime jobs and participate in after-work leisure activities. A staff person either lives nearby or is responsible to check in regularly.

The most independent adults with DS live and work on their own without supervision. Their parents live the dream they have for their children without DS.

Jason Kingsley provides the best summary of the future for teens with DS: "I will do my shopping. . . . I will do my cleaning. I will pay my bills. Intellectually in my brain I am very excited. In my feelings I'm still a little bit nervous. And someday I will get married and start my own history of being my own family."[20]

Resources

Organizations

Family Resource Center on Disabilities
11 East Adams
Chicago, IL 60603
312-939-3513
frcd.org

Government-funded information and training center with recent material about the most effective education for individuals with disabilities, accessibility laws, financing, college readiness, bullying, and resource links to other helpful organizations.

Global Down Syndrome Foundation
3300 East First Ave, Suite 390
Denver, CO 80206
303-321-6277
www.globaldownsyndrome.org
International organization dedicated to improving the lives of individuals with DS through research, medical care, education, and advocacy.

International Down Syndrome Coalition
PO Box 121
New Plymouth, ID 83655
901-413-2047
www.theidsc.org
Provides information, education, and connections to local resources, including meetups. The group coordinates seven national organizations for DS for the Random Acts of Kindness campaign to celebrate teens with DS on World Down Syndrome Day that occurs each March 21.

International Mosaic Down Syndrome Association
PO Box 321
Stow, MA 01775
855-IMDSA-21
www.imdsa.org
Group that offers support, information, and research about individuals affected by mosaic DS.

National Lekotek Center
2001 North Clybourn Avenue, First Floor
Chicago, IL 60614
773-528-5766
www.lekotek.org
International organization that hosts sixty centers in twenty-two states. The Swedish name means *lek* for "play" and *tek* for "library," and the group promotes social health that effects physical, cognitive, and emotional well-being. Lekotek provides a toy lending library, workshops, play sessions for kids with disabilities and their families, consulting, and programs in hospitals and community health

organizations. The group organized Compuplay, a program that provides computer-based play with adapted equipment and targeted software and has a toy evaluation program. The group may be a tad young for high-functioning teens with DS, but it may be beneficial for families with teens who are more disabled.

National Down Syndrome Adoption Network
c/o DSAGC
4623 Wesley Avenue, Suite A
Cincinnati, OH 45212
Birth parent line: 513-213-9615
Adoptive parent line: 513-709-1751
http://www.ndsan.org/
A free nonprofit program that provides support, information, and registry of families from throughout the United States who are interested in adopting for the parents whose baby received a diagnosis of DS and may be considering adoption.

National Down Syndrome Congress
30 Mansell Court, Suite 108
Roswell, GA 30076
800-232-6372
www.ndsccenter.org
Offshoot of the National DS Society with focus on national and legislative action in addition to educational and professional resources, a national convention, and a camp and program to help teens advocate for themselves.

National Association for Down Syndrome
1460 Renaissance Drive, Suite 405
Park Ridge, IL 60068
630-325-9112
www.nads.org
Oldest national organization serving individuals with DS and their families, providing family support, information, referrals, resources, public education, advocacy, and a conference.

The "R" Word Campaign: When You Say "Retard" Someone Hurts
www.therword.org
National campaign to change attitudes and reduce prejudice toward people with disabilities founded in 2007 by parents of a daughter with disabilities after she became the target of unkind words. The campaign has a blog, videos, and products designed to spread the word that "retard" is the same as every minority slur.

Special Olympics of North America
3712 Benson Drive, Suite 102
Raleigh, North Carolina 27609
919-785-0699
www.specialolympics.org
An international organization that supports individual and team sports training and competition for children and adults with developmental delays. The organization includes Unified Sports, where people with disabilities play on the same team with nondisabled players, and Best Buddies, a program that matches college students with teens and young adults who have a developmental delay to meet, share activities, and become friends.

U.S. Department of Education, Office of Special Education Programs
Center for Parent Information and Resources
35 Halsey Street, Fourth floor
Newark, NJ 07102
www.parentcenterhub.org
Site for information about the Individual with Disabilities Education Act and other laws affecting anyone with developmental delays.

Books

Brian Chicoine and Dennis McGuire, *The Guide to Good Health for Teens & Adults with Down Syndrome*, Bethesda, MD: Woodbine House, 2010. An easy-to-read reference guide with great tips that brings understanding to someone living with DS and living with someone who has Down syndrome.

Woodbine editors, *A Room of Golden Shells: 100 Works by Artists and Writers with Down Syndrome*, Bethesda, MD: Woodbine House, 2013. Collection of art produced by artists with Down syndrome ages fourteen to early fifties who created paintings, ceramics, poetry, and prose.

HEMOPHILIA: THE ROYAL BLOOD DISEASE

Healthy teens produce blood that clots. Clotting means blood cells form thickening masses that interfere with loss of blood. This process allows the body to heal from everyday scrapes and cuts that cause breaks in blood vessels. Clotting blood protects the body from lasting injury from trauma, whether inside the body or on the surface.

Usually, the clotting process begins with tiny, sticky particles in blood, called platelets. Platelets containing a substance called fibrin stem the flow of blood by

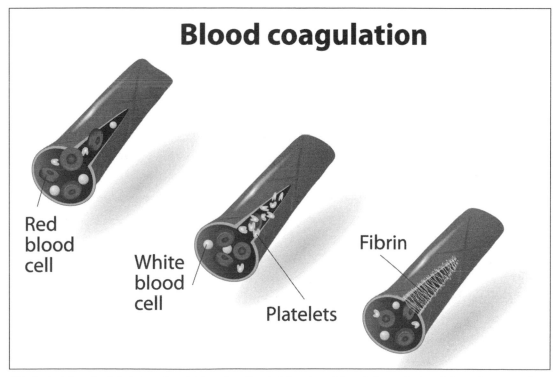

Blood coagulation

Red blood cell

White blood cell

Platelets

Fibrin

Fibrin in blood platelets of red blood cells clot to stop blood flow during injury to vessels.

Shelby

When I was two, an unusually large bruise developed across my back and refused to heal. My parents were confused. How can this be? This bruise isn't normal. . . . Necessarily, their concern carried them (and me) to the emergency room—a site that will become commonplace to me as I age. Three days later, a test returned positive for hemophilia, and my problem was solved. I was treated with a plasma product; the bruise healed; but I went home a hemophiliac, a free-bleeder. And my life changed forever.[a]

---

surging to the source of the bleeding. Once at the injured area, platelets release chemicals. In turn, the chemicals trigger other blood proteins to strengthen the clot and block bleeding.

Some chemicals attract more platelets, while others help platelets stick together. These proteins are known as clotting factors. Your body produces twelve different clotting factors that act together to seal wounds.

Teens with hemophilia experience difficulty with their blood clotting. They are born with few or none of certain clotting factors. Without the ability to clot properly, a teen may bruise more easily or bleed longer, even from the smallest injury. Even minor injuries can trigger life-threatening blood loss.

Bleeding from external injuries can be a problem. But these are not the most serious. More difficulties result from bleeding inside the body. With internal bleeding, blood seeps into tissues, muscles, and joints, particularly in elbows, knees, and ankles. You may not realize internal bleeding occurs until organs or tissues signal serious damage. For example, bleeding in the brain can appear as headaches or trouble focusing. These and other symptoms signal bleeding that can be life threatening.

"I was born in the Philippines; there wasn't any treatment where we lived," Jamie explained. "When I had a bleed, the treatment was to wrap it up, put ice on it, and keep me immobile. I missed a lot of school—about three or four months every year—because I was getting a lot of bleeds. I'd take a wheelchair to school while I was recovering from a bleed."[1]

Clotting problems affect the most basic traditions and body functions. Females may have longer, heavier periods. Males may bleed excessively after circumcision. Going to the dentist becomes a major ordeal because bleeding from the mouth may be difficult to stop. Similarly, cutting or losing a tooth can trigger extreme bleeding.

At first, hemophilia may not appear obvious in babies, especially boys who are not circumcised. Parents may not notice signs of bleeding in their babies for years, if hemophilia proves mild. Often, the first signals are frequent or large bruises that develop after little bumps or falls, such as from learning to walk. Other red flags alert parents when children bleed heavily after dental procedures, during surgery, or from an accident. These are signs to have children tested for hemophilia.

Types of Hemophilia by the Numbers

Hemophilia falls into two main categories based on which clotting factor the body lacks. Both are rare. Only one in ten thousand people worldwide live with hemophilia.[2] In the United States, hemophilia occurs in about one in five thousand, mostly male, births. Currently, only about twenty thousand people in the United States experience hemophilia.[3]

Researchers classify clotting factors by assigning them different Roman numerals. More teens, or about eight out of ten, with the condition have hemophilia A. Teens with hemophilia A either lack or produce low levels of the protein called clotting factor VIII. Teens with hemophilia B represent about another two in ten cases. They produce little or no clotting factor IX.

Doctors identify types of hemophilia by one of three levels: mild, moderate, or severe. The levels correspond to how much clotting factor measures in the bloodstream. If you have normal factors VIII and IX, your numbers should range between 50 and 100 percent.

"With prophylactic [preventive] treatment I worry less about having bleeds as I go through my daily activities," Trevor said. "My annual bleed rate is about one or two bleeds a year. It's really been a while since my last bleed, and I haven't had to miss any school for hemophilia-related emergencies."[4]

With mild hemophilia—and numbers slightly below this range—the person rarely bleeds. The body produces 2 to 5 percent of the specific clotting factor. In this situation, most bleeding occurs after severe assaults to the body, such as from surgery. Some teens with mild hemophilia A never discover their diagnosis until they reach adulthood.

"My family moved to the United States permanently when I was twelve," Jamie said. "When I was thirteen, I learned how to self-infuse. I infuse every other day now. I can't imagine going back to on-demand treatment. When I was getting treatment on demand I could feel my muscles getting really sore, which indicated the start of a bleed for me. I would have frequent bleeds, which made me stop each time to treat them."[5]

Severe hemophilia is not so subtle. Seven out of ten teens with hemophilia A experience the most severe form. With a clotting factor of less than 1 percent, bleeding creates a risky situation that needs immediate attention. Delaying treatment results in bleeding that lasts longer, is more difficult to stop, and takes longer to heal.

Long History of Hemophilia

Hemophilia is a clotting condition with a colorful history. The first writings about abnormal bleeding appeared in the second century. Jewish rabbis recommended that a baby boy need not be circumcised, part of Jewish law, if two brothers already died from cutting their penis foreskin.

Later, the New Testament mentioned a woman who bled excessively for twelve years until she touched Jesus's garment. A tenth-century Arabian physician, Abulcasis, explained how males in one family died from bleeding after injury.

In 1803 a Philadelphia doctor, John Otto, published the first article that described a family with men who bled excessively. Otto traced the disease back to 1720 and a female relative who lived in Plymouth, New Hampshire, indicating inherited disease. In 1828, student Friedrich Hopff first named the condition *heamorrhaphilia*, which later became hemophilia.[6]

The most well-known hemophilia carrier of the then-deadly disease was Queen Victoria of England. During her reign (1837–1901), her physicians

Sad Days for Teens with Hemophilia

In the 1970s nobody knew much about tainted blood that infected kids with hemophilia. Doctors only knew the name of the disease that accompanied this bad blood, Acquired Immunodeficiency Syndrome (AIDS). At the time, the public believed AIDS spread through body fluids, including blood, and it meant certain death. But blood transfusions were a lifeline for many teens with hemophilia.

Thirteen-year-old Ryan White required two or three blood injections each month to boost his blood's clotting power. Injections allowed him to feel healthy, maintain good grades, enjoy time with his girlfriend, and play baseball. But soon after injections began, Ryan experienced bouts of weakness and sickness. Tests later showed that Ryan had contracted AIDS through his blood transfusions.

Ryan's Kokomo, Indiana, community panicked. Parents worried their child could catch AIDS by being in Ryan's classroom. School administrators misunderstood how unlikely chances were that Ryan could transmit AIDS by touching another child. Despite medical facts, the school district barred Ryan from attending public school. Since this was way before home computers and Skype, Ryan received his seventh-grade education by telephone at home.

Kokomo turned against the entire White family. They pelted the family car with eggs. They slashed tires and broke windows in the house. After someone shot a bullet through the living room window, the Whites moved to Cicero, Indiana. By then, the entire nation knew of Ryan's dangerous, unreasonable treatment in Kokomo. Celebrities, such as musicians Elton John and Michael Jackson and Olympic diver Greg Louganis, befriended Ryan and assisted with his growing medical bills.

Cicero schools welcomed Ryan. Administrators went out of their way to educate the community about hemophilia and AIDS. Even though Ryan craved a normal life, he welcomed opportunities to advocate for other children with AIDS. He appeared on television and at benefits. He granted magazine interviews. He addressed a White House hearing about AIDS. Throughout his painful physical ordeal, he maintained a message of hope and faith.

On April 8, 1990, Ryan White died. His funeral brought together about 1,500 mourners, including friends, family, and famous people. Everyone came to honor the courageous teen who lived with hemophilia yet spoke up for others with AIDS. Ryan's efforts led to discovery of manufactured blood products that do not rely on blood donations. And blood products now receive thorough testing before being prepared for injections.[b]

discovered that she was a carrier, which means she inherited the affected X gene from her mother, Princess Victoria (1786–1861). Queen Victoria unknowingly transmitted hemophilia to her son Leopold and two daughters. The daughters, in turn, became carriers who affected their offspring.

As royal families intermarried across Europe, which was common during the nineteenth century, so went hemophilia. The Russian royal family included young Alexis (1904–1918), heir to the throne before he was killed, who descended from

Victoria and had hemophilia. With so many family members across Europe and Russia having hemophilia, subjects crowned the condition the royal disease.

Nothing is royal about this serious genetic disorder, however. In fact, the condition knows no boundaries. Rich, poor, different races—it doesn't matter, although hemophilia affects males more often. Some females acquire hemophilia, but most are carriers who may or may not experience bleeding symptoms. Essentially, anyone with the wrong genetic code can acquire or pass on hemophilia.

A Genetic Problem—Mostly

Hemophilia usually passes from parents to offspring through genes. You already read (see chapter 1) how individuals have twenty-three pairs of chromosomes. This number includes two sex chromosomes: X and Y. Mothers inherit two X chromosomes, while fathers possess one of each. The problem for females comes when one X chromosome contains the gene for hemophilia. Mothers who pass on a defective X gene for hemophilia have a 50 percent chance of giving their sons bleeding problems.

"I am here because . . . I was a boy who received a defective X chromosome from his mother," Shelby Smoak wrote in his memoir *Bleeder*. "Of course it is not her fault, for until I was born, she didn't know she carried the defect. In fact, I am the only proof of it."[7]

Daughters are more complicated as far as X and Y genes go. They rarely receive the disorder, but it's not impossible. If full-blown hemophilia does happen, symptoms would probably be mild. For a daughter to develop hemophilia, she has to be born with an altered X chromosome from each parent.[8]

More often, daughters who possess one defective X chromosome become carriers. Therefore, they can pass hemophilia on to their offspring. In a weird twist of genetics, boys cannot inherit the defective chromosome from their fathers; only girls can. According to the National Hemophilia Foundation, a female carrier passes one of four possible scenarios on to her infant:[9]

- the baby girl is not a carrier
- the baby girl is a carrier
- the baby boy is healthy
- the baby boy has hemophilia

In rare cases, hemophilia is acquired later in life, rather than from birth. Such a form of nongenetic hemophilia is thought to result from an autoimmune response. The body manufactures antibodies that attack certain blood clotting

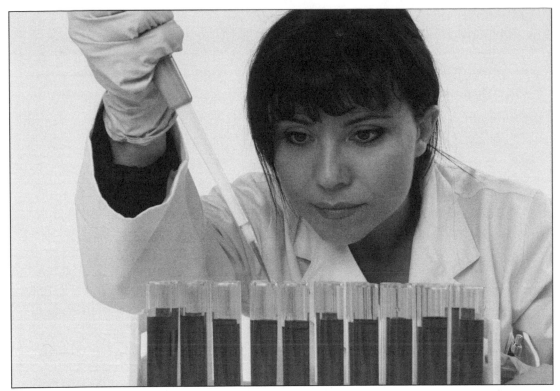

Testing blood for HIV prevents teens with hemophilia from acquiring the disease from tainted blood.

factors. When clotting factors cannot do their job, hemophilia occurs. But most information about hemophilia refers to inherited forms.

Diagnosing Blood Disorders

Seeing your regular doctor is the first step toward finding a diagnosis. As with most conditions, the doctor will want a careful medical and family history. Knowing other relatives have a bleeding disorder will alert the doctor to request a blood test for you. The test evaluates your clotting ability and the time it takes to form a clot. The clotting factor test is called an assay, and this test establishes the type of hemophilia and how severe it is.

If the test proves positive for hemophilia, you and your parents will probably be referred to one of the federally funded hemophilia treatment centers around the country. Here a team of blood specialists, or hematologists, and other trained staff assist in your treatment plan and follow-up. Teens and their parents should receive genetic counseling from a trained professional to assess risks of giving birth to another child with hemophilia.

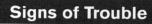

Signs of Trouble

● Abnormal bleeding is the first sign that someone needs to be investigated further. Head for the doctor when you or someone you know experiences any of these signs of excessive or frequent bleeding:

External bleeding

- mouth bleeding from a cut, bite, or losing a tooth
- sudden nosebleeds that won't quit
- massive bleeding from a minor cut
- repeat bleeding after flow stopped

Internal bleeding

- blood in urine (bladder/kidneys)
- blood in stool (stomach/intestines)
- unusual/large bruises (muscles)
- bleeding without injury (joints)
- painful head or neck pain/stiffness; repeated vomiting; sleepiness; behavior changes; double vision; seizures; sudden weakness/clumsiness (brain)[c]

Treating Hemophilia

The first line of defense for preventing hemophilia bleeding episodes is replacement therapy. Teens with hemophilia receive clotting factor either dripped or injected into their veins. Injections replace whichever clotting factor is low or missing.

Clotting factor products may or may not come from human blood. With human blood, donations are screened and treated to avoid spread of other diseases. Blood sources are tightly controlled, compared with when Ryan White (see page 84) contracted AIDS from his transfusions. Blood that is genetically engineered reduces this risk. Synthetic clotting factor is less fragile than human blood. Processed blood is easy to store, mix, and inject at home.

Your doctor may recommend replacement therapy on a regular basis or as needed, whenever bleeding won't stop. The main problem with on-demand

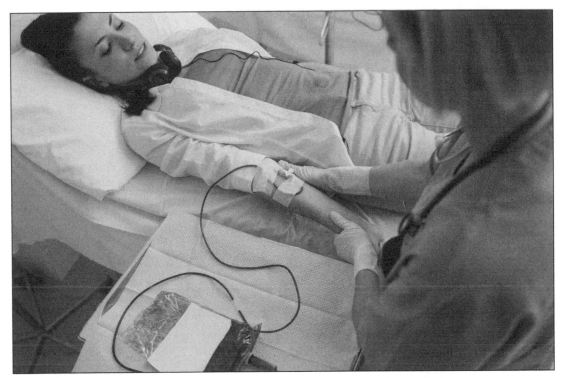

This nurse at a blood bank is removing the needle from a blood transfusion.

therapy is you might not be aware of internal bleeding. So you risk damage before you notice the need for treatment.

Another problem develops when teens produce antibodies to their clotting factor. In this situation, antibodies react to the clotting factor once it enters the bloodstream. Antibodies attack and destroy the clotting factor, so it cannot do its job. Researchers are working on ways to prevent an autoimmune reaction to clotting factors.

Many teens prefer to receive therapy at home. At-home injections offer less delay in treatment and fewer doctor office visits. Home therapy reduces cost and allows you to eventually take control of your own treatment, if you haven't already.

"I don't like to have to infuse, but prophylactic treatment [ongoing rather than when crisis hits] has helped me worry less about having bleeds, so I can enjoy doing the things I like," Trevor said. "I recommend it. My philosophy is: Be careful, but go out and enjoy each day."[10]

To ease the injection process, your doctor might suggest implanting a device in a vein. The needle goes into the device instead of your skin. That way, you never have to stick yourself repeatedly. Many teens prefer this way of receiving replacement therapy. The main drawback is when the device clogs or becomes infected. So you need to explore all the alternatives and how to handle problems before making a decision.

Shelby

In his autobiography, Shelby describes what happened to him during his freshman year of college:

Before the first week of classes ends, I develop a knee bleed. . . . "Bleed" is a hemophiliac's jargon for what doctors call a hemathrosis: the accumulation of blood in the joint. . . . Bleeds also hurt and, when in the knees, make walking difficult.

I . . . limp gently to my door, lock it for privacy, then hobble to the refrigerator and remove my factor. Before infusing, it must come to room temperature, a process that takes about half an hour. Once I infused with it fresh from the fridge, and soon I felt my heart turn into a block of ice. . . . After this, I retrieve the supplies hidden underneath my bed. . . . I pump my fist and search for a vein. I feel like a junkie. Like an addict's veins, my own have become bruised and callused from constant dependence. . . .

I extend my arm, tighten the tourniquet above my elbow, pump my fist, stick the needle in my arm, and then I wait for the familiar blood return in the plastic tubing. . . . I begin infusing, one CC at a time, so that the process takes about twenty-five minutes. Yet factor is not an instant cure: it takes time to work. . . . So I fluff my pillow underneath my swollen knee, and suppress its full throb with Tylenol.[d]

Your doctor should be able to suggest pain medication and physical therapy to help reduce reactions to the injections, both at the injection sight and to the blood product itself. In addition, scientists are testing methods to correct faulty genes that result in hemophilia. The science isn't there yet, but it's close.

Living with Hemophilia

Most teens with hemophilia live a pretty regular life, even with all the extra activities surrounding the condition. You go to school, have a job, and engage in activities for fun with friends. You might have a special friend. You may also be at a point in your life when you feel it's time to pull away from parents and become more independent. These are all part of growing up. But you still need to pay particular attention to your health to ensure these activities happen as they should.

General Tips to Remember

You already know the usual suggestions for maintaining good health (see chapter 11). Well, they are even more important for teens with hemophilia.

For example, exercise. Always a good thing to do. For teens with hemophilia, strengthening muscles helps lessen bleeding from injuries. But not all exercise works with your condition. Leave contact sports, such as football, lacrosse, hockey, and boxing to teens who never experience life-threatening bleeds. Instead, focus on less risky bicycling, swimming, hiking, or other low-impact activities. Swimming in particular puts less stress on joints while exerting all muscle groups.

"I don't sit around, afraid to be active because I'm concerned about getting a bleed," Trevor said. "I'm as active as any teenager, except I know I can't play football or hockey or other contact sports. I usually run or swim. I was on the swim team this year in school."[11]

Weight is an issue for any age person. But for teens with hemophilia, extra pounds can increase bleeding by stressing parts of the body. If weight is an issue for you, talk with your doctor about healthy ways to manage diet and exercise.

Pain control can be more difficult with hemophilia. You cannot take the usual over-the-counter products that contain aspirin, ibuprofen, or naproxen sodium. These ingredients prevent blood from clotting, which will increase your bleeds. Ask your hematologist which medications you can take for pain relief.

Teen years are a time to gain more control over your life. Becoming independent can be stressful in the best of circumstances. With hemophilia, independence becomes more than time management, homework, handling finances, and separating from parents; there are also health concerns, which means your parents might have more difficulty letting go of you. Have patience with them.

Your job is to show your parents you can handle your own factor injections, order your supplies, manage doctor appointments, and keep logs your doctor requires. If you are trying to figure out how to live away from home, say in a college dorm, you also need to take responsibility for your own laundry, schedules, room cleaning, and possibly preparing meals.

Remember, you don't have to manage everything on your own. You can talk with your parents. You can consult with your hemophilia team or contact someone at the local hemophilia association. If you're still in grade or high school, try to get away to camps with other teens who have your condition. Camp provides the support to help you learn to cope with injections and other medical activities,

---

Craig

Hemophilia runs in my family. Both my younger brother and I have hemophilia. We started going to the Midwest Hemophilia Association's Wilderness Camp. . . . It was comforting to be around kids like myself. It is amazing what can happen when a seventeen-year-old talks to a seven-year-old who is afraid to self-infuse. I am an advocate that with proper training a kid can begin to learn to self-infuse and start the journey to becoming self-sufficient. The camp community helps kids understand that hemophilia is something they can take charge of and learn to manage.[e]

---

while allowing you to be a regular teen with others who understand what you're experiencing.

First Aid for Bleeds

One way to show you're more independent is to handle minor bleeds *and* know when to seek professional treatment. Living with Hemophilia, a Canadian website, offers a handy way to remember how to manage bleeds. The site authors call its first aid plan RICE. This stands for Rest, Ice, Compression, Elevation.[12]

- **R**est: If you have a bleed, make sure you rest that part of your body. Use crutches or a cane for a knee or ankle injury. Tape a splint onto the bruised part of your body to immobilize it.
- **I**ce: Ice reduces swelling and pain. Apply either a plastic bag of ice, wrapped ice in a towel, or bag of frozen vegetables for ten to fifteen minutes at a time. Too long an application may weaken the muscle. Reapply ice about every two hours.
- **C**ompression: More severe bleeds benefit from applied pressure to close off blood vessels. Pressure slows bleeding and allows your clotting factor to work. Use an elastic bandage wrapped in a figure-eight pattern. Look out for the injured limb becoming numb, cool, or changing colors. This is a sign you wrapped the bandage too tightly.
- **E**levation: Raise the injured body part above your heart, if possible. This position helps decrease pressure in blood vessels and slow bleeding. Elevate with cushions or pillows to be more comfortable.

Famous People with Hemophilia

Hemophilia may be life long, but it doesn't have to limit what you do. Besides Ryan White and Queen Victoria and her royal descendants, several well-known people have lived—and prospered—with hemophilia. Many more, like humanitarian Mother Teresa, were rumored to have the condition. (But history never confirmed this diagnosis.) Here is a sampling of people you might recognize who have had hemophilia:

- Richard Burton (1925–1984) acted in sixty-one films and earned seven Academy Award nominations. He lived for fifty-nine years and then died of a stroke in 1984.
- Jesse Schrader (born 1985) was a left-handed pitcher in an independent baseball league. With a 92 mph pitch, he earned the strikeout record for nine innings from Tiffin University. In 2015 he competed on two amateur baseball teams. At times, he iced his arm after each game.
- Alexandra Borstein (born 1973) is an actor, comedian, and film writer—and carrier of hemophilia. She is the voice of Lois Griffin in the television show *Family Guy* and participated in the *Power Rangers* and *Barbie* cartoons. Borstein acted in several films, including *Good Night and Good Luck* and *Bad Santa*. She speaks on behalf of people with hemophilia.
- Alex Dowsett (born 1988) is an English professional racing cyclist who won several British championships in 2011 and 2012. Before he could compete in the 2012 Olympics, he was sidelined by a broken elbow—not his hemophilia.
- Barry Haarde (born 1965) became in 2013 the first person with hemophilia to bike across the United States to bring attention to and raise funds for the condition. Haarde contracted HIV and hepatitis C from blood during hemophilia treatment and suffered total knee replacement from nerve disease as a result of his illnesses. Yet, he traveled 3,456 miles from Costa Mesa, California, to Amesbury, Massachusetts, to fund-raise for "Wheels for the World," an international organization that brings medical supplies to patients in developing countries.[f]

Remember, if you cannot control heavy bleeding or you experience signs of internal bleeding, call your hemophilia team or doctor. Or head for the emergency room at the nearest clinic or hospital.

Resources

Organizations

Hemophilia Federation of America
820 First Street NE, Suite 720
Washington, DC 20002
800-230-9797
www.hemophiliafed.org
Group that claims to be the largest patient-focused organization to provide programs, services, consumer advocacy, and forums for community members to learn and support each other. Its website hosts a special young adult hangout with teens discussing different relevant topics from dating and relationships to travel overseas. The organization hosts Hemophilia Awareness Month in March.

Hemophilia Treatment Centers Network
www.cdc.gov/ncbddd/hemophilia/HTC.html
National network of twelve regional centers that has teams devoted to improving outcomes for families dealing with inherited bleeding disorders. Centers offer complete and specialized health care, including dentists, social workers, therapies, nutritionists, and experts in financial assistance who help coordinate with schools, insurance companies, and pharmaceutical companies and conduct the latest research.

National Hemophilia Foundation
7 Penn Plaza, Suite 1204
New York, NY 10001
212-328-3700
800-424-2634 (resource information center)
Organization begun in 1948 that is dedicated to finding cures and treatments for blood disorders and hosts local chapters with programs and fund-raising, supportive walks. Contact the National Hemophilia Foundation for brochures (some according to age) and information at 800-424-2634 (800-42-HANDI).

World Federation of Hemophilia
1425 Boulevard René Lévesque O.

Bureau 1010
Montreal, Quebec
H36G 1T7 Canada
514-875-7944
www.whf.org
Fifty-year-old global organization that supports professional and patient education, advocacy, and research. The site has a special children's section complete with activities and a picture book explaining the role of blood and the effects of hemophilia.

Books

Not much has been written for teens about hemophilia. A book, or two, is old, and there are many self-published accounts that need verifying. Here are two credible resources.

Stephen Pemberton, *The Bleeding Disease: Hemophilia and the Unintended Consequences of Medical Progress*, Baltimore, MD: Johns Hopkins University Press, 2011. General look at hemophilia and its long history.
Michelle Raabe, *Hemophilia*, New York: Chelsea House, 2008. Comprehensive account of hemophilia in the Diseases and People series for teens.

MELANOMA AND OTHER SKIN CANCERS: SKIN DEEP AND NO FUN

Skin cancers seem to appear out of nowhere. They can show up any place skin covers the body. And they can have different degrees of severity. Some cancer growths are easily cut out. Others, like more serious melanoma, spread beyond the original sight to different parts of the body. Often, the spread causes deadly results. Each variety creates its own level of anxiety.

Skin Cancer by the Numbers

The Skin Cancer Foundation reports that skin cancer touches hundreds of thousands of Americans each year. One in five people will develop skin cancer during their lifetime, up sharply from three decades ago. More people have been diagnosed with skin cancer in the past three decades than with all other

Kody

I'm a senior in high school. I was first diagnosed almost two years ago. I had this thing on the bottom of my foot that was misdiagnosed. The doctor thought it was a Plantar wart [rough patch on the sole of the foot caused by a virus]. Not long after, my glands swelled up. That's when the doctor did surgery. He cut out the thing on my foot, then the lump on my groin. Each was sent for testing. Then sample results came back. The diagnosis was stage 4 melanoma.[a]

Natalie

I tanned indoors for the first time when I was sixteen but not regularly until my freshman year of college, when I went about once every two weeks. I tanned because I felt it made me look prettier and skinnier. My grandmother begged me not to tan because she was scared I'd get skin cancer. I was like, "No, it's not going to happen to me."

During my sophomore and junior years, my friends and I usually tanned twelve to fifteen minutes at least once a week. During summers in Florida, I just lay out. I never used sunscreen, just lathered up with tanning oil. I don't think I used sunscreen once in seven years!

Since the end of my teens, I've been vigilant about getting my skin checked once a year because I'm pretty mole-y. The first time I went [to the doctor] it was fine. [But] when I was twenty-one, the doctor biopsied one suspicious lesion on my back, and another on my foot. The spot on my back turned out to be a melanoma in situ, meaning it hadn't gone past the skin surface, so it was 100 percent curable with surgery. But I couldn't believe I had done that to myself by tanning—there was no one else to blame. I had to tell my mom—and hear her cry.[b]

---

cancers combined. That's nearly five million Americans treated each year for skin cancer.[1]

One rare form of melanoma, pediatric melanoma, strikes children as young as newborn. As children age, numbers of melanoma cases increase. While pediatric melanoma accounts for 2 percent of childhood cancers, numbers increase to 8 percent of cancers for teens.[2] What's equally scary is melanoma, the most deadly variety, "is the most common form of cancer for young adults 25–29 years old." Melanoma is also "the second most common form of cancer for young people 15–25 years."[3] A video about melanoma, "Dear 16-Year-Old Self," calls melanoma a "young person's disease."[4]

Chronic Disease or Not?

Technically, skin cancer isn't a chronic disease. Under the best circumstances, whatever spots you find can be removed. But if they appear when you're a teen—

or younger—skin cancer becomes something that requires lifelong watching. A diagnosis means you always require regular doctor visits to check and recheck that new skin growths never form, causing cancer to return. And you must follow medical guidelines to care for your skin to make sure cancer stays away. Of course, the best plan is to protect your skin *before* anything can happen.

Your Protective Covering: Skin

To understand skin cancer, you need to know something about your skin. Skin has several important jobs to help your body function smoothly. This protective outer tissue covers the body. Because it stores water and fat, skin seals in body fluids and helps regulate body temperature. Skin also protects against infection and injury to internal structures and other tissues.

Your skin is a massive sensory organ, one loaded with nerve endings. These extensive nerve endings let you feel touch, pressure, heat, and cold. Pretty impressive for an organ that measures one-tenth of an inch deep, more or less depending upon location.

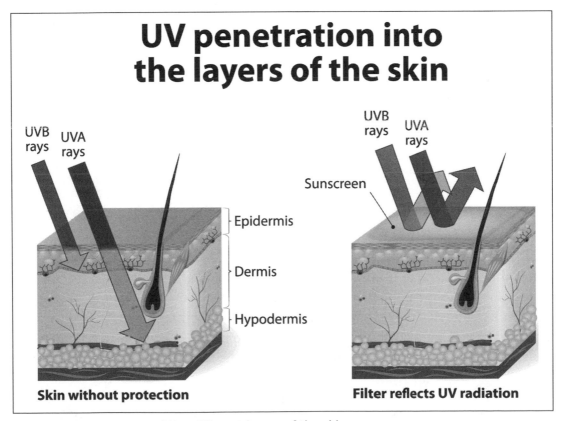

Sun rays penetrate any of the different layers of the skin.

Skin contains three separate layers, each with a different job. The layers are called epidermis, dermis, and subcutaneous. The epidermis is the thin outer skin layer. Mostly, this layer is made up of flat cells called squamous cells and deeper basal cells that control skin color. Their surface, which sloughs off dead cells, is covered with sweat, oil, and fine hairs. These components help the body resist germs and limit light damage from the sun.

Under the epidermis is the thicker dermis layer. This layer contains blood vessels, lymph vessels, and oil and sweat glands. The glands produce substances that extend to the surface of the skin through tiny openings called pores. Glands and the substances they produce give skin its strength and flexibility. The bottom skin layer, or subcutaneous layer, contains fat cells that absorb shock between the skin and tissues and organs inside the body.

What Is Skin Cancer?

Before focusing on cancer of the skin, it's important to understand what cancer is. Normally, healthy cells grow and divide, creating new cells whenever the body needs them. With time, many cells age or become damaged. These usually die and are replaced with new healthy cells. Sometimes, this process changes. Cells that should die don't. Or cells multiply faster than normal, causing cells to form larger masses.

Any uncontrolled, abnormal growth of cells is a sign to check for cancer. Usually, the unwanted cell cluster is benign, meaning free of cancer. But you still need to be watched because sometimes abnormal cell clusters can spread and turn troublesome. With skin cancer, however, these changes cause skin cells to grow out of control. If left to spread, they can invade other parts of the body, causing harm, even death.

Types of Skin Cancer

Scientists define three main types of skin cancer, although there are several uncommon varieties. Types of cancer correspond to the layer of skin where cancer originates. Basal cell cancer is the most common form of skin cancer in the United States. It shows up in the basal cell layer of skin. Basal cell cancer commonly begins in parts of the body that are exposed to the sun. At first, the cells look like small, pink bumps or flat, scaly red skin. When the bumps are cancerous, they may show blood vessels in the spot or surrounding skin. They may bleed easily when bumped or scraped. The good news is basal cell cancer grows slowly. With relatively simple surgery, it can be completely cured.

What to Look For

Figuring out if marks on your skin are cancerous can drive you crazy. Leave a diagnoses to the pros. Head for the doctor if you notice any changes in color, size, shape, or texture of an existing mole. To help you remember what to look for, the National Cancer Institute says to consider your ABCs.

- *Asymmetry*: Does one side of the mole look different from the other?
- *Border*: Check if mole borders appear irregular. Are the edges blurry, notched, or ragged? Did pigment/color spread to surrounding skin?
- *Color*: Is mole color uneven? Are there shaded patches of black, brown, or tan? Do you see specks of blue, gray, red, pink, or white sprinkling your little mole?
- *Diameter*: Has width or length changed since you first noticed your mole? Some skin cancers are tiny. But most melanomas grow larger than a pea.
- *Evolving*: Have you noticed any other changes over weeks or months? If not in A, B, C, or D, what about texture? Some melanomas harden skin, look lumpy, or ooze or bleed easily. Some teens complain of itching, tenderness, or pain. Take these signs seriously, and seek another opinion if your first doctor isn't impressed.[c]

Squamous cell skin cancer is more serious than basal. When untreated, squamous cells move slightly faster than basal cells into nearby lymph nodes, sending cancer elsewhere in the body. But if treated early, this form of cancer has a high cure rate. Squamous cells look red and scaly and can develop from precancerous lesions. The lesions usually appear on parts of the body most exposed to sunlight, such as backs of hands, ears, and face. Squamous cell cancer needs to be surgically removed, too.

Melanoma presents the most health risks. This serious form of cancer can be cured if treated early. But if left untreated, it quickly spreads to other organs of the body, such as liver and lungs. Although melanoma is relatively uncommon, it causes the majority of deaths from skin cancer. Melanoma cells originate in parts

Chelsea

I'm surrounded by people who have always loved tanning salons. Both of my grandmothers tanned indoors and my aunt actually had a tanning bed in her home. I visited my first tanning salon at age fourteen. For about six years, I tanned for approximately twelve minutes three to four times a week for a month before major events, like prom. Tanning was a social event for me: my college friends and I would carpool to the salon. I just wanted to have a "healthy glow." (I hate that phrase now!) I thought if I only went a few times a year, I'd be fine.

When I was 23, I scratched an itch on my back that felt like a scab. My boyfriend looked at it and said that the mole on my left shoulder had scabbed over and was leaking a clear fluid. I knew that wasn't normal, so I called the dermatologist the next day. The dermatologist did a full body check and thought I was okay, but decided to remove the suspicious mole, just to be safe. Ten days later I was having the stitches taken out and joking with my boyfriend when the dermatologist walked in and blurted out that I had melanoma. He . . . prepared me to hear that the melanoma had spread and that I would need treatment.[d]

of the epidermis that contain pigment that gives skin color. The cells cluster into irregular moles that can range in color from brown to black to blue. To make detection more complicated, they can appear in areas not usually exposed to direct sun, such as the back or soles of feet. When moles show irregular outer lines or change color, they need a doctor to inspect them for definite diagnosis. Sometimes, a teen can have between ten and forty moles at once. The same as with other skin changes, early detection of melanoma provides the best chance for a cure.

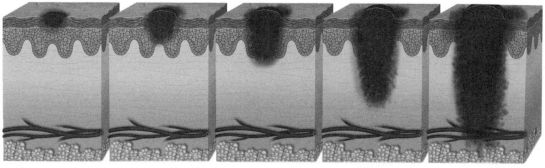

Different stages of melanoma are based on how deeply the cancer extends.

Defining Stages of Skin Cancers

Doctors treat skin cancer based on which stage it is. Identifying stage determines what treatment will work best. The National Cancer Institute suggests staging based on growth size, its depth into the skin, and whether cancer cells have invaded other parts of the body.

- Stage 0: This stage involves only the top layer of the skin. With melanoma, the name is melanoma in situ. With other skin cancers, the condition is called carcinoma in situ.
- Stage I: The growth is less than one millimeter thick (about the width of a sharp pencil point) with a broken surface with melanoma or as large as two centimeters wide (about the size of a peanut) with other cancers. Melanomas can also grow between one and two millimeters thick without a broken surface.
- Stage II: The growth measures between one and two millimeters thick or more than two millimeters. Either size exhibits a broken surface.
- Stage III: Cancer cells have spread to nearby tissues or at least one lymph node, the body's drainage system that sends fluids throughout the body and back to the bloodstream.
- Stage IV: Cancer cells, either squamous or melanoma, have spread to other parts of the body. Melanoma cells can reach into the lungs or other organs, skin areas, or distant lymph nodes. Usually, melanoma first spreads to other parts of the skin, tissue under the skin, lymph nodes, and lungs. The next path is to other organs, such as the liver, brain, and bones, where it gets particularly nasty.[e]

Who Gets Skin Cancer?

Skin cancer is an equal opportunity invader. The disease doesn't care about your age, gender, or nationality. Once common wisdom suggested that dark-skinned people never got skin cancer, but that turned out to be untrue. What is true is the lighter your skin, the greater your chances are that skin cancer develops. Similarly, skin cancers appear more often in people of color on areas with less pigment, such as palms, soles of feet, and nail beds.[5] More teens who are fair skinned and have red or blond hair and blue or green eyes are at risk of skin cancer than their dark-skinned, dark-haired friends.

Family history plays a role, too, especially for the most serious cancers. Anyone whose mother, father, sister, or brother experienced melanoma has a greater likelihood of developing the disease. The same with some rarer forms of skin cancer. Altered genes can transform into a deadly mix with repeated X-rays or exposure to chemicals in arsenic, coal, tar, paraffin (used in candles), and certain heavy oils.[6]

But the greatest threat of skin cancer comes from exposure to sunlight, with its ultraviolet (UV) rays. At one time, teens sat in the sun for hours, just to get a tan. If anyone burned or freckled, well, that was the penalty for beauty. Over the years, studies proved that sunlight and UV rays cause skin cancers. This was especially true in light-skinned teens who burned easily. What's worse is tanning is cumulative. This means that risk increases each time your body is exposed to more sun every year—no matter what type of skin you have. Certain medications enhance the danger, increasing the possibility of burning. So read labels on all medications you are given. Cover up when outside, particularly if you take sulfa

Kate

At sixteen I was legally permitted [in Canada] to tan indoors. My parents were against it, but I started tanning anyway, at first weekly, then 2 to 3 times a week. I ended up tanning up to sixteen times a month for approximately 12 to 15 minutes a session.

After graduating high school, I went straight to the salon to apply for a job. When I was hired I signed a contract saying I would maintain a tanned appearance. . . . I believed in what I was doing. We [salon staff] were sent to seminars with scientists who told us that tanning beds prevented cancer. I worked at this salon for two-and-a-half years. [When in college] my mother noticed that the freckle on my stomach had changed. . . . I went to a dermatologist who thought it looked fine. But he did a biopsy, and left an inch-long scar. Three weeks later the doctor called to tell me that the "freckle" was a melanoma, the deadliest kind of skin cancer. I dropped the phone and broke down. I had truly believed what I'd been taught by the industry. . . . I was brainwashed.[f]

drugs, tetracycline, thiazide diuretics, nonsteroid anti-inflammatory medications, and certain antidepressants.

Sunlamps and tanning booths cause the same skin damage from UV light as sunshine that can lead to skin cancer. The danger is so great that the International Agency for Research on Cancer that works with the World Health Organization lists UV tanning devices as a primary cause of skin cancer.[7] By 2014, Brazil and New South Wales, Australia, had banned all indoor tanning. Eleven other nations prohibited tanning for teens under age eighteen.[8] Tanning and tanning beds cause that much harm!

Even if your lawmakers refuse to take on corporations supporting these establishments and products, you can. Stay away from indoor tanning no matter how safe companies' advertisements say they are. Remember: advertisements are designed to entice you to the product, and are not necessarily true statements.

Diagnosis

The best way to detect skin cancer is to examine yourself regularly, particularly if you frequently must remain outdoors in the sun, such as for work or to play or compete on a team or in an individual sport. Ask a parent or sibling to check unusual moles. If you find changes, consult a doctor.

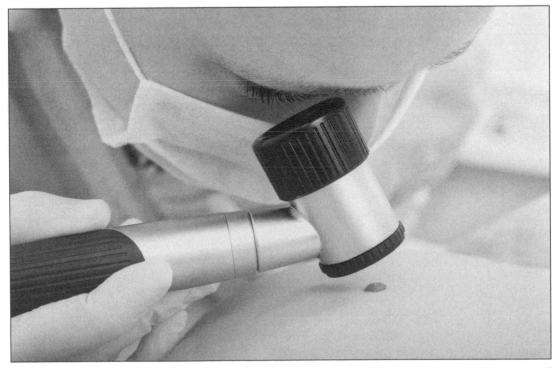

The dermatologist carefully examines each birthmark or other skin growth for signs of melanoma.

The doctor, usually a dermatologist (skin doctor), looks at size, shape, color, and texture of your growth and the rest of your body. Dermatologists also want to know if there is any family history of skin cancer. After gathering information, either a sample slice of the mole or the entire growth is taken off to biopsy. A pathologist examines the biopsy sample under the microscope to check for abnormal cells that may indicate the presence of cancer. Many teens find that waiting for test results is the worst part about a biopsy.

You may receive a local anesthetic to prevent you from feeling pain during the biopsy. Doctors perform one of four types of biopsies:

1. A shave biopsy involves the doctor using a fine sharp knife to scrape off abnormal cells.
2. A punch biopsy is when the doctor removes a circle of tissue from the growth with a sharp hollow tool.
3. An incisional biopsy requires a scalpel to cut part of the growth.
4. The excisional biopsy allows the doctor to remove any abnormal tissue and tissue around the growth with a scalpel. Doctors reserve this type of biopsy for when the growth looks obviously suspicious.

Michelle L.'s Dad, Bo

My daughter was diagnosed at age seven. Now she's fifteen. She had a mole on the left thigh of her leg for quite some time. It didn't meet the typical criteria for melanoma. We took her to a dermatologist who removed it.

The biopsy went to pathology, and it took longer to get a report back because when the pathologist looked at it under the microscope he didn't believe a seven-year-old got it. He sent the sample to another pathologist who confirmed melanoma, and we needed to deal with it.

The doctor removed the mole and a large section of tissue around it to make sure they got all cells in the vicinity. In her case melanoma had spread to several lymph modes, which were removed. Once they had wide incisions and nodes removed, they could better stage her cancer. She was 3B with a lesion depth of 3.6. Hers was also ulcerated, so they had to take another layer of tissue. Generally, if melanoma is ulcerated, outcomes tend to be worse. But following surgery, she recovered. A couple weeks later, Michelle started immunotherapy with interferon.[9]

Childhood melanoma may require imaging to check inside the body for cancer cells. These may include CT (computerized tomography) or CAT (computerized axial tomography) scans. MRI (magnetic resonance imaging) scans, PET (positron emission tomography) scans, ultrasound, or X-ray. None of these hurt, but they may require you to lay still or inside the scan tube for an uncomfortable length of time. And MRIs give off creepy clanging sounds, but these are harmless.

Treatment

According to the National Cancer Institute, the goal of treatment is to remove, cure, and kill the cancer forever.[9] Treatments for skin cancer vary, depending upon the type and level of cancer and whether cancer cells have spread to other organs. Size and location of the growth and general health and medical history also play a role. Given all these circumstances, one or more treatments may be needed to do the job.

Most skin cancers, when found early, can be removed through surgery. If there is spread or the cancer is considered a future threat, you may need additional therapies. These often require a team of specialists in other areas to work with your dermatologist to create the best plan for you. *Remember: get another opinion if you are uncomfortable with the treatment choices suggested to you. It's your body.*

Surgery

A surgeon usually performs surgery beyond the biopsy. A common type of skin cancer surgery is called Mohs surgery. With this procedure, the doctor first numbs the area. Once it's numb, the doctor shaves away thin layers of the tumor. Each shaving is then examined under a microscope. If cancer cells appear, another layer is removed from the skin. This process continues until all the cancer and only small areas of healthy cells are removed and healthy tissue remains.

If the skin cancer indicates there might be migrating cells, the surgeon will remove nearby lymph nodes to check for the extent of the spread. For large skin removal, the surgeon will take healthy skin from other areas of the body to patch the area. Should this situation be necessary, make sure your surgeon works with a plastic surgeon whose job is to minimize scars and other disfiguring results from surgery.

Cryosurgery

Another form of cancer removal is cryosurgery. This technique involves the doctor spraying liquid nitrogen on the area with cancer cells. The hope is that

Kody

I've been on chemo pills. Immune therapy. More surgery. Every once in a while, when I have surgery, it puts me back. Some surgeries take a lot of recovery. I've had about seven surgeries: foot, back of knee, groin, lungs, and brain to put a port in the back of my head to send drugs into the brain.

It's rough sometimes. The hardest part? I don't know. Sometimes the treatment and stuff. It just sucks.[h]

direct applications of this extremely cold substance will freeze and kill the cancer cells. While the treatment benefits patients unable to undergo other forms of surgery, it can cause swelling, nerve damage, and loss of feeling in the applied area. Check out the National Cancer Institute free fact sheet about "Cryosurgery in Cancer Treatment" at www.cancer.org to see if this treatment is an option for your situation. Several fact sheets are available from the National Cancer Institute website that can help you make other choices in your information and treatment journey.

Photodynamic Therapy

Similar to cryosurgery, this procedure relies on a drug combined with a strong light source, such as laser light, to kill basal or squamous cell skin cancers. First, the drug is injected or rubbed into the skin, where it is absorbed by cancer cells. The drug remains longer on cancer cells than healthy cells. After hours or days,

Kate

I always have new spots appearing and changing. I recently had a couple of biopsies and one came back last week as precancerous, but they got it. I'm going for surgery soon on my left breast, as my doctors recently found two spots they are very concerned about. I'll never forget going to the surgeon's office the first time with my mom—he thought she was the patient. When he realized I was the patient, he told me I was the youngest person he'd ever treated for melanoma. I'm only 21.[i]

a technician focuses light directly on the questionable tissue. The light activates the drug to destroy cancer cells. The plan has relatively few serious side effects. But it can cause burning or stinging in the area. Skin may redden or swell, and healthy nearby tissue can scar. The National Cancer Institute prepared a fact sheet called "Photodynamic Therapy for Cancer" to help you evaluate this procedure and compare it with others.

Radiation

A common therapy combined with other therapies is radiation. This form of treatment involves beaming high-energy rays directly at the cancer sight. Normally, you go to a hospital or clinic for radiation therapy, usually as an outpatient. A radiologist prescribes a series of treatments. More often, radiation is chosen for difficult-to-reach cancers, such as growths on the eyelid or nose. Radiation adds to other therapies when cancer cells are deep, or melanoma has spread to other parts of the body.

Radiation, though painless, can take a toll on the body, depending upon dose and treatment frequency. Skin in the treated region may redden and burn, and radiation can cause fatigue. You can read more about radiation in the National Cancer Institute booklet "Radiation Therapy and You."

Chemotherapy

Teens with varying degrees of cancer may be treated with chemotherapy. This means your doctor will prescribe any number of drugs to be ingested or spread like lotion. Early and thin basal or squamous cell skin cancers respond to certain drugs in creams or lotions that kill cancer cells on the top skin layer. Deeper growths or cancer that has spread may require drugs by mouth or injection. These drugs go directly into the bloodstream to reach hard-to-detect cancer cells.

Benefits of chemotherapy drugs are their reach and the lack of a scar from treatment. Problems can develop, however, with really strong drugs. Their reach may also include healthy cells, causing infection, fatigue, and sometimes other cancers. Some drugs reduce your appetite, make you nauseous, or give you mouth sores. Your doctor can give you added treatments—creams or medications—to minimize these side effects. Remind yourself that these side effects will diminish as your treatment lessens. At least at first, you want strong drugs to do their job and rid your body of skin cancer.

Hair loss can be a huge—and embarrassing—problem for some teens. The important thing to remember is hair grows back. Your hair may change in color and texture, but it will return. In the meantime, you can buy a wig, shave off all your hair to minimize the awkward stages, or wear a hat or scarf. Or you can wear the hair loss as a badge of courage, which you deserve.

Biological Therapy

Advanced melanoma requires strong treatment. Biological therapy works to boost the body's natural defenses by encouraging the immune system to do its job. With this therapy, a drug is injected under the skin to slow or kill the growth of melanoma cells. A doctor gives the injections in a hospital or clinic. Sometimes, these treatments can take days in the hospital.

Two biological drugs used more often are interferon and interleukin-2. Both can cause side effects of rash, swelling, fatigue and muscle aches, and fever. Other drugs are often given to minimize these reactions.[10] The National Cancer Institute covers the range of this treatment in "Biological Therapies for Cancer."

Michelle L.'s Dad, Bo

The way these treatments work, she [Michelle] had a yearlong protocol. First four weeks she received high doses. Medications were given in the hospital through infusions five days straight a week. She was admitted for the first three days of the high-dose period. Her reaction to the first dose wasn't bad. On day two, she had a bad response, so they kept her a third night. Then her body started to tolerate it. Part of the infusion she received had Benadryl, fluids, and Tylenol to lessen side effects. Prior to the injections, they inserted a picc line, a tube threaded up the arm to use for injecting medication and draws for daily blood testing. Michelle's side effects were flulike symptoms—high fever, chills that looked like seizures they were so extreme.

The last forty-eight weeks, it's a lower dose phase. She received injections at home three days a week for forty-eight weeks. Same side effects but not as severe. During treatment she received blood work once every couple weeks to check her liver and kidney function. When her white blood count went low, they gave her an infusion of medication to prevent pneumonia. One of the things we learned through this process is how to advocate for yourself and navigate the medical world.[j]

Prevention

Hindsight is always informative. One suggestion that came up during interviews with skin cancer survivors is to be conscious of preventing future growths. The most obvious recommendation is to limit time in the sun. That includes sunlamps and tanning beds in addition to outdoor activity.

Breakthroughs on the Horizon

Ken Burns, television producer and author, talked about the Human Genome Project on his April 2015 show. He featured scientists who discovered complex cancer cells that change genes. These changes allowed cancer to spread and suppress other cells. Now the hope is to target other cells that control and suppress these cancer cells.[k]

Not all advances result from genetic study. Here are some other areas that are creating considerable excitement in melanoma research.

Scientists are investigating a new test for cancer called liquid biopsy. Instead of cutting tissue from the tumor for a biopsy to test for melanoma, doctors test blood samples. Research shows that tumors shed cancer cells, or DNA, into the blood. Study continues to confirm the value of blood tests to identify cancers. Hopefully, they will prove accurate at pinpointing specific cancers, such as melanoma. If so, blood tests will be a less invasive way to profile cancers. They could target drugs that might fit the cancer type, and test that a treatment actually works.[l]

Researchers are exploring immunotherapy to treat cancer. Doctors believe that a person's own immune system may have the ability to destroy cancer cells. T-cells of the immune system are attack cells. They typically recognize foreign invading cells, such as virus or bacteria, and kill them. Scientists are testing the idea of training T-cells to work the same way with cancer cells. If that happens, teens will be able to forgo the usual treatments, such as radiation or poisonous chemicals that destroy cancers.

The most promising results have been with advanced melanoma. A recent long-term study of five thousand patients with advanced melanoma receiving immunotherapy found that 22 percent live for ten years or longer compared with similar patients who live only seven months to a year. The exciting result is that immune cells seem to stick around in the body and remember the invader. If the invasion reoccurs, it is quickly spotted and destroyed.[m, n]

CBS television news reported in spring 2015 about a new study that suggests vitamin B_3 can keep skin cancers under control. Patients in the study experienced a 23 percent reduction in their skin cancer and a similar reduction in its recurring. The study also cited fewer lesions in nonmelanoma skin cancers.[o]

But staying out of the sun completely isn't realistic, especially if you're an athletic teen. So here are some other suggestions from the National Cancer Institute:[11]

- Remember that sun beams the strongest rays in the middle of the day between 10 a.m. and 4 p.m. Save some midday activities until later, if possible.
- Sun rays reflect off sand, water, snow, ice, and pavement. And rays shine through light clothing, windshields, window, and clouds. If you think a cloudy day will protect you, you're wrong.
- When in bright sun or sun for a long time, cover up. Wear shirts with sleeves and made from tightly woven fabrics and long pants. Consider a wide-brimmed hat that shades your face, neck, and ears. Hats can be fun and attention getting.
- Wear sunglasses to protect skin around your eyes from UV radiation.
- Always lather up with sunscreen, especially if the preceding recommendations prove impossible to follow and especially on really sunny, hot days. Buy a sun protection factor (SPF) of at least 15. Higher than 30 SPF is unnecessary. Companies just want you to pay more for higher SPF. Don't fall for the ploy. Apply sunscreen before going outside and again every two hours. Don't forget to reapply after swimming or sweating activities, as lotion may be gone.
- Decide if using one of the newfangled electronic reminders to apply sunscreen would help you remember. It may sound like science fiction, but there are a couple apps and devices you can wear that measure UV rays and remind you to apply sunscreen.

There are more gadgets on the invention horizon. Check out the wearable device called JUNEcan, which is similar to exercise monitors. You can download the free iOS app to check the daily sun forecast and add sunZapp to your

SKIN CANCER PREVENTION

DO NOT BURN/TAN

Nulla luctus neque et turpis commodo tincidunt. Maecenas sem dui, venenats in egestas eu, posuere eu libero.

SEEK SHADE

Praesent nec ex ante. Pellentesque auctor interdum diam sed mollis. Curabitur elementum libero non molestie hendrerit.

GET VITAMIN D SAFELY

Donec at euismod purus, sit amet porta magna. Nullam at consectetur ex, dapibus condimentum quam.

ENJOY OUTDOOR LIFE

CAUTION REFLECTIVE

Sed sit amet elit nec ex laoreet semper quis ac urna. Cras tincidunt ipsum leo, eu consectetur sapien rutrum id.

APPLY SUNSCREEN

Mauris quis lectus ut ex porta accumsan in a ipsum. Maecenas ut libero ultrices felis bibendum euismod massa.

PROTECTIVE CLOTHING

Donec auctor et nibh in blandit. Sed ac velit tellus. Morbi ut nisi ex. Cras quis felis nunc. Fusce ullamcorper massa.

Check out different ways you can prevent skin cancer.

smartphone as a sun warning system. Or try a disposable wristband or sticker (UVSunSense) that changes colors to signal that it's time to either get out of the sun or reapply sunscreen.[12]

"Obviously apply sun screen when outside," Michelle suggests. "Sometimes I forget, but my dad says to pile it on. At games. Any time I'm outdoors. Be careful."[13]

Resources

Organizations

Adolescent and Young Adult Program
MD Anderson Children's Cancer Hospital, University of Texas

1515 Holcombe Boulevard
Houston, TX 77030
877-632-6789
www.mdanderson.org/patient-and-cancer-information/care-centers-and-clinics/
childrens-cancer-hospital/support-programs/aya-program.html
Medical and support services for teens at a premier cancer center for teens in the United States. The program sponsors Kim's Place, a lounge area for patients ages fifteen to thirty to hang out and, if they choose, enjoy games, a jukebox, Internet and videos, counseling services, and crafts and theater. It also sponsors Cancer180, a network that coordinates social outings for young adult patients in their twenties and thirties and their family and friends.

Cancer Care
275 Seventh Avenue, 22nd Floor
New York, NY 10001
800-813-4672
www.cancercare.org
Free professional support services (financial, counseling, education, daily activities assistance) to anyone affected by cancer. Services are primarily for New York, Connecticut, and New Jersey families.

"Dear 16-year-Old Me"
David Cornfield Melanoma Fund
www.youtube.com/watch?v=_4jgUcxMezM
Excellent quick video that condenses the hazards of melanoma, its problems for teens, and how to prevent the illness.

First Descents, World Headquarters
3001 Brighton Boulevard, Suite 623
Denver, CO 80216
303-945-2490
www.firstdescents.org
Group offering young adult (18–30) cancer survivors a free outdoor experience designed to empower them to climb, paddle, and surf beyond their diagnosis and reclaim their lives while connecting with others.

Melanoma International Foundation
250 Mapleflower Road
Glemoore, PA 19343
866-463-6663

melanomainternational.org
National organization begun in 2003 to offer support, resources, and education.

Melanoma Research Foundation
1411 K Street NW, Suite 800
Washington, DC 20005
877-673-6460
www.melanoma.org
National organization for research, advocacy, and education. The group also spon-sors an awareness campaign for hair stylists called Mark the Spot. The campaign was first started by Mark Samitt, a man who died of melanoma but wanted to bring awareness to the hairstyling community about cancer. Samitt believed hair stylists could help detect melanoma on the scalp, where his began. But they needed to know what to look for and how to tell clients, if they were embarrassed to say anything. Check out informative videos at www.melanoma.org/get-involved/melanoma-awareness/mark-spot and get your hair stylist involved in this simple yet important program.

National Cancer Institute (NCI), Department of Health and Human Resources
BG 9609 MSC 9760
9609 Medical Center Drive
Bethesda, MD 20892-9760
800-4-CANCER (800-422-6237)
cancer.gov
Reliable and recent cancer information for patients and their families, profession-als, and the general public. For immediate assistance, you can instant message with NCI staff on LiveHelp at livehelp.cancer.gov.

Skin Cancer Foundation
149 Madison Avenue, Suite 901
New York, NY 10016
212-725-5175
Educational foundation started in 1979 to educate the public about prevention and early detection of skin cancer.

Stupid Cancer: The Voice of Young Adults Cancer
40 Worth Street, Suite 808
New York, NY 10013
877-735-4673
www.stupidcancer.org

Charity started by a cancer survivor that addresses young adult cancer through advocacy, research, support, outreach, awareness, mobile health, and social media.

Financial and Travel Assistance

The American Cancer Society's Road to Recovery Program
250 Williams Street NW
Atlanta, GA 30303
800-227-2345
www.cancer.org/treatment/supportprogramsservices/road-to-recovery
National program that gives teens rides to treatment when parents and friends are unavailable, and they cannot drive themselves.

Cancer Financial Assistance Coalition
www.cancerfac.org
Coalition of fourteen member organizations that coordinate to reduce financial challenges experienced by cancer patients.

Books

Bellenir, Karen, ed., *Cancer Sourcebook: Basic Consumer Health Information about Major Forms and Stages of Cancer*, Detroit: Omnigraphics, 2011. An overview of cancer information.

Fogelson, Hillary, *Pale Girl Speaks: A Year Uncovered*, Berkeley, CA: Seal Press, 2012. A humorous, readable memoir about a young woman who faced melanoma.

National Cancer Institute, *What You Need to Know about Melanoma and Other Skin Cancers*, CreateSpace, 2014 (but free online at www.cancer.gov/publications/patient-education). The most up-to-date review of skin cancer, its treatment, and prevention. Check out the related government books that cover treatments and other pertinent issues more extensively.

Shea, John, *Frequently Asked Questions about Skin Cancer*, New York: Rosen, 2013. Review of skin cancer information in a format that focuses on questions teens may have about skin cancer.

MULTIPLE SCLEROSIS: NERVOUS SYSTEM ATTACKS

Multiple sclerosis (MS) is an autoimmune disease that attacks the nervous system. Because this system controls all movements and can affect the body anywhere, MS strikes each person differently. Flare-ups can come and go. Symptoms can linger between attacks or change without warning. With each attack symptoms can alter the same or different parts of the body. Incidents can be as mellow as mild numbness or severe enough to inhibit movement altogether.

Many doctors believe multiple sclerosis is one of the more mysterious diseases of the nervous system. That's because no one knows for sure exactly what produces symptoms and their attacks. Research points to MS being an autoimmune disease—in this case the body attacks its own nervous system. But scientists are still working to confirm that assumption. What doctors do know is MS causes any number of problems from defects in the nervous system.

Sean

I was in third grade and noticed vision in my left eye getting blurry. At first, I didn't know what was going on, so I went to an ophthalmologist [eye doctor], and he said my lazy eye could be the problem. He didn't recommend a patch. Instead he said we'll just see if the blurry eye can correct itself.

I continued living life, then went to get a driver's license at age sixteen. When the guy evaluated my vision, he said my optic nerve looked pale, and I needed to check it out. Normally, the nerve does not appear pale. I went to a neural ophthalmologist and was told I had optic neuritis. The doctor said this could maybe be related to multiple sclerosis or many different diseases.

My vision wasn't that bad, so I didn't care much at the time. That summer, we went to Colorado, and I hiked up the mountain. When we decided to come down the mountain, my knees would not support my body weight. So my dad carried me down the mountain.

Sophomore year in high school, I started experiencing foot drop in the left foot. I compensated by swinging my foot around, so I didn't trip over my foot, which messed up my gait and balance completely. Bummer! Because of that when I was a senior swinging my leg around, I started using a walker. It worked for me, but I wasn't expecting to use a walker when I was a senior in high school.[a]

The Healthy Nervous System at Work

Think of your nervous system as the body's control center. It consists of the brain, spinal cord, and network of nerves that radiate throughout the body. Nerves from the brain tell different body parts what to do, much like a remote controls a television. In turn, body parts send signals back to the brain for interpretation and action.

The nervous system is made up of billions of nerve cells called neurons. You can only see these tiny units of living matter under a microscope. Neurons carry messages back and forth from the brain into the spine and other parts of the body through complex lines of interconnected nerve fibers. Fibers connect the brain to muscles, skin, other organs, and senses. These control how you move your hands and feet, breathe, and see. For example, when you touch something sharp, nerves in your fingers relay a message of pain through your network of nerves to the brain. Your brain signals your fingers to respond by pulling your hand away from what is causing the pain.

By sending these messages to and from the brain, nerves help you perform an enormous range of behaviors that allow you to move, talk, think, behave, and sense your world. Nerves also keep your body systems and organs functioning without your realizing how hard they work. So you breathe, digest and eliminate food, and receive sensations from your skin and sexual organs because of a properly functioning nervous system.

A fatty coating called myelin protects nerves as they relay messages. The myelin sheath works similarly to rubber casing around electrical wires. This covering ensures that high-speed messages travel directly to where they should go to help you perform a variety of daily activities. Scientists estimate that healthy

Michael

I was nineteen years old and in the army. And I stressed myself in basic training. My feeling is that stressing myself brought on my first episode. I couldn't get out of my cot. My superior yelled at me to get up, and I said I can't. He screamed until he understood I wasn't faking.

I was brought to the army hospital. They didn't have correct equipment for an MRI, a neurologist, or specialists. They thought I had an ear infection. Dizziness. I stayed down trying not to throw up. I kept falling because I was dizzy. It was difficult to see what I had.

I got better over a period of a month. The army put me into another unit. I was in military police and went to do a two-mile run and kept falling. I had drop foot. Electrical impulses got blocked from the brain to the leg, and the leg only moved part of the way. So I tripped and fell. I was bleeding by the end of the run. I finished it, got home, and most of the problem was gone. But I had numbness in my hand, which I still have today.

A year went by and I had the next attack. I got dizzy again. I had drop foot, and I couldn't pee when I had to. I went to the doc to see what was wrong. From there I was sent to a neurologist who gave me an MRI. And I got diagnosed. I thought most people who get multiple sclerosis (MS) are females around forty years old, not twenty-year-old men.[b]

teens shoot messages up and back along their nervous system at a rate of about 225 miles per hour. Usually, you never notice the nervous system functioning. It just performs much like flipping a switch to turn on the light.

The Nervous System with MS

Imagine what happens when the rubber casing in light switch wiring frays or becomes blocked. The light won't turn on. Or you feel sparks from the wires. No matter what you do to the wiring, it will not produce light unless you rewire the switch with new casing.

The problem is much the same with MS. The myelin sheath frays or becomes blocked, which interferes with smooth transmission of signals to and from the

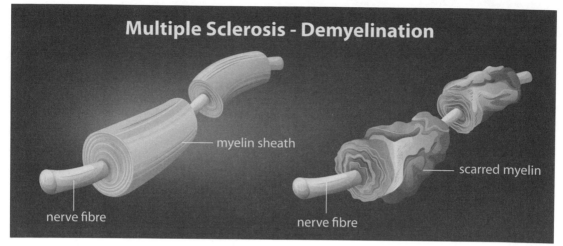

Scarring in the protective myelin sheath causes problems with sending messages to and from the brain.

brain and spinal cord. Messages slow or become interrupted or distorted. Such was the case when Michael became dizzy and Sean experienced blurriness in his left eye.

Sometimes signals become totally blocked, as with both boys' inability to move at all. Depending upon the extent of nerve damage and where it occurs, one person with MS may lose eyesight, while another feels weak or numb in the hands. Sometimes, damage repairs itself. But if damage lasts a long time or turns extreme, complete nerve loss may develop. The process of damaging the protective covering of nerve cells is called demyelination.

Should MS progress, hard patches of tissue grow over damaged areas. When patches cannot be eliminated, scars form, further interrupting or distorting the flow of information throughout the body. These patches produce visible scars on the brain and spine. The term *multiple sclerosis* comes from the Greek term for scarring, or sclerosis. *Multiple* refers to the many scars that can occur throughout the nervous system.

Types of MS

MS progresses differently with each teen. In 10 to 20 percent of MS cases, illness disappears completely after the first attack. For a few, the disease never progresses. For others, damage to the nervous system flares in locations that never obstruct functioning. In rare cases, once MS strikes, the disease progresses quickly, and you become disabled in areas touched by the disease.

Specialists identify the type of progression as following one of four main disease patterns. But these categories are not neat and tidy. Sometimes the label changes over time; sometimes not.

Common Signs of MS

Teens with MS exhibit a range of symptoms. You may notice some signs, such as trouble walking or talking. But many symptoms, such as tingling or memory loss, are usually invisible to others. Each case is individual. Not every teen with MS experiences all the following possible problems identified by the National Multiple Sclerosis Society:

- tiredness
- vision problems
- pain
- walking difficulties
- dizziness
- inability to move arms or legs
- difficulty urinating
- changes in ability to think
- memory loss
- sexual performance problems
- numbness

- weakness
- tingling
- loss of balance
- muscle cramps
- problems speaking or swallowing
- loss of bowel control
- attention problems
- emotional changes (mood swings)
- headaches

Depending upon which nerves are involved, teens can also experience the following:

- speech difficulties
- swallowing problems
- breathing problems
- itchy, burning, stabbing sensations

- tremors
- seizures
- hearing loss[c]

Relapsing-Remitting

About 85 percent of MS cases begin with occasional relapses, or flare-ups. In between relapses, teens with this type of MS experience remission, a complete or near-complete return to functioning before the relapse occurred. Some symptoms, however, never return to original functioning.

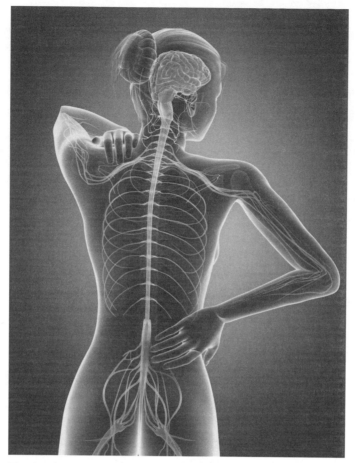

The brain can send painful messages anywhere along the nervous system with MS.

Each attack, or relapse, comes from swelling around the site where myelin is destroyed. The swelling is similar to what happens from a cut on your skin, and skin swells to protect the wound. Only with MS, swelling blocks messages sent through the affected nerves, which triggers an episode. Once swelling eases, nerves send messages again, thereby relieving symptoms and often resulting in remission.

Usually with this type of MS, relapses appear every few years or a couple a year. As the cycle of relapses and remitting continues, nerves become more damaged and cannot work properly. Then MS follows a more severe path with more symptoms and fewer disease-free periods.

Secondary-Progressive

After about ten years, one in every two cases of relapsing-remitting develops secondary-progressive MS. With secondary-progressive MS, symptoms worsen

---

Suzi

My first sign was inflammation behind the optic nerve. I went from 20–20 to 20–40 vision. I went straight to the doctor, who diagnosed the nerve problem.

About a year later, I started feeling numbness around the abdomen area. Really strange place to notice. I must have leaned against something cold and realized I could feel one side but not another. Again I went to the doctor. He said it could be MS. Turns out I have relapsing-remission, which means MS symptoms come and go. I go from attack to attack.

As soon as you hear MS you think of the worst cases. There are so many varying degrees that MS could be like a cold is to pneumonia. The doctor said don't worry. I asked if I could still have children and was told that would be okay.

One time, I started having trouble with my hands in the thumb area. The doctor said don't think everything you have is MS. I had carpel tunnel syndrome [when the median nerve to the hand compresses, causing hand or wrist tingling, numbness, and weakness]. I was lucky all I needed was a brace on my wrist, and that corrected the problem. But every time MS returned, it affected a different area.[d]

---

with or without periods of recovery. Progression can be slow or fast. But symptoms generally worsen to the point of no remission after about twenty-five years.

Primary-Progressive

One in ten victims of MS finds their illness worsens after the first attack. With primary-progressive MS, there are no relapses and hardly any remitting, at least not with improvement. Inflammation damage to the brain and spinal cord destroys nerve cells from the beginning. Disease progression can be slow or fast. Symptoms may level off for a while. But this form of MS develops without a break in symptoms. For now, current treatments work less with this form of MS.

Progressive-Relapsing

Less than 5 percent of people diagnosed with MS find their symptoms advance steadily after the first episode. Unexpected attacks may or may not worsen the

Teens who fall often benefit from using a wheelchair and service dog for assistance.

disease. But damage progresses between the attacks without a return to a previous level of functioning. The speed of worsening depends upon the individual but always looms high.

Who Gets MS?

The National MS Society investigated the frequency of MS. But numbers are difficult to confirm. One problem is MS can be tricky to diagnose. Symptoms appear as other conditions, they come and go, or they change with each attack, making confirmation challenging. Another problem is the national government. It does not require reporting or keeping track of MS cases, as with other diseases. So no one agency takes responsibility for requiring doctors to report instances of the disease or collecting figures for MS.

That said, the National MS Society has conducted research to figure out how prevalent the disease is and who is more likely to acquire the condition. Reports estimate that more than four hundred thousand cases of MS exist in the United States and 2.3 million worldwide. About one hundred new cases appear every week (about one hundred thousand per year).[1] Although total numbers remain small compared with other diseases, MS counts as the most common disease of the nervous system.

Most people receive their diagnosis between ages twenty and forty. But between eight thousand and ten thousand kids and teens up to age eighteen get MS. Another ten thousand to fifteen thousand might endure symptoms but not know what they represent.[2] The National MS Society believes 2 to 5 percent of individuals with MS probably experienced some form of symptoms before turning eighteen.[3] Either they thought nothing of it, the signs were not severe enough, or their doctors never recognized the symptoms as MS. Now doctors diagnose children as young as four with signs of MS. Moreover, they see numbers of new MS cases in young children rising.

For unknown reasons, gender and location play a role in who acquires MS. The disease affects women at more than twice the rate of men.[4] These numbers are especially true at younger ages. As teens age into young adulthood, however, the number of new cases comes closer to balancing between genders.

Another factor that affects new cases is location. Five times the new cases of MS arise in colder climates than hot. Therefore, higher rates of MS exist in the northern United States, Canada, and northern Europe than in tropical climates.

Interestingly, teens who move to low-incidence areas take on the same low risk of developing MS as residents of the new region. This is especially true for teens under age fifteen. Studies show that teens who move from tropical regions to cold climates before age fifteen increase their risk of developing MS.[5] After age fifteen, however, the move rarely increases risk beyond what others from their homeland experience.

Study findings point to the environment as a factor in developing MS. But researchers cannot pinpoint exactly what in the environment raises red flags for MS. Does lower temperature, less sunshine, more rainfall, or higher altitude increase risk? Does the lack of vitamin D in cloudy regions play a role? Do families in high-risk areas eat different foods? Or are residents more exposed to germs, as in large cities? Many organizations continue to investigate these and other questions about MS.

The last possible risk factor for MS is ethnic background. MS rarely appears in Asians, Inuits, and Africans. Instead, white families from northern Europe comprise most cases of MS. Some evidence shows that MS runs in families. When a parent has MS, children face fifteen to twenty times the risk as the general population of acquiring the disease.

The Long History of MS

Most likely, MS existed since the beginning of time. Count Jan Van Bieren of Holland wrote the earliest written record of MS symptoms in 1395. He told of a fifteen-year-old girl with terrible face pain. After a short time, she experienced leg weakness that caused her to fall when she ice skated, her favorite sport. Gradually, she began losing the ability to walk, feel her legs, and see out of one eye. As she lost these abilities, the Count marveled at how this young woman continued to help others despite her progressive suffering. After her death in 1433 at age fifty-three, she reached sainthood and was called the Saint of Ice Skaters.

Four centuries later, doctors began noticing unusual changes in the brain and spinal cord. They wondered whether small brown and white patches in the nervous system related to mysterious symptoms in some patients. Yet, the doctors never connected the two with a specific disease.

New Discoveries: Good and Questionable

In 1868 Jean-Martin Charcot, a French professor, first linked changes in the nervous system to a specific disease. For the next few years, he examined thousands of patients before and after their deaths at a Paris institution. His investigations verified a match between MS and changes in the nervous system. He wrote about *la sclerose en plaques*, or scarring in patches, that interfere with how the nervous system functions. He tried many treatments, from injecting patients with gold and silver to electric shock to arouse the nervous system. Nothing worked.

Over the years doctors treated MS patients by inducing sweating, vomiting, and bowel movements. Other doctors recommended herbs and bed rest. None of these treatments cured MS.

The nineteenth century brought identification of the body's myelin by French doctor Louis Ranvier. His discovery led to other investigations of the nervous system. In 1925 British scientist Lord Edgar Adrian recorded the first electrical activity in nerves. Doctors now understood how nerves conducted messages to and from the brain. Adrian later established the role of myelin in transmitting messages and how blockage along pathways from swelling interfered with the body processes.

During the early twentieth century, doctors found MS in abnormal fluid from the spine. But they had no idea what that meant for a cause or cure. They believed men suffered more from MS than women. But that was because doctors assumed MS symptoms in females came from hysteria, nervousness, or madness. Thankfully, this sort of thinking is gone—hopefully!

Recent Revelations

In 1935, American Dr. Thomas Rivers discovered that nerve problems caused MS symptoms, rather than an outside agent, such as virus or bacteria. His discovery led to focus on allergies that might produce an autoimmune reaction. Doctors treated MS patients with allergy-reducing drugs and vitamins, only to see little improvement in symptoms or disease progression. But with improved hospital care and infection control, patients with MS started to live longer. More research confirmed that the body's immune system goes crazy and attacks its own myelin. Why is still a puzzle.

Investigation Continues

Studies report that family history may play a role in MS. The National Multiple Sclerosis Society claims the average person in the United States has a 1 in 750 risk of developing MS. Numbers rise sharply to 1 in 100, if you have a sibling with the disease, or 1 in 40 cases, if a parent has MS.[6] Being an identical twin who shares the same DNA raises the risk to 1 in 4. Even twins reared in different families in different locales face the same percentage risk.

Twin studies are important as controls for the study of environments and ethnic background. Other research focuses on customs and habits, such as smoking or work conditions. Since 1980, when the first report targeted a child, more emphasis has been on studying the rising number of MS cases in children and teens.

This helps researchers know where to focus new research—on environments and backgrounds as contributing factors to immune system errors. Scientists know babies are not born with the disease, only harbor an inclination toward getting it. Several theories point to a combination of genes and the environment as risk factors for developing MS. Researchers continue to struggle with how to identify MS earlier and prevent the disease.

Diagnosing MS

Currently, no single symptom or laboratory test confirms a diagnosis of MS. Instead, doctors follow guidelines outlined by an international panel studying diseases related to MS. These are a series of steps to rule out other disorders and pinpoint signs of specific disease. The process involves personal accounts and laboratory and invasive tests.

Sean

After several years, I went to a different neurologist. He officially diagnosed me with MS. He didn't use a test. He could tell by the symptoms and signs, like the mountain trip, optic neuritis, and foot drop in my left foot. He said most likely it was MS.

At first, I put it off. I didn't care about it [MS]. But my parents were torn up. I, however, was lucky number one. It took a while to kick in. I would say my junior or senior year of high school depression started kicking in much more. I started seeing a therapist that helped a little, but it didn't solve the problem. My family, friends—just being able to go out with friends and have them help me out—has helped me so much throughout this journey.[e]

Even with these guidelines, identifying MS can be difficult and take time. In some instances, MS can be discovered easily. More often, detection can take months or years. Teens and their families often become discouraged. They want to be taken seriously. They want answers about why they feel crummy.

Doctor's Appointment

The first thing doctors want to learn about is you—in detail. They need to learn about previous illnesses, medications you take or have taken, and family history of nervous system disease. Your doctor might ask you to keep a diary to document your attacks, if possible at least two. Next comes the general physical exam to check for other illnesses and signs of MS. Diagnosing MS is often a ruling-out process.

If findings suggest a nervous system problem, your regular doctor will recommend a neurologist, a doctor who specializes in nervous system problems. Neurologists check coordination, sensation, and strength. They test face and eye movements. Results of these exercises determine whether further nerve tests are necessary.

Magnetic Resonance Imaging (MRI)

This photographic scanner detects patches of myelin loss in the nervous system by taking pictures through the skin and inside the body. These images travel to a computer that translates magnetic information into multiple slices of the brain, spinal cord, or other body parts.

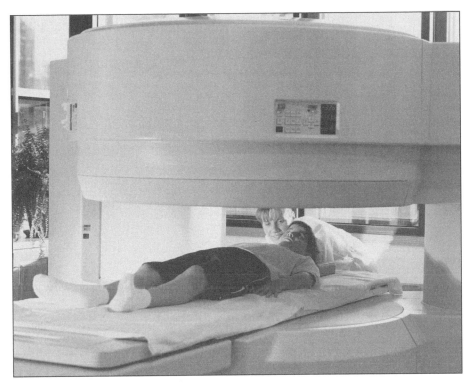

This patient is about to receive an MRI scan.

An MRI is painless. The hard part is lying still long enough for multiple images to be processed. Early MRIs were long, narrow tubes that caused stress in some patients who hated closed-in places. Newer models are more open. They still make a loud clanging noise, so don't be surprised. Sometimes, testing clinics pipe in music to mask the sounds.

Another problem is the test's ability to identify MS. Twenty-five percent of MS cases are invisible to the MRI. Sometimes, the pattern of disease shown through MRI mirrors other diseases. So doctors order different tests to guide them in making a diagnosis when MRI fails to confirm MS or results seem borderline, meaning no definite answer.

Evoked Potential (EP)

With this test, the technician places wires on your head, neck, and limbs. The wires link to a computer that records results from stimulating different nerve pathways, such as through eyes, ears, and skin. For example, you may be asked to watch a pattern on a television monitor to check your eye nerves. As you respond to the visual stimuli, or pattern, the computer records your responses and how quickly they occur. When MS is involved, your response will come slower because demyelination interferes with nerve signals.

Evoked potential tests cost less than MRI scans, and they detect early MS in 65 percent of the cases.[7] Like MRI, they are not painful. That said, you may feel tingling in your arms and legs as these parts are stimulated.

Cerebrospinal Fluid (CSF) Test or Spinal Tap

This is the most intrusive test for MS. A doctor inserts a long needle into the back to draw a sample of cerebrospinal fluid to test for proteins that typically appear in spinal fluid of people with nervous system diseases, like MS. Cerebral spinal fluid is a clear liquid that surrounds the brain and spinal cord.

The test can be uncomfortable. Pain during the test can be extreme, although the test is quick. Afterward, you must lie still to allow the needle site to close and CSF fluids in the spine to rebalance. If you sit up too quickly, expect a headache.

Treating MS

Although researchers are inching closer to a cure for MS, none currently exists. Treatment centers on relieving and preventing symptoms. The type of treatment depends upon how severe the symptoms are and how often they appear.

Until the 1990s, effective medical treatments were only a pipedream. Now medications alter the course of MS, reduce the size of demyelinated patches, and prevent new blockage from occurring. Improved ability to identify MS and devise targeted medications offers hope that teens will one day be able to control and beat their disease.

Teens with sudden, serious attacks wind up in the hospital for injected high doses of corticosteroids. These improve symptoms for the short term. They act quickly. They shrink swelling and immune system responses. But they can cause scary side effects, so your doctor needs to know how to monitor your doses.

"Usually with steroids, you need to reduce doses gradually," Suzi said. "Once a doctor ended my injections cold turkey. I got numbness all over, tingling, hives, and diarrhea. My whole system went out of whack. With time, my system returned to normal. But the reaction lasted about a week."[8]

More recent medications target symptoms that appear and disappear. Medications that you can inject yourself work on all types of MS except primary-progressive, which never causes relapses or remissions. Several medications in the interferon beta category work to neutralize antibodies in the immune system to prevent attacks. These injections successfully treat many teens with MS.[9]

But interferon doses and medication need to be monitored carefully. Some teens with a history of depression may grow more depressed. And interferon may

Suzi

When I had long spans, say five years, between attacks, the doctor treated me with the oral steroid prednisone. Then attacks came every three years, then two years in a row. One time it affected my walking. All of a sudden I couldn't walk.

I switched doctors. This one put me into the hospital right away after an attack. I received high doses of a different steroid intravenously. Nurses hooked me up for several hours, and I had to stay in bed for a couple hours for a few days. I left the hospital in a wheelchair. I had a hard time walking five houses down the block. My leg was dragging.

Gradually, I started walking and exercising. Each day I'd increase distance. The doctor said exercise was good for MS to improve strength and balance.

After my second hospitalization, the doctor suggested a Betaseron (interferon beta-1b) shot every other day to lessen attacks. The frustrating thing about MS is you don't know if the shot is working or not. When I started getting attacks every year, I consented to the shots. I was told to take Advil before each shot to minimize flulike symptoms. I also gave myself shots in different parts of the body. That was to prevent hard spots, called cellulitis, I once got on the skin from too many injections in one area. When I went three years without an attack, I realized the shots were working.[f]

start losing its ability to prevent relapses and new central nervous system lesions. Always check with your doctor before taking any type of supplement or medication. It can affect more than your motor skills.

"I did get moderate to severe depression," Sean said. "With me, it wasn't sadness: I was just really angry. I would get angry at stupid things—at myself and my foot when it wouldn't lift. I would yell at my foot, 'Stupid foot, why don't you lift up?' It tore me up inside. I would suppress the anger, and it would turn into rage. Something would tick me off a little, and I would explode."[10]

Newer medications can be swallowed instead of injected. These are much easier to administer and way more convenient. The problem is all MS medication must be strong in order to block reactions that trigger episodes. Side effects, some serious, may appear with pills, too. Contact your doctor as soon as you feel something that isn't right with your body—or mind.

Most medications have not been approved for children. But doctors prescribe them anyway, rather than allow kids and teens to go untreated. Reports so far indicate that young patients suffer the same range of side effects as older patients. Therefore, doctors believe it is better to do something than allow relapses to advance the disease.

You can do your own research on medications. Contact the National MS Society (800-344-4867) with questions about approved medications. The organization updates a brochure of current medications and their side effects. It also lists clinical trials for stubborn symptoms. Clinical trials provide relief in controlling cost. Multiple sclerosis drugs are expensive. The society can help you find assistance paying for drugs outside clinical trials, too.

Managing Symptoms

About 50 percent of teens with MS find some form of pain accompanies their disease.[11] Pain can range from sharp jabs in the face and shooting pain in the limbs to achy muscles, tingling, and burning. Some prescribed medication calms painful nerves. So can over-the-counter painkillers and cold packs.

An alternative is to ask the doctor to recommend a physical therapist, a trained professional who can plan exercises to relieve your specific discomfort. Physical therapists draw from different techniques, such as stretching, deep breathing, and refocusing thoughts onto something pleasant. These activities can help you manage symptoms outside therapy sessions.

Another option that some teens with MS claim reduces pain and stress is smoking or eating products prepared with the cannabis plant. Most teens know it as marijuana, and it's still federally illegal to grow, sell, and ingest. But many states have passed local laws that allow medical marijuana use with a doctor's approval. Some teens with MS find cannabis helps relieve tingling sensations, urgent bladder responses, shaky legs, and depression. They also find cannabis protects against medication side effects. When cannabis provides relief, patients require fewer medications, which saves them money. Efforts continue to open doors to acquiring or being allowed to grow cannabis for personal use to ease symptoms of MS and some other conditions in this book.

Brighter Future: Keeping Up Spirits

Genetic testing, stem cell therapy, new medications, vitamin D research—all these options are being studied to prevent or relieve symptoms of MS. New research appears daily. What can you do in the meantime to help yourself feel better? Teens with MS say to stay positive and find activities to help you feel better about yourself when you cannot do what you did earlier.

Sean

Talking with individuals is really a big help—people with and without MS. For teens who have MS, they need to know life is not over. It's just a minor hurdle in your life. Life could be worse. You are not alone.

You really realize who your true friends are. Who is there for moral support. Being helpful, being someone who offers their arm if someone with MS is falling. I didn't get much teasing. My real friends still give me a call. Once I stopped driving, having friends pick me up taught me who my true friends are.

I didn't date before because I thought walking with a walker isn't that attractive to a girl. I thought women saw me as an old man. But once I came out of my shell and understood that it's MS not the walker that's important, I realized I was still me—Sean.[9]

Successful People with MS

People used to try and hide their MS. Today, not only do noted people with MS talk about their disease, but they actively campaign to raise research funds. Many offer themselves as role models for teens who need hope that they can achieve whatever they choose in spite of their illness.

- Julie Roberts, country music singer
- Tyler Campbell, NFL prospect turned MS spokesperson and successful businessman
- Joan Sweeney, children's book author
- Clay Walker, country music singer who speaks and raises funds for the National MS Society
- Richard Cohen, television news producer and author of books about his journey with MS: the memoir *Blindsided: Lifting a Life above Illness* and *Strong at Broken Places: Voice of Illness, a Chorus of Hope*
- Alessandra Ambrosio, model
- Kiaran McLaughlin, Belmont Stakes–winning horse trainer

- Tamia Washington Hill, R&B singer
- Jordan Sigalet, goalie for the Falcons hockey team
- Stephanie Stephans, golfer
- Montel Williams, talk show host and motivational speaker
- David Osmond, singer on *American Idol* and entertainer who wrote an inspiring song about battling MS
- Sharon Elliott, actress, realtor, engineer, founder of Women Standing in the Gap to uplift females of all ages with MS
- Courtney Galiano, professional dancer in episodes of *Glee* and *Dancing with the Stars* plus other television and stage shows
- Kayla Montgomery, former high school track star and one of the fastest long-distance runners in the nation, diagnosed with MS at age fifteen
- Wendy Booker, mountain climber who reached peaks of six of the world's highest summits

Resources

Organizations

Multiple Sclerosis Association of America
375 Kings Highway North
Cherry Hill, NJ 08034
800-532-7667
www.mymsaa.org
Nonprofit begun in 1970 that seeks to improve lives of all-age people with MS and their family/caretakers through regional offices nationwide that offer resources, education, publications, online webinars and videos, insurance and prescription assistance, and a toll-free hotline.

Multiple Sclerosis Foundation
6520 North Andrew Avenue
Fort Lauderdale, FL 33309
800-225-6495
www.msfocus.org
Organization begun in1996 that offers a helpline, local resources, education programs, and support.

Myelin Repair Foundation
20111 Edinburgh Drive
Sarasota, CA 95070
408-871-2410
www.myelinrepair.org
Research-focused organization that investigates and promotes clinical trials for
MS treatment and cures.

National Multiple Sclerosis Society
733 Third Avenue, Third Floor
New York, NY 10017-3288
800-FIGHTMS (800-344-4867)
www.nationalmssociety.org
National information, support, and research organization that works to reduce
and eliminate effects of MS.

PatientsLikeMe
www.patientslikeme.com
A health information website with personal stories about MS, health data, and
support forums and conversations about MS and related illnesses. But read all
the disclaimers carefully before posting any private information. A for-profit
company hosts the site, and it shares information with other companies that offer
drugs, equipment, and insurance to families dealing with MS.

Books

Kathleen Costello, *Navigating Life with Multiple Sclerosis*, New York: Oxford
University Press, 2015. A comprehensive overview of MS for the newly
diagnosed and long-term diagnosed.
Rosalind Kalb, *Multiple Sclerosis for Dummies*, Hoboken, NJ: John Wiley & Sons,
2012. An overview of MS written for the lay reader.
Lindsey Leavitt, *Sean Griswold's Head*, New York: Bloomsbury USA, 2012.
Novel about how a teen deals with her dad's new MS diagnosis.

PHENYLKETONURIA (PKU): NEWBORNS ON A DIET

Teens with phenylketonuria (PKU) learn about this condition as soon as they are old enough to make food choices. But few others know what PKU is. This seems strange since PKU touches everyone. Each newborn in the United States receives a screening test for PKU within a day or two of birth. Most likely, you did too.

Doctors order that babies receive this test before they leave the hospital. Physicians realize that knowing about PKU early is important. Although rare and debilitating, this condition is treatable. For teens who test positive for PKU, one heal prick changes the course of their life forever.

"I can't remember a time not knowing I had PKU," Olivia said. "As soon as you understand yes and no, and you have to eat food, you become aware of PKU. It's been engrained in me since the beginning."[1]

What Is PKU?

PKU is a genetic condition that appears at birth. The disease results from the body's inability to process the protein phenylalanine, or phe. Processing problems develop when a faulty liver cannot produce the enzyme phenylalanine hydroxylase (PAH). A deficiency of PAH leads to extremely high phe levels in blood and tissues. Excess phe levels eventually prove toxic to the central nervous system. This is the situation with phenylketonuria. If left untreated, even for a few weeks after birth, PKU causes mental retardation and other neurological problems.

Phenylalanine is the amino acid necessary for overall normal growth and development of infants and children. Amino acids are organic compounds that comprise all proteins. They occur naturally in plants and animals and are present in their earliest development. The body gets amino acids from proteins in the diet.

When Phe Levels Soar

Heightened phe levels effect teens differently. Here are two accounts by teens whose diet wasn't working.

I vividly remember times when my level was high. The littlest things would upset me, and I'd have a big temper tantrum. The ones where you feel the world is after you, and you are full of anger. . . . It was not abnormal for throwing, screaming, and flailing around to accompany these fits. I'm normally not like this.[a]

If I don't follow the diet, or I have too much phe, I will notice it's hard for me to focus. That has rarely happened. I'm pretty good at sticking with my diet. When I can't, I feel fuzzy and can't think.[b]

Then the body uses them for growth, maintenance, and repair. As an essential building block of protein, phenylalanine remains necessary to maintain normal metabolism throughout life.

You consume sources of phenylalanine in meats, eggs, grains, and dairy products. At correct levels, this protein helps break down fats, carbohydrates, and other proteins from food into smaller chemical elements that can be absorbed into the body. Excess phenylalanine causes serious deficiencies in the ability to use foods that contain it. Welcome to a lifetime of different eating.

Ranges of PKU

Teens experience varying levels of PKU based on how their specific gene regulates phe levels. Different levels cause a range of symptoms, too. Blood tests measure levels of PKU from slight to severe. Where teens are on the scale helps them plan treatment that best suits their form of PKU. Organizations differ about how many types of PKU are identified along a spectrum. Some, like PKU.com, define four levels of PKU. Others, such as the National PKU Alliance, prefer three simpler designations.

Both groups define classic PKU as the most severe and common form. This is when teens must live with the smallest phe intake in their diet, which is less than 350 to 400 mg per day. That's because PAH activity is less than 5 percent. There is no going off diet here. The body has the least ability to tolerate cheating with foods not allowed on the treatment plan.

Babies without Treatment

No symptoms usually appear in newborns, as the mother's prebirth phe lingers in the baby's system. This residue helps balance proteins in the baby. Still, parents need to discover PKU as soon as possible after birth. Otherwise, problems develop within a few weeks or months without immediate treatment. Sadly, most of these problems never go away.

The Mayo Clinic lists several mild to severe symptoms that may appear in children who never receive treatment or whose treatment is delayed more than a few weeks:

- abnormally small head
- delayed development
- slow intellectual ability
- problems with behavior: irritability, swinging emotions, and social maladjustment
- psychiatric disorders
- neurological disturbances, including seizures
- hyperactivity
- skin rashes
- poor bone strength
- visibly poor tooth enamel
- vomiting
- earthy-smelling breath, skin, or urine from excess phenylalanine in the body
- blue eyes and fair skin due to the inability of phenylalanine to change into the pigment melanin needed for hair and skin tones[c]

Moderate PKU is when liver production of the enzyme PAH is less than 10 percent. This results in the body's ability to tolerate phe levels of between 350 to 600 mg. These figures are slightly better but still not great in terms of diet. Doctors recommend not cheating with this treatment plan either.

With very mild PKU, some levels of PAH activity, less than 5 percent, can be measured. Phe levels remain only slightly above normal. With these levels, teens have few or no dietary restrictions, that is, if they experience no symptoms.[2]

Discovery of PKU

PKU has a relatively short but troubled history. Famous author Pearl Buck wrote in the 1920s about her lovely daughter who failed to progress after a few months. Her book, *The Child Who Never Grew*, describes how her first infant showed such promise. But at about three months, the light—and intelligence—went out of her blue eyes. Although Buck took her daughter to several doctors, none could diagnose that her child had PKU.

According to the PKU News, Norwegian Dr. Asbjorn Folling first identified two children with the disorder—and severe mental retardation—in 1934. Dr. Folling's discovery first linked serious mental problems with abnormal amounts of phenylpyruvic acid in the urine of these children. He found that elevated levels of the acid in urine correlated with the inability to process phe.[3]

Throughout the 1930s, several scientists experimented with low phenylalanine diets. Although infants improved with the diets, they never caught on. The diets turned out to be expensive. Doctors and their egos battled each other to find answers.

In 1951, the first recognized diet treatment for PKU was developed. Experimenters realized that children could never reverse the mental capacity they had lost. But those with PKU who were identified as infants and started on the new commercially made formula showed promise. The first calls for testing newborns for PKU began.

Testing created more controversy. Initially, doctors tested infant urine, checking for its characteristic musty odor. But urine testing was unreliable until after babies already exhibited irreversible brain damage. In 1960 the microbiologist Robert Guthrie devised an inexpensive blood test. His heal prick test proved reliable within a few days after the baby's birth. A race began to require blood testing for all newborns.[4]

Initially, the medical community resisted testing. Dr. Guthrie took his case to the public. With backing from the National Association of Retarded Citizens, the leading advocacy group for people who had developmental delays, and the U.S. Children's Bureau, which field tested screening, the push was on for national screening. Even with professional backing, some people worried that screening would take away funds for education and treatment of older people with disabilities.

In 1963, laws for mass screenings of newborns passed in a few states. By 1967, thirty-seven states enacted newborn screening laws for PKU. Twenty years after screenings first began, in 1983, Dr. Savio Woo isolated the gene for phenylalanine hydroxylase.[5]

Since then, the PKU community has focused on better treatment options. A protein drink enhances the allowed diet. A new pill lowers blood phe levels for some teens with PKU. And genetic treatments and enzyme replacement therapies are in clinical trials. The future looks brighter for teens with PKU.

PKU Screening

The test for PKU is really simple. Between twenty-four hours and a week after birth, technicians prick a baby's heel or arm and take a few sample drops of blood. The blood sample goes to a laboratory to be tested for phenylalanine levels and other metabolic disorders.

At this point, infants with PKU appear normal. But some may feature fairer skin and hair than other family members. With time, babies with untreated PKU may develop early signs of vomiting, a rash, smelly urine, and fussiness. More

---

Olivia

Every once in a while when my diet isn't totally controlled, I get sleepy and moody. Most symptoms when diet isn't in control I haven't experienced. More common symptoms are trouble concentrating, mood swings, and mild bipolar disorder [extreme mood swings between depression and over-the-top joy]. When getting worse, teens experience attention deficit disorder [inability to focus that effects activities and learning].

Last year I was at the National PKU Conference. One scientist said that every week off the diet you can lose one IQ point. They showed footage of this two-year-old who was unable to say anything that was coherent. She couldn't follow objects around the room. By age four or five, most patients who are newly diagnosed are severely handicapped. The researcher found kids he studied in homes for children who are mentally disabled.[d]

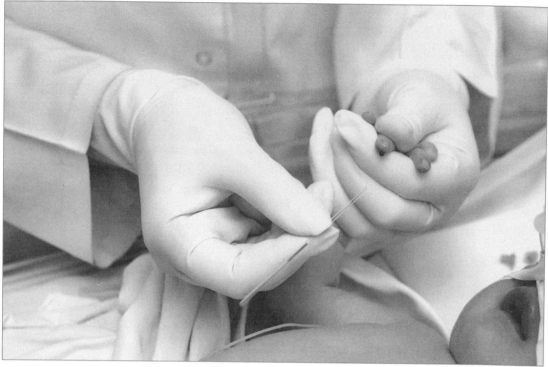

Newborn blood tests occur between twenty-four hours and one week after birth.

visible symptoms mentioned in the Mayo Clinic checklist (in "Babies without Treatment," page 139) emerge should PKU be left untreated.

If an initial blood test indicates PKU, additional blood tests are needed to confirm the diagnosis. The baby may also receive a urine test, and both parents and infant may benefit from genetic testing to pinpoint gene changes.

Those Pesky Genes Again

PKU is a rare, inherited condition. The condition originates in a recessive gene. That means parents can carry—and pass on—the PKU gene yet not have the disease themselves. Carriers never show signs of the condition, so parents rarely

Leah

No one else in my family has PKU. Both parents are carriers with one PKU gene. They gave them both to me. My little sister only has one PKU gene, so she's just a carrier.[e]

think to be genetically tested before conceiving. In fact, one in fifty to sixty people has the mutant gene that causes PKU, a huge number.

Even with these high numbers, genetic makeup causes only one in ten thousand PKU cases in newborns. A PKU diagnosis requires both parents to have the defective gene that alters how the body processes phenylalanine. Chances of two carriers mating are only 1 in 2,500. When both parents are carriers, however, their chances of giving birth to a baby with PKU are one in four, or 25 percent.[6]

Like several conditions in this book, PKU is an equal opportunity offender. Male and female babies receive the diagnosis equally. For some unknown reason, PKU is less likely to appear in blacks than whites or Asians. Incidence varies in different countries. In the United States, 14,500 people live with PKU.[7]

Women who have PKU are at greater risk of giving birth to children with the condition. High levels of phe harm the developing fetus, leading to serious birth defects. Still, babies born to moms with PKU can develop normally. This just takes planning ahead. And you need to maintain strict control of low PKU levels. Even if your food choices have been relaxed, this is the time to eat a restricted diet again. One study suggests starting the stricter diet before conception and following it through the entire pregnancy. The recommended diet should keep blood phe levels below 6 mg.[8] Once born, the hopefully healthy baby will receive a blood test to confirm no PKU and normal development.

Robin, Mom of Matthew, a Teen with PKU

Matthew's mom, Robin, remembers the first days with her newborn and discovering PKU.

PKU babies are born looking and acting normal. My body kept him from excess phenylalanine buildup. After he was born and had something to eat, his body couldn't process food. But in the first twenty-four hours, PKU doesn't show up. That takes a couple days. We found out that he failed the heal prick test. The doctor did a second test, and he called in a week with the news.

The first six months after the news, I was totally devastated. Our first child was a beautiful, healthy girl. She was born normally, and we don't know if she's a carrier yet. We have a third son that we know is a carrier. We had to map our genes and know he's a carrier but doesn't have PKU.

We had a lot of learning to do [after Matthew was diagnosed]. Besides having the condition, you have to figure out how to handle it. I was sad. My pediatrician said, "You are mourning the loss of the child you expected."[f]

Matthew

It hasn't been a big deal. At home I don't get extra attention for PKU. My dad can't eat sodium, so I'm not getting special attention. The biggest thing in high school is I never have to wait in line for food. My mom orders special food and sends it to the cafeteria. I would order my food in the morning and get it at lunch. I could walk past the food line in the cafeteria.[g]

Treating PKU

The only sure-fire treatment for PKU is a phenylalanine-free, or controlled, diet. This is a lifelong diet that severely limits foods with protein because they contain phe. But the body needs protein to develop. So people with PKU must drink a nutritional supplement daily to get enough nutrients to keep them healthy and growing. That's the only way to keep symptoms away and you healthy.

For some teens keeping to the diet is easier than for others. In the beginning, parents take the lead in securing and preparing meals for their baby. As children

---

Leah

I think there's been ups and downs. The main thing to deal with is the strict diet designed to keep your brain healthy. When I was young and my brain was developing, my diet was super strict. My diet has gotten less restrictive as I grew older.

Elementary school and junior high was my worst time for PKU. It's so different and so rare. When you're a kid you can't understand it. You have to eat this special diet and take formula.

What you don't like is being different. I would get made fun of for eating part of my lunch from school and part from home. I got made fun of for drinking formula. It smelled bad, so kids said I smelled bad. And I drank it from a bottle. Kids joked that it was a baby bottle.

By fourth grade, I finally reacted by getting more private. I stopped taking two lunches, so people wouldn't see what I was eating. I drank formula out of sight. I got more comfortable with myself by the end of junior high.[h]

and teens mature and become involved in more activities outside the home, responsibility for maintaining the diet to stay symptom-free is theirs.

The idea is to eat only a safe amount of phe—no more, no less. That amount varies over time and with every person who lives with PKU. Therefore, your doctor will keep records of your recorded diet and your growth. The doctor will also require frequent blood testing to monitor phe levels, particularly during growth spurts, puberty, and pregnancy.

Choosing Foods and Reading Labels

Since the sanctioned amount of phe is so low, blood levels between 2 and 10 mg, doctors advise teens to skip proteins altogether and drink supplements to replace lost nutrients. But the foods that contain protein may surprise you. Milk, eggs, cheeses, meats, fish, poultry, and nuts and soybeans are definite candidates to avoid. Did you know that potatoes, grains, and certain vegetables can cause problems, too?

"Most people with PKU are counting how many cherry tomatoes they eat because cherry tomatoes have protein," Leah said. "You are counting cereal or protein, so you don't have too much. A slice of wheat bread has three grams of

Teens can usually find PKU-friendly foods to eat with friends.

protein. I know people who can only have one gram of protein a day. Basically, you bake your own bread or buy it online."[9]

The best way to learn which foods work for your diet is to consult a nutritionist or trusted health-care worker. These professionals teach you how to read protein amounts on food labels. They help you discover which cereals, starches, fruits, and vegetables are acceptable and which measured amounts maintain your phe levels. They can recommend a milk substitute, synthetic phe-free formula, and specially prepared breads and other food substitutes online and where to find them.

At one time, doctors thought that by teen years the PKU diet could be relaxed. That advice changed after physicians observed patients who began having discomforting PKU symptoms after easing diet restrictions. Doctors also saw how difficult it was for teens who stopped to begin the diet again. Now doctors recommend restricting phe for a lifetime.

What Other Teens Say about Handling PKU

In the beginning, parents set the standard for sticking with treatment. They choose your food. They—and your medical team—teach you what you can and cannot eat and how much.

But dealing with unusual meals eventually falls to the person with PKU. Through the years, teens have devised ways to account for what they eat. Basically, following treatment involves planning ahead, learning what works best to help you stay focused on treatment, and being comfortable with yourself.

Olivia

I'm a big planner. I think you have to be. When you don't have any food issues, you don't think about how food centric our society is. Parties, sleepovers, pool parties, family gatherings. We're food centric. I definitely learned to be a big planner and that has translated to pretty much everything else in my life. For example, if I visit a friend out of town, I arrange to go between meals. Or I pack a lunch. I never eat meals in the cafeteria at school. I started a trend in high school by bringing my own lunch.

My parents were great when I was little about contacting parents before I'd go to friend's homes. Not everyone needs to know the details, but they need to know, "Hey, my daughter can't eat everything, so expect her to have a cooler in the refrigerator when she comes over."

I've learned that there are bits and pieces at most meals I can eat. For example, I can't eat cake, but I can eat the icing. At a restaurant I can get a bowl of fruit or salads or baked potatoes. Pretty much I order from the side menu. It's about picking and choosing. You have to make your diet fit your needs.[i]

Planning Ahead

School lunches can be tricky, especially if you struggle with who to tell what. When you're younger, your parent probably makes your lunches or calls ahead to work out food choices with cafeteria workers. With time, you learn to prepare your own lunches. Brown-bagging food and packing acceptable snacks to bring along is common among teens with PKU. It's just easier.

Some teens find the low-phe diet keeps them hungry. Substitute foods don't always provide a full feeling. With a mainly vegan diet of fruits and vegetables

Teens with PKU need to carry snacks that fit their diet, especially when exercising.

Leah

My diet has gotten less restrictive as I grew older. Since my PKU is mild, I can eat more foods than most people with PKU. About a year or so ago, I started taking a new medicine called Kuvan that helps enzymes metabolize phe. I responded to the medicine, so I can eat more protein. A year ago I had my first burger, which was odd. Then I had my first milk shake. Whoa! That was amazing!

I still have to eat less protein and watch what I eat—every day. I am still on formula. I run track, so I need protein. I wake up, have breakfast, go to school, have formula with lunch, have formula before running, and have formula and Kuvan for dinner.

I make formula bottles to take with me. It's easier to transport that way. I put powder in the bottle and take it to school. I mix the powder with water at school. It's gross if warm. It's one hundred percent amino acids and it tastes like it.[j]

with some substitute breads and pastas, teens often complain they never feel 100 percent full.

The trick is to keep low-phe snacks handy to give you an energy boost. A few teens mentioned spending a block of time preparing dishes and storing portions in plastic containers and freezing them. They bake snack crackers, rolls, breads, and pizza. They buy baked pretzels and low-protein pasta and prepare several different sauces to vary meals with different added vegetables.

"Whenever I make green beans or eat pineapple or peaches, I always put the leftovers in single service containers, so that they are ready to eat when I am hungry later on. Sticking to the low phe diet is SO much easier if you have

Brittany

Usually, I pack my own lunch with both low-pro foods and some of the other higher foods as well. I usually would bring an apple or some other type of fruit, a sandwich or crackers of some kind and then something else like a rice crispy square. I would also take a fruit cup or free jello or pudding that my mom would make for me. I feel that it is much easier dealing with the diet once you get older. . . . You kind of know what you can and can't eat. Also, when you are older you know more about the diet and you know about how much you can eat.[k]

> ### Larry
>
> Our Taco Bell will make me a taco with only lettuce and tomato and salsa or hot sauce [check phe levels for the shell beforehand]. If we go to Kentucky Fried Chicken I eat from the food bar potatoes, veggies, fruit, and salad. Otherwise we go to a buffet and there's always lots of fruits, vegetables, Jell-O, and baked potatoes. We eat Oriental sometimes, and when we do I eat the strawberry-covered bananas and the vegetable dishes.[l]

premeasured food in the fridge just waiting for you every day," PKU teen Kristi Eichorst wrote on National PKU News.[10]

Teens with PKU often complain that eating out can be a pain. But it's part of getting together with friends. You meet at restaurants. You hang out at the local pizza place or in someone's kitchen. Several teens offer these suggestions: Call ahead to see if there are acceptable foods. Sometimes, you aren't sure where you are going, so sticking some snacks in your pocket or backpack can let you join your friends without having to order from a sketchy menu. Usually, teens with PKU can be creative and find something satisfying—and social—to eat.

Tricky Traveling: Discovering What Works for You

Being away from home for more than a school day involves extra planning. You might be on some traveling sport or debate team, or vacationing with friends or family. You wonder if you should pack or send food ahead. You consider what to do with your necessary formula. Here are some tips from teens on the go who wrote suggestions to PKU News:[11]

- "I always try to find out as much as I can about the place I am visiting. [Call or e-mail ahead.] What is available? What foods are commonly eaten? How clean and safe is the water? Will I be able to keep my formula cold or

> ### Olivia
>
> Every once in a while if there was a kid I didn't know or was annoying asked about what I ate, my response was, "I'm vegetarian, vegan, lactose intolerant, and have nuts allergies." I am those things but none of those things.[m]

not? Does the hotel have a refrigerator? The more information I have, the better I can plan the easiest way to take care of my diet."

- "When traveling by plane, I ALWAYS pack my formula in my carry-on. Formula is expensive and hard to replace. If luggage is lost or stolen, I can replace things or manage without them, EXCEPT for my formula."
- "When I'm traveling short distances in the states, I usually take a cooler with ice to keep my formula cold. However, when I traveled internationally, I put the dry powder in my cups and mixed it with water later."
- A product called techni-ice keeps food cold for up to two days.
- "I don't ever take food [low-protein] with me when I travel. I might put a few crackers or cookies in my carry-on with a couple apples for snacks. I've learned to eat salads, vegetables, fruit, and other low phe content foods."

Being Comfortable with Yourself—and PKU

Having PKU can become complicated with family and friends—but it doesn't have to. For some, like Matthew, "it hasn't been a big deal."[12] Others experienced more problems during elementary and junior high years when all kids are more self-conscious and hate to be different.

One activity that helps is to share feelings with others going through similar problems, like sticking to a low-phe diet. Check resources at the end of this chapter to find a local group that might connect you with others your age.

Think about staying at a camp for kids and teens with PKU. Teens report loving the camp. You hear about other teen challenges and successes growing up

Leah

Most people I talk to are other teens. For casual friends, they know Leah doesn't eat a lot of protein. Other friends, like my boyfriend, know what it's called and everything. To a majority of people I say I don't eat meat or protein and might be bringing my own food to their house. I still don't like to talk about it much around other teenagers because others don't get it. They ask if it's an allergy. If I get hardcore and sit you down and explain PKU, it means I trust you and you're going to be my friend.

People with PKU generally don't want to talk about it. If they do, please listen. Really listen. If you can't, don't be a jerk about PKU and call it weird. That goes with any chronic disease.[n]

Olivia

In first grade, I remember PKU affected my social life. I can remember that I felt like this weird kid with a lunch box and food. Kids can be harsh. A first impression at six affects your life. After that I don't think it affected my social life too much. I think it made me closer to friends more quickly because it's usually a question I get early in a relationship. It's not so personal that it's intimate, but it's become a nice ground to build off of.

I would say my parents might have babied or coddled me a little bit longer. I think it was for my own good, so I would learn more how to advocate for myself. They would show me. Especially at restaurants. On vacation my mom is first to say, "Olivia, do you see that they have this on the menu?" Sometimes I get snappy.

By high school, most teens with PKU find their stride. They actively participate in the same range of activities that any teen does. They realize everyone has something that makes them different. They figure out whether they feel comfortable sharing that they have PKU and with who. PKU might cause them to eat differently, but they are like any other teen—wonderful traits, warts, and all.°

with PKU. You can eat everything and to your heart's delight, as meals are specially supervised and prepared for PKU diets. The National PKU Alliance lists PKU camps across the country at npkua.org/Portals/0/PDFs/camps/2015%20 Summer%20Camp%20List.pdf.

Leah

If you got PKU don't give up, man. It's going to be every day, but it's going to be your life. PKU is not you: it's this thing that you have, like a pesky sibling. Deal with it, and don't let it consume you. Cry or throw things at a wall when you need to, if that helps. But don't give up. There will be days when you say you can't do this anymore and other days when it's no big deal. *You're Beautiful! We're still us.*[P]

Resources

Organizations

National Institute of Child Health and Human Development
National Institutes of Health
www.nichd.nih.gov/health/topics/pku/conditioninfo
Government agency started in 1962 that conducts research and clinical trials and supports professional training that examines how different diseases, including PKU, affect individuals and their families. A good place to look for the latest PKU research.

National PKU Alliance
PO Box 501
Tomahawk, WI 54487
715-437-0477
www.npkua.org
National support and educational organization that has local programs and access to PKU camps for teens and their families.

National PKU News
6869 Woodlawn Avenue NE, Suite 116
Seattle, WA 98115-5469
206-525-8140
www.pkunews.org
Nonprofit founded in 1989 by a dietician working with PKU patients. PKU News is dedicated to offering current news and information to families and professionals who deal with PKU. The founder, Virginia Schuett, has written several information and recipe books for readers of all ages.

PKU.com
www.pku.com
An online community that includes everything about PKU—education, resources, support discussions, even recipes. One caveat: the site is run by a pharmaceutical firm, so research product recommendations thoroughly before buying.

Books

Virginia Schuett, *Low Protein Food List for PKU*, Madison: University of Wisconsin Press, 1997, revised and updated 2010. This book's author founded the National PKU News in Seattle, Washington, and dedicated this title to helping figure out what a family member with PKU can eat.

U.S. Government, *Comprehensive Medical Encyclopedia with Treatment Options, Clinical Data, and Practical Information* (Two CD-ROM Set), Progressive Management, 2009. A "book-on-disc" that is designed to be user friendly and a reference and educational tool for patients and their families dealing with PKU.

SICKLE CELL DISEASE: THE INVISIBLE PAIN

What makes sickle cell disease (SCD) less visible than other conditions in this book, such as Crohn's or celiac? The answer lies in the fact that this lifelong illness alters red blood cells. These cells transport life-giving oxygen throughout the body. When a problem with blood cells exists, the situation can create havoc anywhere in the body. The pain just appears without warning. Scary. Really scary.

Understanding What You Have

Sickle cell disease is an inherited blood disorder. A glitch in genetic makeup alters the shape of red blood cells. The different shape causes these cells to function abnormally. Because the disease is chronic, it can cause lifelong suffering and many complications.

The specific problem with SCD lies in hemoglobin, red pigment in red blood cells that transports oxygen. The defective gene, named hemoglobin S, creates an abnormal shape of the red blood cells. Under a microscope, diseased red blood cells look like tiny sickle, or banana-like, forms.

Heidy's Story

Heidy reported in the book *Hope & Destiny* that by age ten she had been hospitalized more than one hundred times for intense [SCD] pain. She hated all those trips to the emergency room, even though they were the only way to ease her pain. Sometimes, pain was bearable. Other times she thought she would die. Treatments weren't much better. Strong drugs. Medicines given through needles poked into her veins. She just wanted to be a regular kid with regular issues. She wanted to live a normal life. Over and over she asked: "Why me?"[a]

In a healthy teen, red blood cells easily pass through blood vessels. For some reason, sickle cells without oxygen tend to be stiff and sticky, causing them to clump. Their unusual shape plus clumping of cells impedes blood flow through small blood vessels. Sometimes sickle cells get caught, or they break apart. Whichever the situation, sickle cells reduce the amount of oxygen and blood flow to body tissues. Without enough oxygen, tissue and organ damage results, along with painful episodes in the affected areas.

The medical community also calls the painful episodes crises. Symptoms of crises can be mild enough to remain undiscovered for years or severe enough to require parents to make frequent trips to the hospital with their babies. Depending upon how severe the episode and how quickly the body responds to treatment, crises can last hours or days.

"You can get slow throbs, and it builds and then feels like someone is punching you, then stabbing you. Then a building is coming down on you," Eric Williams, a teen with SCD, told NBC News[1] during September Sickle Cell Annual Awareness Month.

Another complication results from the life span of blood cells. Healthy red blood cells usually live about 120 days, while sickle cells survive only 10 to 12 days. Because the body cannot replace sickle cells fast enough, the number of red blood cells declines. This reduction often causes anemia, a condition when

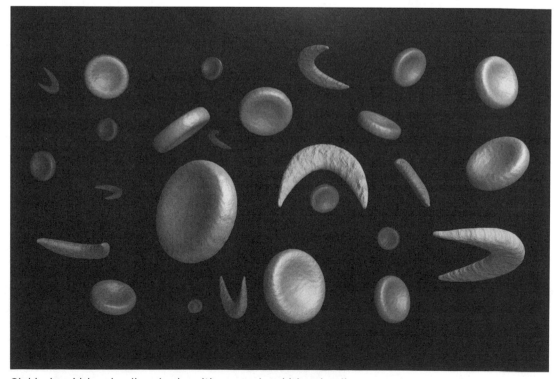

Sickled red blood cells mingle with normal red blood cells.

reduced hemoglobin triggers fatigue and other weakening symptoms. Some medical professionals refer to SCD as sickle cell anemia.

Range of Symptoms and Complications

How sickle cell develops differs from teen to teen. Symptoms can be mild or severe. They can first appear about four months of age or not until years later. More often, one of the first signs results from blockage of small blood vessels in hands and feet. This blockage causes swelling and pain in the affected areas.

As someone ages, growth and development may be slower than normal. Teens with SCD might have experienced puberty later. The disease touches other areas as well. Chronic anemia results in fatigue, pale skin, and weakness. Even mild exercise causes shortness of breath from lack of oxygen to the lungs. When sickle cells collect in the lungs, they can produce illness that resembles infections, such as pneumonia.

Because bone marrow works overtime to boost red blood cells, bones thin. Thinning bones makes them more brittle and prone to fracture. Speedy breakdown of red blood cells may result in yellow-colored skin and whites of the

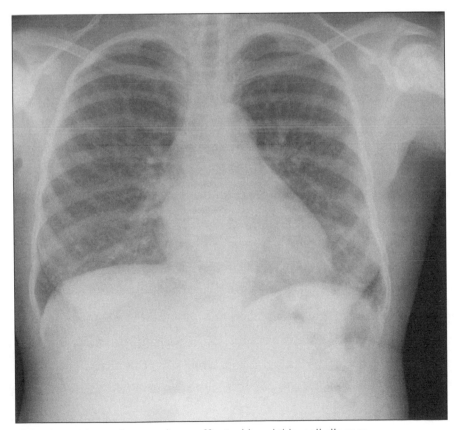

This chest X-ray shows a lung affected by sickle cell disease.

eyes. Without enough oxygen flowing to light-sensitive tissue of the eye, vision can deteriorate. Sickle cells that clog blood vessels to the brain can trigger strokes. Strokes damage the brain by interrupting blood flow to the brain or by leaking blood from vessel walls. Either situation can be life threatening.

Teens may feel sudden pain in any part of the body—organs or joints—where sickle cells block blood flow. If pain isn't trouble enough, complications occur when SCD harms internal organs. A liver can stop working and require surgery. The heart can enlarge, which may lead to more severe heart disease later. Damage to the spleen, which filters bacteria from the bloodstream, can leave you open to infection.

Episodes of pain can result from any situation that raises demand for oxygen. So teens need to watch out for high altitudes, infection, strenuous exercise, and stress. As a woman with SCD, even delivering a baby can trigger crises.

You Don't Have to Be Black

Probably SCD has been around for centuries. But Dr. James Herrick first wrote about sickle-shaped cells in 1910. He told of a patient who complained about

Geno Atkins, National Football League Player

The first time I learned I carry the sickle cell trait was as a freshman at the University of Georgia. . . . Having the sickle cell trait does not exclude an athlete from participating in sports, however, the training staff and coaches need to take precautions to ensure the athlete is not put in dangerous situations. In high school my coaches would get on me because I was always in the back during running drills, and I often got very tired. I think back now and realize that it could have been a dangerous situation for me if I had over-zealous coaches or I had pushed too much during those hot days in South Florida. . . .

I knew from my research that it would not be good for me to play in high altitudes, so I prayed I wouldn't get drafted by Denver, which is at a high altitude. I ended up in Cincinnati and have played at a very high level without any adverse effects of the sickle cell trait. During the 2011 season, we did travel to Denver to play the Broncos and that was the first time I can truly say I felt the effects of the trait. I could not breathe after a 10-play series and had to be given oxygen on the sideline.[b]

pain episodes and signs of anemia. Because Herrick used the term "sickle shaped cells"[2] to describe what he saw under a microscope, the name stuck.

In 1927, studies revealed that depriving red blood cells of oxygen caused them to take on the characteristic sickle shape. These results linked oxygen deprivation and sickle cells to a specific disease. Later research determined that some relatives of patients who carried sickle cells never experienced symptoms of the disease. They could pass on the disease without actually experiencing symptoms. What they showed became known as the sickle cell trait and linked SCD to a genetic condition.

Fast forward to the twenty-first century and more information about SCD. Forget the myth that you have to be black to be born with sickle cell disease. It's wrong. Your likelihood of acquiring SCD is more a matter of geography. In regions where the disease malaria runs rampant—think hot-weather places— SCD appears more often. Mosquitos thrive in hot places—including sub-Saharan climates—and when they bite humans, malaria gets into the bloodstream. Over many centuries, human bodies have adapted to fend off malaria. Turns out that blood with sickle cells protects against malaria. A problem develops when this same sickle cell blood causes SCD, a different potentially deadly concern.

! Myths about Sickle Cell Disease

● Few teens have ever heard of sickle cell disease or anemia. But many who have harbor misguided ideas about the disease and teens who experience it.

Myth: Only African Americans get SCD.
Fact: Geography plays more of a role in inheriting SCD than skin color.

Myth: All female teens who make frequent trips to the bathroom are pregnant.
Fact: Frequency of urinating depends upon many conditions—what and how much you drink, how large your bladder is, whether you are pregnant, and your general health. Girls who have SCD need to drink lots of water. That means they urinate often, not that they're pregnant.

Myth: Teens with SCD are drama queens.
Fact: Think again before you joke about someone who doubles over or grimaces in pain. Sickle pain is real—and it can be intense. Sickle cells

can travel anywhere in the body. When they get lodged somewhere, pain occurs, sometimes great pain. No drama intended: it just hurts.

Myth: Teens with SCD pretend to be sick to get out of gym activities.
Fact: Sickle cell disease and pain accompanying it can drain anyone. Many cannot physically handle sports and exercises that are part of gym class. Teens with SCD would much prefer joining class activities and not be singled out.

Myth: Sickle cell anemia is catchy.
Fact: Sickle cell is a genetic disease that teens acquire at birth. You cannot catch SCD by touching, kissing, or anything else with someone who has the condition.

Myth: Teens with SCD are dumb.
Fact: Teens with SCD are the same as you and your friends in school. But some sick teens have been more prone to strokes when younger. These teens might talk differently or have learning disabilities. But they still have brain power to learn with an extra boost. Another issue is repeated hospitalizations. Teens with SCD may spend considerable time in and out of the hospital. That may slow them down in school from missing many class days at a time. So be kind—and helpful to classmates with chronic disease.

More recently, malaria has come under control in many steamy places but not all. India reports the highest rate of malaria—and SCD. The United States wiped out malaria in the early 1950s. But millions of people worldwide carry malaria and SCD. Teens whose ancestors moved from the Middle East, India, Mediterranean countries, and Africa inherited SCD from their ancestors. Sickle cell disease rears its ugly head in the United States when travelers return or migrate from these other nations.

According to national figures,[3, 4] one hundred thousand people in the United States have SCD, with millions more worldwide. Eighty thousand Americans with the disease represent different backgrounds. One in 172 Hispanic Americans carry the sickle cell trait. The largest number of cases happen among African Americans—one in five hundred births. Equally troublesome, one in twelve blacks carry the sickle cell trait.

Types of SCD

According to the St. Jude's Research Department of Hematology,[5] sickle cell disease is actually a group of disorders. In the United States, doctors identify three common types of SCD. You receive one hemoglobin gene from each parent. Differences depend upon the makeup of your two hemoglobin genes.

Teens with SCD inherit an abnormal hemoglobin gene from each parent. If you have one copy of the gene that causes SCD from one parent, you will probably live a life without symptoms. You are, however, said to carry the sickle cell trait. That means you can be a carrier who may give the disease to your children. If you find a mate with the same trait, you would pass on SCD to your offspring. Or the trait could be one factor in combining with another hemoglobin gene to cause other medical complications.

Hemoglobin SS Disease

Rather than normal hemoglobin A in red blood cells, teens with this form of SCD show mostly hemoglobin S. The SS comes from both parents who have the sickle cell trait. That combination results in the most common form of SCD, hemoglobin SS disease.

Sickle-Hemoglobin C Disease (also Hemoglobin SC Disease)

With this form of SCD, teens display both hemoglobin S and hemoglobin C in their red blood cells. Both are irregular types of hemoglobin and result in medical problems. Hemoglobin C by itself usually does not cause illness. But coupled with hemoglobin S, disease results. In this case, one parent carries the sickle cell trait and the other contributes hemoglobin C. Therefore, offspring will be born with hemoglobin SC disease.

Sickle Beta-Thalessemia Disease

With this form of SCD, one parent has the sickle cell trait, while the other has the beta thalessemia trait. Together they risk the range of SCD symptoms.

Testing

Since 2012, all states now test newborn infants for sickle cell anemia. The most common method is called hemoglobin electrophoresis. This test measures blood oxygen levels in hemoglobin.

Any teens touched by SCD need to get genetic counseling before starting families of their own. Genetic counseling helps both partners better evaluate the risk of passing on the disease. Even if you do not exhibit signs of SCD but have relatives who do, it's worth getting a simple blood test to make sure you are not carrying the trait. Your information could have an impact on your future family's reproductive choices and chances of passing on the disease.

Treatment Options

At one time, kids with SCD died before their teenage years. Now they live to fifty or beyond. Longer and better life spans come from medical advances and access to more knowledgeable professionals. Still, there is no cure for SCD yet, although studies are promising for gene therapy.

Treatment options do exist, however. These focus on preventing episodes and reducing the effects of those that occur. Mild attacks can usually be controlled at home. Doctors recommend taking ibuprofen every six hours for one or two days to relieve pain.[6] Drink lots of liquids, preferably water. Rest. Use warm (not icy or hot) compresses to expand blood vessels in painful areas. And try to distract yourself.

If pain gets worse, ask your doctor for stronger medications that reduce pain. Increase fluids and keep busy, for example, with calling a friend, computer games, or a favorite television show. Diversions sometimes help you control pain.

If pain becomes severe, you spike a fever of 101 degrees or higher, or you have trouble breathing, strongly consider a trip to the nearest doctor's office, clinic, or hospital. You may need fluids injected into your bloodstream, stronger medicines to reduce the pain, or oxygen to help you breathe. In some cases, the medicine hydroxyurea is offered to reduce chest and joint pains. Studies indicate that hydroxyurea also reduces the number of return hospital trips and need for blood transfusions.[7]

Some teens find that red blood cell transfusions give them better quality of life. With transfusions, a technician exchanges abnormal red blood cells with healthy ones donated by another person. Transfusions are most successful in situations when teens have had strokes, become anemic from lack of oxygen in the blood, or have difficulty breathing due to low oxygen levels.

Recent successes have resulted from bone marrow (stem cell) transplants. Marrow in bones of teens with SCD produces red blood cells with disease-causing hemoglobin S. If your doctor can find a perfect match, diseased bone marrow can be replaced with healthy bone marrow of a donor without SCD. Doctors find the exchange often produces a cure. But exact matches are rare, which limits how many teens can find the cure they desire.

Life with SCD

Several general tips for living with chronic conditions are offered in chapter 11, "Taking Care of Everyday Business." But there are many times when teens with SCD find their condition causes specific problems that might benefit from other suggestions:

- Anything that makes your blood vessels constrict should be off limits. That means taking a pass on smoking—cigarettes and marijuana. Blood

Drinking plenty of water helps blood flow with sickle cell disease.

vessel constriction only heightens pain. Nicotine reduces oxygen in the lungs, which can trigger an episode. Why take a chance on smoking?

- Same with alcoholic beverages. Alcohol speeds up your loss of fluids. If you get dehydrated from too little fluids, pain occurs. Better to drink eight to ten glasses of water that will help reduce pain.

- Thinking of trying harder street drugs? Think again. Cocaine stimulates heart and breathing rates as well as raises blood pressure. Any of these changes can cause a SCD episode. Caffeinated drinks, such as colas and coffee, create similar situations in the body. This is in addition to addiction problems street drugs cause. Street drugs are dangerous for anyone, but more dangerous for teens with SCD.

- Exercise moderately but keep moving, if you can. Regular exercise helps keep your mind and body healthy. But start slow and build up gradually. Make sure you drink plenty of water while exercising.

- Remember to avoid any activity in high altitudes, so mountain climbing probably wouldn't be the best choice for outdoor fun. If you have any questions about what your body can handle, consult your doctor or nurse first. Remember to keep your coach or gym teacher up on your health. You may think speaking up isn't cool, but whatever promotes a healthier you is the best choice.

- Teens with SCD deal with a lot more than non-SCD teens. If the worry and stress of your disease grows too great, seek professional assistance.

AJ Green Has Goals

Teenager AJ loves to sing. He sang for presidents Bill Clinton and Barack Obama and has performed with many well-known stars. One day AJ hopes to win a Grammy for his talent. His other main goal is to advocate for teens like himself with SCD. As he told the Center for Disease Control, he hopes to "put sickle cell on the map" by raising awareness of the disease. So far, he has talked with other kids about SCD, spotlighted the need for minority blood donors, and urged healthy minority teens to donate blood.

"For the most part I have been able to meet my goals," he wrote, "but I always strive for bigger goals in life, so everything's not complete just yet. My first aspiration was to be known as a singer and also as an advocate for sickle cell disease. . . . People don't have to be afraid of it [SCD]: they don't have to be held down by it. Try to find triumph in the situation."[c]

- Ask your trusted doctor for a referral. Check out a support group, one familiar with SCD, at your local clinic. Find a friend or family member who will listen to you and give you a much-needed hug. You don't have to journey with SCD alone.

Resources

Organizations

American Sickle Cell Anemia Association
DD Building at Cleveland Clinic
Suite DD1-201
10900 Carnegie Avenue
Cleveland, OH 44106
216-229-8600
www.ascaa.org
The oldest sickle cell research and educational group in the United States. Services include diagnostic testing, counseling, family counseling and support, and screenings at local health fairs.

Centers for Disease Control and Prevention
1600 Clifton Road NE
Atlanta, GA 30329-4027
800-232-4636
www.cdc.gov/ncbddd/sicklecell/index.html
National resource for the latest information and research about treatments and clinical trials.

Children's National Sickle Cell Disease Program
111 Michigan Avenue NW
Washington, DC 20010
202-476-5000
childrensnational.org/~/media/cnhs-site/files/departments/sicklecelldisease
program/bmt-brochure.ashx?la=en
Treatment center for patients birth through adolescence that includes peer support, transition to adult care services, and pain therapy. Link here leads to a brochure on the program.

National Heart, Lung, Blood Institute
PO Box 30105

Bethesda, MD 20824-0105
301-592-8573
www.nhlbi.nih.gov/health/health-topics/topics/sca
Department run by the National Institutes of Health that offers the latest explanations and resources for research and other organizations that deal with SCD.

Sickle Cell Disease Association of America
3700 Koppers Street, Suite 510
Baltimore, MD 21227
800-421-8453
www.sicklecelldisease.org/
A group that advocates for families experiencing SCD and searches for a cure. The site includes a kids' network with teen ambassadors and general information.

UIC Comprehensive Sickle Cell Center
University of Illinois Hospital and Health Science System
1740 West Taylor Street, Suite 5E
Chicago, IL 60612
866-600-CARE/312-996-5680
www.uicscc.org
University-sponsored health center that offers care, treatment, and social support for teens with SCD.

Books

Allan Platt, James Eckman, and Lewis Hsu, *Hope and Destiny: The Patient's and Parent's Guide to Sickle Cell Disease and Sickle Cell Trait*, revised 3rd ed. Indianapolis: Hilton Publishing, 2011. Overview of living with SCD, including complications, research, and treatment.

U.S. Department of Health, *The Management of SCD*, CreateSpace, 2014. Up-to-date research, health management information, and treatment options for SCD.

TOURETTE SYNDROME: ITS VARIED FEATURES

Tourette syndrome is one of the more misunderstood conditions. One reason involves the puzzling movements, or tics, teens produce as part of the disease. Another oddity is how tics erupt seemingly without cause or warning and at any time. This mix of varied characteristics taken together adds up to a syndrome, Tourette syndrome (TS).

Every teen with TS exhibits an individual range of uncontrolled symptoms. Tics can be obvious and distracting, like shouts, or barely noticeable, such as occasional blinking. Each type of tic has the potential to interfere with activities someone with TS tries to execute. Often, tics bother people around them, too.

Equally troubling, tics can form the basis of how others perceive teens who tic. You know that adolescence can be a time of feeling extra self-conscious. Imagine how embarrassing it would be to stand out because of some odd movement or sound you produce. Others with little knowledge of TS may wonder whether you're safe to hang around. They may tease or fear you because you have Tourette. By learning more about the disorder, hopefully, you and others will understand that TS has no effect on how smart, agreeable, or safe someone with TS is.

Each year, thousands of children and teens receive a diagnosis of TS. Researchers estimate that two hundred thousand Americans exhibit forms of TS so severe they can be life altering. Those with milder signs, such as occasional twitches or facial movements, account for as many as one in one hundred individuals. Countless others struggle with feeling something is wrong but never discovering what it is. The bad news is tics tend to worsen in early adolescence, a difficult time for any preteen. The good news is tics subside by the late teens and early adulthood. Doctors continue to investigate the causes and treatments of this challenging disease.

Ryan

My mom says I started sniffing a lot when I was five years old. Thinking something was wrong, she brought me to the doctor. He tested for allergies and prescribed medication. Then other movements started—head jerking, eye blinking, and more embarrassing, grabbing my testicles. I was ten years old before another doctor diagnosed me with TS. By then other kids noticed how I acted.

I would get teased constantly. People never asked why I was doing these things. They just made fun of me. Some seemed scared. I'd hear them talking about me behind my back. I cried a lot. And I acted out and hit kids.

My symptoms changed as I got older. My hands and toes jerked. My fingers tapped on desks and tabletops. I repeated phrases other people said. Unusual mouth sounds came and went. Test-taking triggered grunts and smacking noises that bothered classmates who needed quiet to think.

In seventh grade, I started asking questions, even when I knew the answers. I did this at home and at school—often. I'd raise my hand constantly to ask what others found obvious. Teachers thought I took up too much class time. Classmates found me weird. My mother yelled at me to stop. I had no friends.

In high school, everything improved. A school counselor helped me organize and adapt to various situations, like taking tests in another room. I gained confidence. I joined the soccer team and ran track off-season. I still jerk my head sometimes or make strange sounds. But I learned to mask the movements to look more natural. My grades improved, so I feel less stress about schoolwork. Now I have a shot at a good college to train as an engineer.[a]

A Complicated Condition

Tourette syndrome is a physical disorder involving the nervous system. The brain tells one or more muscles to contract. These muscles can be anywhere in the body. Muscle messages result in unwanted sounds or movements called tics. Faces contort without context. Feet kick. Noises and inappropriate words explode out of nowhere. Signs of TS involve these repeated, involuntary movements and sounds. Symptoms can change over time in intensity and variety.

What makes tics so frustrating is they are beyond anyone's control. Tics happen despite the situation. They appear suddenly and quickly and repeat without

Lillian

My harsh symptoms of TS started when I was in grade three. No one, including myself and my parents, knew what was wrong with me. Worst of all, my symptoms included blurting out and repeating profane [foul] and inappropriate language. I couldn't control it at all. I felt horrible about myself. I used to get punished every day for uttering bad language. I got teased and was despised by a few people. Back then, I used to cry myself to sleep every night, wondering if I was crazy and why I said horrible language. A year later I was diagnosed with TS.[b]

warning. Not surprisingly, tics worsen when someone is under stress or excited. But most teens who tic find outbursts improve during calm and focused activities. The most important thing to understand is that a diagnosis of TS does not mean someone has mental illness or is less smart than anyone else.

"Usually, my symptoms worsen when I am nervous and under pressure, or when I eat too much sugar. On the other hand, my symptoms lessen when I concentrate on one thing really hard, for example, if I read or draw," Lillian[1] wrote in *That Darn Tic: A Newsletter by and for Kids with Tourette Syndrome*.

Classifying Tics

Doctors talk about TS symptoms as either motor or vocal tics. Vocal tics begin in muscles that control speech and sound. Examples of vocal tics include everything from barking, sniffing, or smacking sounds to swearing and shouting words or phrases—all at odd times. Motor tics can arise in any other muscle of the body. Examples of motor movements can be as basic as eye blinking or as dramatic— and painful—as punching yourself.

Either type of tic can be simple or complex. Individual movements of one body part, such as eye blinking, are called simple tics. Tics that are simple involve individual sounds or movements, such as snorting, throat clearing, or grunting. For example, simple vocal tics arise from air moving through either the nose, throat, or vocal cords, rather than from more than one organ or passageway.

Complex tics engage several muscle groups at the same time. These muscles act together to provoke patterns of movements. For example, jumping or tapping walls are complex motor tics because the coordinated muscle pattern requires more than one muscle group to carry out the movements. More embarrassing are motor tics that affect other people. Some teens with TS feel the urge to touch someone else, imitate other's actions, which is called echopraxia, or make offensive gestures, named copropraxia.

Complex vocal tics produce their own share of unease. With echolalia, a person repeats that last sound, word, or phrase uttered by someone else. For example, your mother says, "Pick up your underwear." You might follow immediately with, "Pick up your underwear." Palilalia is similar. With palilalia, you repeat your own words or sounds. You might say, "I'll pick up my pants, pants, pants," or "I'll pick up my pants-s-s-s." Imagine how frustrating this repeating can be for both you and someone on the receiving end.

The most well-known symptom of TS is coprolalia, which Lillian mentioned. This form of vocal tic causes cursing or uttering socially inappropriate words or phrases for their specific situation or culture. Think about swearing at a funeral service or shouting odd phrases in class or a quiet movie theater, and you can assume how problematic—and inappropriately attention-getting—this form of TS can be.

Because coprolalia seems so outrageous, this is usually where media focuses, if it portrays TS at all. Television and movies that highlight people with TS usually feature someone who blurts out a torrent of swear words or sexual terms without prompting. Yet, less than 15 percent of teens with TS struggle with coprolalia. With such popular negative attention, many people assume that anyone with tics also swears, which is untrue.

Lessening Tics

Many teens report that their tics ease when they exercise. Rhythmic physical activity helps refocus energy required to generate tics. In much the same way as Lillian suggested, tics often disappear when concentrating on an absorbing activity. Some teens find their tics subside while they listen to music, read, or draw.

Sandy

There is much more in public about really severe cases. Kids feel they have the right to brand every kid who has it [TS] as a freak. If anyone is different, kids say they have TS. Television shows say things like, "These poor traumatic kids [with TS] are learning to cope with disabling things in their lives." It's not very disabling at all from my experience, but my experience is not very consistent with everyone else's. Somehow people have drawn conclusions. Not sure where people get their information.[c]

Neurologist and popular science author Oliver Sacks noticed how focusing reduced tics for a surgeon with TS. Sacks observed the surgeon as he went through his daily routine, including surgery. At home the doctor sometimes tossed objects, such as saucepans, a rolling pin, or an iron. Onlookers might think he was angry, but he wasn't. The surgeon also said he felt compelled to perform activities three or five times, numbers he couldn't understand. At the hospital he walked down hallways skipping each fifth step. Without warning, he bent over and touched the ground. In meetings, the doctor tapped coworkers with his fingers or rolled on his side to reach their shoulders with his toes. But in surgery, Sacks watched in fascination as the doctor skillfully used his tools on a patient, despite all his

Table 10.1 Simple and Complex Motor and Vocal Tics

Simple Motor Tics	Simple Vocal Tics
toe bending	throat clearing
finger moving	barking
tongue thrusting	grunting
eye blinking	lip smacking
leg jerking	belching
shoulder shrugging	sniffing
head jerking	coughing
neck twisting	hissing
muscle tensing	yelping
nose wrinkling	tongue clicking
Complex Motor Tics	**Complex Vocal Tics**
biting, rubbing, hitting, or other self-destructive actions	spitting
	stuttering
leaping	saying words or phrases out of context
spinning	
producing unusual faces	producing animal sounds
smelling objects	saying offensive words or phrases
imitating others' actions	repeating one's own words or sounds
producing offensive gestures	repeating a sounds word, or phrase
touching other people or things	after someone else

Jeremy

I have vocal tics, grunting, teeth grinding, rapid hand movements. It's like a ball of energy builds, like having to go to the bathroom. Eventually you have to go. This massive amount of energy has to come out. For me, I can hold it to a certain point. Then I have to go some place private and let a couple [tics] loose. Afterward, there is this sense of relief. I feel less anxious. During puberty, when my hormones were raging, there were tics coming out of nowhere. Now that I know what tics are, I can subdue them until I'm alone when others can't see them. There are tons of different types of TS.[d]

touching and jumping before surgery. He couldn't understand how the surgeon performed such delicate work.

"B. took the knife, made a bold, clear incision—there was no hint of any ticking or distraction," Sacks wrote.[2]

Stopping Tics

The first signs of TS usually appear between three and ten years. Common initial signs are eye blinking or throat clearing, although children may exhibit a range of tics. With time, different tics may emerge. Or the intensity of tics may change.

Between nine and thirteen years of age, tics may worsen. This is when new and increased hormones kick in. Along with hormones and accompanying body changes comes emotional concerns about maturing and what other preteens think about strange TS movements. Since worry increases stress and stress contributes to more ticking, approaching adolescence can seem like a minefield with a seemingly out-of-control body.

As distressing as these changes can be, the upside is TS makes teens more aware of their bodies and how different parts perform. Increased body image allows many teens to feel when a tic may happen. This information helps teens identify what triggers their tics. Once a trigger is identified, the teen can better predict and handle these tics in various situations. Tics may never go away. But teens who have them can gain at least some control over when and where they occur.

Many teens report they can suppress their tics. Suppressing doesn't work for everyone with TS, but for those who can, controlling their tics lessens the stigma of odd movements and sounds. Some teens maintain they can hold back tics for up to thirty to sixty minutes. Holding them in allows time to find a private place to let the tics out.

> ### Cindy
>
> Sometimes if I try to hold them [tics] back, I can feel it inside of me building up. I want to let it out. It's just like a certain area where the tic is. If I'm really self-conscious, I can hold the tic back and let it out an hour later. Sometimes, I don't think about it, so it goes away. It just sort of disappears. But other times, it gets worse if I hold it back. Like after I'm out of a self-conscious place and I'm in a safe place, I let it out until I feel relaxed.[e]

And let the tics out they must. Try to stop a sneeze or hiccup. It works for a while. But you need to express it eventually to release the tension inside your body. Same feelings with tics. Eventually, teens with TS need to relieve the tension created by a tic. For some teens, when tics are delayed they explode with greater force and for longer time periods than if they could express the original urge to tic.

Finding a Diagnosis

One of the problems with TS is discovering it exists. Not everyone who tics has TS. Reactions to medication, some mind-altering drugs, and other nervous system conditions can cause tics that mimic TS. Any brain injury, such as a blow to the head during a car accident, can leave someone with tics.

Most new parents don't realize that there is a normal range of childhood tics that develops as the nervous system matures. These may appear and disappear on their own and are in no way considered TS. As many as one in five children exhibits some type of tic. These can last from a few months to a year, depending upon whether a child is nervous or under stress. Childhood tics are usually mild or barely noticeable. Mild tics rarely limit routine activities enough to cause worry. In most cases, ignoring the tics prevents reinforcing, and continuing, their presence.

Once tics last more than a year or become so severe they disrupt school or play, parents need to consider a doctor's visit to see if TS is the reason. Physicians usually begin the visit by asking parents about family history and what they see in their child. Doctors talk with the patient about unusual movements or sounds and how these interfere with daily activities. The doctor wants to develop a picture, or case study, of what the family and patient are experiencing. Physicians who agree that a problem exists may suggest a body scan or blood tests to rule out other health conditions.

Until recently, families commonly went from physician to physician because so few recognized signs of TS. A typical time frame before a confirmed diagnosis

Guidelines for Diagnosing TS

After ruling out other conditions, doctors follow guidelines for TS from the American Psychiatric Association in their *Diagnostic and Statistical Manual of Mental Disorders*, fifth edition (*DSM-5*). The *DSM* is updated regularly, the last edition published in 2012. The reference book helps mental health professionals in the United States and Canada identify mental and neurological conditions. According to its guidelines, "a tic is a sudden, rapid, recurrent, nonrhythmic motor movement or vocalization."[f] Doctors making a diagnosis of TS look for

- multiple motor tics and at least one or more vocal tics;
- tics that may come and go in frequency but persist for more than a year since the first tic appeared;
- tics that arise before age eighteen years;
- tics that cannot be explained by any other medical condition or effects of a body-altering substance, such as medication or addictive substance.

was five to ten years. Now more doctors know how to identify symptoms of TS, although the journey to diagnosis can still be frustrating.

Accepting there is a problem and visiting a doctor is the first step toward identification. Once a physician is consulted, a time frame of six months to a year before determining TS is not unusual. Ruling out other conditions takes time and many tests. As more positive and accurate information becomes available about TS, people who struggle with tics will seek diagnosis and treatment sooner. And more research and information will alert physicians about how to diagnose the syndrome earlier.

Related Conditions

Discovering TS can be challenging when other conditions complicate the diagnosis. Several behaviors of TS overlap or mimic other disorders. Still others share common symptoms.

Sandy

My first symptoms appeared between ages six and seven. It was biting my lip. My parents thought I had a speech problem, so I was off to the speech pathologist. Aside from not being able to pronounce my Ss and Ps, she could not find anything wrong . . . but she couldn't explain my overbite. She thought, why don't we send him to a psychologist because there must be some reason why he's doing this. For a couple months, I went between a psychologist and psychiatrist. Then I got referred to a psychiatric social worker. They thought the overbite was some type of mental health issue. I spent the next six or seven years with the psychiatric social worker discussing a lot of issues, trying to figure out why I had this overbite that was my first symptom. Then other symptoms started, barking and noises and physical movements. More symptoms developed while I was talking with the social workers. Six months after I stopped seeing her at age thirteen, I was diagnosed with TS.[9]

Recent sources suggest that between 79 and 90 percent of teens with TS also grapple with another disorder in addition to tics.[3] Many teens who tic have trouble paying attention, or are hyperactive, obsessive, compulsive, impulsive, disorganized, or depressed, or experience sleep, mood, and learning problems. Having more than one condition compounds the number of problems a teen must handle to navigate through daily activities. In some cases, the additional condition becomes more disabling than tics.

Scientists believe several overlapping conditions arise from related causes. But not all teens with TS have or will acquire these other conditions. Tics remain the more visible symptoms for most teens with TS.

Attention Deficit Disorder with or without Hyperactivity

The more frequent condition to occur with TS is attention deficit disorder (ADD). If you struggle with ADD you may find focusing your attention difficult. You may be unable to control impulses and behave as expected in school, work, and social situations. Even the slightest movement or sound can distract you from activities and conversations with others.

Without the ability to stay focused, you can lose track of what's going on. Losing track often leads to mounting disorganization. At home and school, others

---

Andy

I can be really hyper and out of control. I ran around making noises—actually sensations that my chest screamed. I used to buy things compulsively. I have more energy than most people, which is a good thing about being hyperactive, and I don't tire easily. I could stay up all night if I had a good TV to watch. I don't like having to be up at a certain time, and I hate mornings. I'm kind of hyper at school, too. I get sent to the principal's office a couple times a day. I have to say over and over, "I will follow directions and respect people's property."[h]

---

think you are forgetful. Teachers and parents claim you cannot follow directions. Others may view you as incapable of completing any job, such as chores, projects, and schoolwork.

You may know friends, coworkers, or classmates who seem fidgety. They talk excessively and move constantly. In class and social situations, they blurt out answers before questions are completed. They interrupt conversations, as if what they have to say is most important. They cannot wait their turn. They never seem to listen, which drives friends crazy, if they have friends at all. More worrisome, they lack the ability to stop themselves. Without the ability to foresee consequences, they thrive on taking dangerous risks. These teens may also be hyperactive and have attention-deficit/hyperactivity disorder (ADHD).

Frequently, signs of being hyper appear before tics when both conditions are present. For some teens, medicine for ADD or ADHD brings out or worsens tics. Similar to TS, teens with ADD find their symptoms appear and disappear. Because signs change, you might assume someone with ADHD or TS can control their behavior, which is untrue.

Obsessive-Compulsive Disorder

The next most common disorder that teens experience with TS is obsessive-compulsive disorder (OCD). About one-third of teens who tic display obsessions and compulsions. Like TS, OCD is a neurological condition. But with OCD, a chemical imbalance in the brain causes a wide range of obsessions and compulsions.[4]

Obsessions are unwanted and often unpleasant thoughts or images. These impulses run through a person's mind repeatedly, turning into worries. An example of a harmless obsession is a child who gets stuck on the same bedtime story.

When obsessions become extreme, they interfere with daily activities. Stress from obsessions is enough to leave you feeling upset and out of control. For instance, you might worry that dirt and germs will infect your body. Moreover, you fear that once infected, harm or sickness will endanger you or your family members.

People with unusual worries can become consumed with thoughts about certain words, objects, or numbers. Worries and superstitions are part of everyday life. But for anyone who is truly obsessed, these uncomfortable feelings bring extreme fear, sickness, or doubt.[5]

"My thoughts raced through my mind so quickly, I had trouble expressing myself. My thoughts were not always related to what I was talking about with my parents," Andy explained. "Part of my frustration was how they couldn't understand what I was saying. My mind kept getting stuck on something, and I needed to see or say it over and over."[6]

Compulsions are actions obsessive teens take to make the discomfort go away. Performing certain behaviors becomes the only way to reduce anxiety that results from unrealistic fears and doubts that are at the heart of OCD. For example, if you fear germs, you may wash your hands until the skin cracks. Or if you worry about keeping strangers away, you may touch a doorknob a specific number of times. Other teens may feel the overwhelming urge to listen to a song over and over again or wear a certain pair of pants to a given location. Or you may know someone who rechecks homework so many times that the deadline for handing it in passes. Or someone who erases work so much to make it perfect that the paper tears.

Teens with OCD already know that their obsessions make little sense. But they are unable to control the urge to satisfy them. It's as if their brain gets stuck on a certain thought or action that prevents them from doing anything else. When obsessions and compulsions become this strong, the person who experiences them receives a diagnosis of obsessive-compulsive disorder.

"An obsession is thinking about something, and a compulsion is doing something," said Mark who has both TS and OCD. "You keep doing it until you get it right. It's like a tic. But when I'm ticking, I don't even know I'm doing it. With a compulsion, I have a thought process. For example, when touching my nose, I keep thinking about the word 'touch.' The compulsion is I *have* to do it."[7]

Many teens with OCD benefit from behavior therapy or cognitive behavior therapy. The treatment involves exposing you to the compulsion and delaying the usual action in response. Gradually, you increase the time between exposure and responding. As you respond less frequently, you experience that the feared consequence does not happen. With practice, the initial worry subsides. Eventually, the unwanted actions—and anxiety—lessen and go away.

Common Obsessions and Compulsions

Obsessions	Compulsions
• fixates on a number or letter	• hoards and saves
• worries about dirt and germs	• practice washing and cleaning rules
• sees sexual images often	
• mentally rearranges letters and words	• tattles or prays excessively
	• repeats actions
• fears scary or harmful things will happen	• seeks continual approval
	• touches self, others, objects
• is consumed by religions/moral thoughts	• erases mistakes repeatedly
	• arranges and lines up items
• suffers unusual worry or doubt	• arranges objects by specific number patterns
• imagines losing control and becoming aggressive	
• needs order and symmetry	

This is not an easy or quick process. Trained therapists ease the journey. Anyone who tries behavior therapy is brave to undertake the series of activities and keep practicing until they notice a difference.

Learning Disabilities

Tics have no effect on intelligence. But teens who have TS may be more prone to various learning disabilities. About 30 percent of teens who tic experience serious learning disabilities. Some result from tics that interfere with learning, such as constant eye blinking, body jerking, and poor control that creates difficulties reading, concentrating, and writing.

The most obvious signs of a learning disability are low grades and poor performance. Teens with a learning disability may be unable to process information they see, hear, or remember in the same way other teens do. Therefore, they struggle learning basic skills needed to read, write, spell, and handle math. Tourette only compounds these problems.

Teens with learning disabilities try just as hard. But they fail tests and never seem to get good grades. Unable to cope with schoolwork, they become frustrated. As the school year progresses, they lose interest and stop trying.

"I have vocal tics—grunting, teeth grinding, rapid hand movements. I also have ADD, which affects people in different ways," Jeremy said. "For me, if I'm not interested, say in grammar school and now high school when I didn't like math or history, I found it hard to concentrate. If I'm interested in something, like a book or film, it's fine."[8]

Sleep Disorders

Tourette syndrome often comes with sleep problems. One reason is relentless tics make falling asleep difficult. Once asleep, teens who continue to tic may awaken frequently during the night or walk and talk in their sleep. Research indicates that some teens with TS display motor and vocal tics when they sleep that are similar to those observed when they are awake. Other teens discover that their tics lessen or disappear during sleep. Either way, taking a chance with a sleepover can be stressful.

"In third grade, Jeremy's most significant problem was related to sleep," Jeremy's father said. "He was having long periods when you could hear him ticking in bed. He would have his action figures under his cover and bang them together to mask his vocal tics. He still has a lot of sleep problems. It takes him a long time to get to sleep because of his tics."[9]

Conduct Problems

One trait in some teens with TS involves huge mood swings. More often, the teen exhibits another condition, such as ADD or OCD, that may play a role. Extreme feelings can overwhelm these teens on a daily, monthly, or yearly basis. Outbursts of rage may far exceed standard temper tantrums and the normal range of personality differences of people you know.

Like symptoms of TS, the outbursts seem to come from nowhere without anyone provoking them. They build into a wild fury. Once begun, rages must follow their course until all energy is gone. One teen with TS explains his outbursts as a need to see or feel things break or the rage isn't satisfied.

Raging with TS is usually not about anger. It's more about someone having a short fuse and needing to let off steam, like a tea kettle. Once the rage has subsided, most teens feel ashamed or guilty about what they have done. You can

> ### Jeremy
>
> I know very well how awful it felt to be stuck in a rage that there was no excuse for. My unrestrained expression of rage was completely disproportionate to the trigger. The horrible part was that I could not get out of it or even indicate in any way to my targets that I knew I was being unfair. I could only wait for it to pass. It was as if a cloud of rage had floated by and seized me, filling me up for a while before it drifted off on its way again. Finding out that, for me, rage is a part of my overall symptoms was a great relief in comparison with the years I spent agonizing over my evilness. I was not born bad. I am neither aggressive nor dangerous. Learning the reason was the gift that promoted me to deal with it.[i]

imagine the toll these outbursts take on family, teachers, and friends in addition to the individual involved.

How Does Someone Get TS?

Classmates may ask how you got TS—or any of these other conditions. What they really want to know is if they can catch it like the flu. The answer is no way! The exact cause of tics remains unknown for now. But researchers do know that TS is never contagious. The most likely explanation for the condition is a tendency toward ticking that you are born with, like eye or hair color. That tendency originates from different causes that are under investigation.

The Brain's Message Center

Researchers have been investigating how different parts of the brain work to produce tics. Recent studies point to faulty communication of nerve cells in the frontal and occipital parts of the brain. The breakdown comes from an imbalance of neurotransmitters. These brain chemicals carry signals from one nerve cell cluster to another. So far, the two neurotransmitters identified as contributing to TS are dopamine and serotonin.

With TS, the frontal portion of the brain produces too much dopamine. The added neurotransmitter interferes with regulating social behaviors. Similarly, serotonin produces feelings of well-being when it's in balance. Usually, the two

History of Tourette Syndrome

Knowledge of TS goes back to ancient Greece. Two thousand years ago, physicians wrote about people who displayed sudden facial movements, barking sounds, and cursing. Scientists in every era since have recorded stories of patients who twitched and shouted without reason.

People who ticked were not always treated kindly. Their actions and sounds often provoked harsh responses. Depending upon local superstitions, people who ticked were worshipped or thought bewitched. Many faced abuse because they were thought mentally ill. Others were tortured, jailed, or burned as witches.

In 1825, French physician Jean-Marc Itard originated the modern understanding of TS as a specific disorder. Itard observed a noblewoman for nineteen years, beginning when she first exhibited motor tics at age seven. As she aged, she added swearing and screams and never stopped odd movements. She spent her life as an outcast, although she eventually married and died at age eighty-six.

Itard's former student and neurologist Georges Gilles de la Tourette wrote about similar strange symptoms in one of his patients. His paper comparing Itard and his patient identified tics as a separate disorder. He offered the first evidence that TS ran in families. Equally important, he claimed that people who ticked could not control themselves, and their illness was mental, not physical. The medical community named the disorder maladie des tics de Gilles de la Tourette, or Tourette syndrome, in his honor.

neurotransmitters work together to control and moderate movements. When one or the other is off balance, nerve clusters become less able to communicate with neighboring cells. The body responds with sudden bursts of uncontrolled movements. Researchers continue to compare brain scans to determine what other neurotransmitters or parts of the brain may be involved in complex movements that result in tics.[10]

Check Your Genes

Scientists believe genes play a role in developing TS. The exact role, however, is still unclear. The Human Genome (gene) Project, a federally funded study that maps genes and traits, found that TS most likely originates in multiple genes. Therefore, one or both parents must contribute the exact combination of genes for TS or related disorders to pass on the tendency to tic.

Tourette traits seem to cluster in families. If a parent has TS, the likelihood of an offspring acquiring some form of the condition is 50 percent for boys and 30 percent for girls. The odds of inheriting serious TS drop to about 10 percent. Family and twin studies provide proof that genes play a role in TS. Links remain stronger when looking at early onset forms of OCD with TS. Parents with TS have a higher than average risk of passing on mild tic disorders and obsessive-compulsive behavior than parents in the general population.

But specific patterns of inheriting TS have proven unreliable. The science leans toward involvement of multiple genes, some undiscovered as yet. Added research continues to investigate interactions between heredity and conditions in the environment that alter existing genes.

Consider Your Environment

Researchers continue to look into the role of infection as a TS trigger. Studies particularly focus on the role strep bacteria plays in increasing abnormal behavior and movements in TS. Scientists link similar problems with strep bacteria to obsessive-compulsive behaviors, hyperactivity, and the range of tic disorders.

Strep is a disease-causing bacteria that invades the body. Usually, during an invasion, the body sends out antibodies. These specific substances attack the offending germs and render them harmless. When antibodies make a mistake and identify the wrong invader, such as strep infections, the autoimmune system attacks itself. Studies indicate that in a small number of TS cases, reactions to strep infection resulted in antibodies attacking healthy nervous system tissue. For someone prone to tics, the outcome from strep or similar infections amounts to symptom flare-ups, changes, or worsening tics.[11]

Treatments to Reduce Tics

The bad news is TS has no cure. The good news is most cases are so mild they require no treatment. Tics are usually mild enough to rarely interfere with normal activities. Slight increases in symptoms can usually be controlled with minor

People with Tourette Syndrome

Sometimes, it might feel like you're the only one with TS. Think again. Check out some of these people who have lived with—and overcome—obstacles of the condition.

- Mahmoud Abdul-Rauf (born 1969), nine-year National Basketball Association guard
- Dan Aykroyd (born 1952), actor, former *Saturday Night Live* comic, and film producer and actor who has mild Asperger syndrome and TS
- Jim Eisenreich (born 1959), former Major League Baseball player
- Lowell Handler (born 1959), photographer and author
- Tom Howard (born 1979), soccer star
- Howard Hughes (1905–1976), film director and aviator with OCD and TS
- Samuel Johnson (1709–1784), author of the first English-language dictionary, who is thought to have had TS
- Howie Mandel (born 1955), comedian with OCD and TS
- Dash Mihok (born 1974), actor
- Wolfgang Amadeus Mozart (1756–1791), Austrian composer and pianist thought to have had TS
- Calvin Peete (1943–2015), professional golfer who won twelve titles in seven seasons
- Jeremy Stenberg (born 1981), freestyle motocross rider whose nickname is Twitchy
- Michael Wolff (born 1952), pianist and jazz musician

lifestyle changes, such as reducing stress and helping others understand TS and allowing adaptations. (See the section Managing Stress: Mind over Illness in chapter 11.)

When tics cause obvious problems, the few people who display them can find remedies to reduce their effects with social life, work, or school. Often a doctor recommends more than one treatment to best deal with all the symptoms. To date, promise for tic reduction lies in behavior intervention techniques and medication.

> ## Dennis
>
> My parents took me to the neurologist (about age five) where I was diagnosed with TS. From then on I started to take a plethora of medicines, which had nasty side effects from weight gain to sadness, happiness, anger, appetite, and sleepiness. My life became busy with doctor appointments, and I never kept the same doctor. My mother started to look for help, and she came upon the Tourette Syndrome Association. They e-mailed us information about TS, which we made into small presentations that I presented to each class every year. I also presented a poem and a book on TS. I became a TS advocate.[j]

Behavior Therapy

Behavior training has proven the most promising treatment to reduce tics. With behavior treatment, a trained therapist teaches teens with TS and other conditions how to manage the intensity, severity, and impact of their tics. The National Institutes of Health has been investigating a behavioral plan they call Comprehensive Behavioral Intervention for Tics (CBIT). This program encourages teens with TS to focus on their type of tics and the situation that makes them worse.

One method of CBIT helps teens take this knowledge and learn to replace problematic tic behavior with a new, competing behavior. For example, when a teen finds hand raising occurs more often in class, he can sit on his hands. Or the teen who rubs her head might replace the rubbing with crossing her arms. These types of alternative behaviors are called habit reversal.

Other strategies of CBIT include relaxation techniques and assistance for parents and teachers. Sometimes, just changing surroundings is enough to provoke a new behavior to replace the tic. CBIT might take practice and persistence for everyone concerned. But enough positive results have been documented that the Centers for Disease Control and Prevention and Tourette Syndrome Association promote these programs for families dealing with TS.[12]

Medication

If behavior methods fail, medication is an effective way to calm tics. The problem is no one medication helps all teens who tic. Doctors often run through several

---

Dennis

Even though kids knew about my sickness, they still avoided me and this continued well throughout elementary and middle school. My TS stunted my social growth and happiness and confidence. I hardly had any friends and I couldn't talk to people.

My first two years of high school things were the same, but in my junior year things changed. My TS hardly acted up. I made a lot more friends, gained more confidence and social skills, got a girlfriend, and found new passion in reading, science, and acting. I also did lots of community service. Soon I received many offers for scholarships, acting positions, program and event offers.

Even though I had a rough childhood, I think my TS has made me stronger and more persevering. I don't think I would be as successful without it. What I've always wondered is if other African Americans have TS like me. If so, I would like to be an advocate for them and kids with TS in general.[k]

---

medicines and different doses before finding the correct match to reduce certain tics. Some teens require a combination of medications to reduce tics and treat other disorders that accompany TS. And these medicines probably will not eliminate tics completely.

Even with the best medications, there are always body changes that make altering the medicine cocktail necessary. Regular doctor visits are part of the treatment plan to ensure your medications work for you. "It helps for me to talk with my doctors about how my medicine is working or not working," Lysso wrote in *That Darn Tic: A Newsletter*. "I take a few different things to help with my tics, hyperactivity, and going to sleep. Sometimes my medicine seems to help me focus better on math, so the brain cramps I get are more bearable. Other times, I'm just talking myself into not getting frustrated and taking walks can help."[13]

Effective medications often come with a range of side effects. These may include fatigue, restlessness, social withdrawal, stiff muscles, or weight gain. Keep a journal of your medications and any side effects to discuss with your doctor to decide together whether you need to make changes.

Resources

Organizations

Association of University Centers on Disabilities
1100 Wayne Avenue, Suite 1000
Silver Spring, MD 20910
301-588-8252
www.aucd.org/template/index.cfm
National network with local branches that provides health care, diagnosis, referrals, research, and educational and academic support for individuals with disabilities.

Centers for Disease Control and Prevention (CDC)
1600 Clifton Road
Atlanta, GA 30329-4027
800-CDC-INFO (800-232-4636)
www.cdc.gov/
Main U.S. public health institute whose primary job is to promote health, including for conditions like TS. The CDC offers free training programs on CBIT for health professionals and referrals to parent training and other information.

CHADD (Children and Adults with Attention Deficit/Hyperactivity Disorders)
8181 Professional Place, Suite 150
Landover, MD 20785
800-233-4050
www.chadd.org
National organization for teens with ADD/ADHD that has a website for information about ADHD, support through local groups or online, professional referrals, and conferences concerning ADHD.

International OCD Foundation
PO Box 961029
Boston, MA 02196
617-973-5801
ocfoundation.org
The IOCDF provides a wealth of information about professional referrals, local groups, educational materials, and conferences concerning OCD.

Learning Disabilities Association of America
4156 Library Road

Pittsburgh, PA 15234-1349
412-341-1515
www.ldanatl.org
National organization that offers information on learning disabilities for parents, teachers, and teens. The website lists state chapters, updates on relevant laws, and upcoming conferences.

National Institute of Neurological Disorders and Stroke
NIH Neurological Institute
PO Box 5801
Bethesda, MD 20824
800-352-9424 or 301-496-5751
www.ninds.nih.gov
National organization that provides information about specific neurological disease and research programs that cover the disorder, including TS.

Tic Disorder Obsessive Compulsive Disorder Specialty Clinic
Yale Child Study Center
230 South Frontage Rd.
New Haven, CT 06519
203-785-2540
medicine.yale.edu/childstudy/ocd/research/tourette_treatment.aspx
University medical center clinic devoted to treatment and research related to TS and OCD.

Tourette Syndrome Association, Inc.
42-40 Bell Blvd.
Bayside, New York 11361-2830
718-224-2999
tourette.org
National organization that offers educational materials, physician and advocacy referral, and research to identify the cause, cure, and treatments to reduce the effects of TS. Local chapters run support groups and camps for families dealing with TS.

Books: Nonfiction

Marlene Targ Brill, *Tourette Syndrome*, Minneapolis: Twenty-First Century Books, 2012. In-depth overview of Tourette syndrome and its causes, treatments, and tips for teens about living with the condition at home and at school.

Josh Hanagarne, *The World's Strongest Librarian: A Memoir*, New York: Gotham Books, 2013. Story of how a boy grew to manhood dealing with a misunderstood condition.

James Matovic and Jeffrey Foxworthy, *Ticked: A Medical Miracle, a Friendship, and the Weird World of Tourette Syndrome.* Chicago: Chicago Review Press, 2013. A journalist's personal journey with Tourette syndrome and the new brain stimulation treatment that helped with his tics.

James Patterson, *Against Medical Advice: A True Story.* New York: Little, Brown and Company, 2008. Story of a family's decades-long battle to discover the reason for a son's odd behavior.

Books: Fiction

Michael Vey, *Hunt for Jade Dragon*, New York: Simon Pulse, 2014. Fourth book in a series about a teen with Tourette syndrome who has electromagnetic powers that allow him to battle evil and save the day in different situations.

DVD

Susan Connors, *I Have Tourettes, but Tourettes Doesn't Have Me.* Home Box Office, 2005, DVD. Documentary that informs about Tourette syndrome through experiences of young people.

TAKING CARE OF EVERYDAY BUSINESS

No matter what your condition, you are probably tired of dealing with differences most other teens never encounter. Too many specialists, medications, treatments, special diets, different classes in school. All potential hassles. Or you remain symptom-free, at least for now, so you naturally think, "Why stir things up?" "Why schedule an annual checkup?" As a result, you balk at yet another appointment, one you view as unnecessary.

Such thinking is totally understandable. But every teen—with or without a special condition—needs to eventually take responsibility for his or her general health, no matter how tiresome. It's part of maturing and being independent.

Remember Those Checkups

Self-care includes regular checkups with an internist or pediatrician who can monitor your overall health beyond whatever your condition requires. Checkups usually involve a schedule of blood tests to inspect general health, weight and height measurement to make sure you are thriving, and vaccinations to prevent other illnesses—the same routines other teens follow. That's in addition to checkups for your specific condition, whether you experience symptoms or not. Whichever condition you have, you need to monitor your health regularly.

"All kids who have had melanoma will be followed for a lifetime, although Michelle isn't chronic in terms of constant treatment, medication, whatever," said Bo, Michelle L.'s dad. "She's followed every couple months and goes to the hospital twice a year. That will be for her whole life."[1]

Advocating for Yourself

An important aspect of self-care is advocating for yourself. Whether you were born with a syndrome or acquired your condition growing up, chances are your

Remember to schedule regular checkups with a doctor who monitors your overall health.

parents or guardians advocated for you. They made doctor appointments, fought battles with schools, took you to treatments and appointments, prepared special foods, and ordered medications to help you feel better. But you are getting older. Now it's your turn to assume these responsibilities—with their guidance, of course.

Your parents or guardians may find it difficult to relinquish their role in your life and health. They may be more overprotective of you than they are of your siblings. That's natural: you've been through a lot together. Letting go as a child ages is always challenging for parents. In your situation it may be even harder. Try to understand their viewpoint. Have patience. As you prove you are ready to take over different aspects of your life, they should back off.

One way to protect yourself—and reassure your parents—is to wear identification. Keep emergency contacts in your cell phone. Wear a MedicAlert bracelet to alert others of your condition, if you cannot tell them. MedicAlert (see Resources at the end of this chapter) items come in an assortment of wearable products from necklaces and bracelets to tags for your jogging shoes.

Another way to protect yourself is to know the law. Understanding your rights is particularly important when needing special accommodations at school, applying to college or for housing, or interviewing for a job. The Americans with Disabilities Act of 1990 (updated in 2010) "prohibits discrimination and ensures equal opportunity for persons with disabilities in employment, state and local government services, public accommodations, commercial facilities, and transportation."[2]

This means you cannot be turned away from school or work because you need some changes in the environment. You will probably need to prove why you need certain modifications. But administrators at public institutions know they must comply. Accommodations could include different dorm foods or a private room or bathroom, a different or longer testing situation, and tutoring or altered deadlines due to absences for health reasons. Speak up for yourself. You have the law on your side.

"I had one teacher [in high school] who wouldn't let me go to the bathroom, and I sat there and was extremely uncomfortable," Carly, who has Crohn's disease, said. "After class I went up to her. I said, 'If you can't let me go to the bathroom I need to find another teacher.' She wrote a medical pass to let me go."[3]

Money and Health Care

Let's face it, finding a diagnosis and identifying the best treatment can take a long time. Then comes the costs of treatment and medications. Or you might have been born with a syndrome that requires extra medical attention, a different education setting, or a special diet from infancy. These can be costly. You may not be in charge of the family budget, but you probably pick up signs at home when finances are stretched too thin, no matter how much your family shields you from money concerns.

Families want the best for their teens. But insurance, travel, taking off work and school for appointments, medication, and other treatments can strain the household budget. Government is trying to ease the burden on families, but the health-care system is in flux. And it may be for a long time.

Tell your parents that you and your family don't have to struggle alone. Several organization and charities assist families with necessary arrangements to ease financial worries. They provide coverage or low-cost travel to treatments and housing at hospitals for families that qualify. They can help you deal with insurance companies and locate lower cost medications. Check out the resources at the end of this chapter to find help for you and your family during what can be stressful times.

Foods and Exercise

You may eat a specially prescribed diet. If so, this next paragraph isn't for you because you already make the connection. For everyone else, please know that diet counts.

Tips to Ease the Family Budget

No condition should drain the family budget. The Cancer Financial Assistance Coalition suggests some ways your family can try to limit financial struggles:

- Talk with a health-care team about the cost of care. A social worker or financial counselor can help your family understand insurance coverage and offer avenues for assistance, whether they be outright financial aid or a special payment plan.
- Ask a social worker about benefits your family can apply for under the law.
- Identify community-based programs that can reduce your financial burden, such as energy relief and housing and transportation allowances for families with illnesses and disabilities.
- Investigate patient assistance programs that offer help with medicines and co-pay relief programs.
- Appeal to your family insurance company directly. Often, insurance companies put up barricades to limit questioning of their policies. But endurance pays off. Tell your parents to keep plugging until they get their rightful payments.
- Consider fund-raising. Many communities (schools, religious institutions, social and volunteer groups) will throw parties to raise money for families in need.[a]

The foods you eat contribute to your general health. Food gives you energy, especially if you have a condition that drains you. A healthy diet offers vitamins and minerals to keep your body running smoothly. But you need to eat a variety of foods to obtain the healthy balance of nutrients. Variety comes from a mix of proteins, carbohydrates, and healthy fats. Food choices should draw from whole grains, vegetables and fruits, and lean sources of protein, such as beans, fish, and fowl.

You've heard this next one before: keep weight under control. In your case, carrying extra pounds only makes your condition worse. Being overweight causes your body to work harder to move at a time when you may need that energy to heal.

Which foods contribute most to an unhealthy diet? Sugars, as in sweetened drinks, unhealthy fats, as in chips and fried foods. These provide no fuel to keep you going. Instead, they boost calories that give you a quick high. Then nutritionally limited foods send your energy level into a nosedive. If you lack energy or have other health issues, consult a dietician or nutritionist. Your health depends upon the fuel a sound diet provides.

Have you ever heard from your parents or grandparents to "use it or lose it?" Makes sense. Even with pain or difficulty moving, staying active helps. The most limited movements boost energy and keep your muscles strong and flexible, sometimes preventing further deterioration. Activity burns those extra calories that might be contributing to weight gain. And exercise of any kind sends a message to your brain to release hormones that relieve stress and contribute to your staying a happy, balanced person.

To Tell or Not to Tell

Most teens interviewed for this book prefer to strike a balance between telling others they have a specific condition and not telling. As with other personal facts about themselves, they are on a need-to-know basis. Health and your makeup are only one aspect of your life. No need to wear a sign letting the world know you live with something ongoing.

But there are circumstances when discussing your condition becomes an issue, sometimes essential. Then these teens are open and honest. No secrets. For example, if diet plays a role in the condition, teens will speak up at a restaurant,

---

Michelle L.

I'm actually at a new school. Obviously my old close friends know I had melanoma. In this school, it's not one of those things that comes up. That might change after I speak at Relay for Life, an American Cancer Society fund-raiser. Last year, I was survivor keynote speaker, so I talked in front of about two thousand people. A lot of people found out about my story. This year, I will be telling the same story at our school.

I get different reactions. A lot of people come up after I speak and tell me I'm strong. My friends treat me the same. There is no difference in how they think of me, which is really nice.[b]

call ahead, or request a restaurant that has food they can eat. Or they choose to bring their own food. No big deal. They prefer to—and must—advocate for themselves to stay healthy, rather than jeopardize their health.

In other instances, a teen might want to share this one aspect of themselves—their condition—with a close friend or new partner. Sharing what plays a key role in your life contributes to a closer relationship. The Crohn's and Colitis Foundation suggests, "When dating or socializing with your friends, you may need to explain that you might sometimes have symptoms and will not always be able to go out, but you don't have to say any more."[4]

At times, you might need to alert an adult at school or work. You don't want those around you to freak out if you have an episode as a result of your condition or have unexplained behaviors, for example, due to Tourette or a Crohn's attack or because you move differently. Offering information about your condition is important for others to know how to help you.

When deciding to share information about your condition, there is another aspect to consider: educating others. Many teens—and adults—harbor myths and misconceptions about a lot of issues, including health. One major myth is that someone can catch what you have, which is untrue. You might not always feel like informing others and dealing with their prejudices. But when you do, you are boosting chances that you are chipping away another wall of prejudice.

Then there is the issue of interviewing for a job. Teens seem divided about whether to tell up front or not. Of course, this depends upon the condition, how much it could interfere with job tasks, and how visible signs are.

Some teens believe that honesty is the best policy. According to the Americans with Disabilities Act, employers are required to make reasonable accommodations for physical and mental conditions. Sometimes, it's better to know up front if employers will claim hardship, which relieves them of making adaptations, or are willing to work with you. Other teens prefer to wait until a second interview or when they are on the job before explaining their condition. Still others don't feel the need to tell at all. These teens probably have no outward signs and require no time off for repeated medical or therapy appointments.

Kody

Every once in a while, when I have surgery [for melanoma], it puts me back. Some surgeries take a lot of recovery. I've had seven surgeries—foot, back of knee, groin, lungs, and brain, where they put a drainage port in your head. I've missed a lot of school. They've [teachers] been pretty good about helping me, so I'm caught up. That's good. I hope to go to college next fall.[c]

Questions to Ask Yourself

Two sides apply to almost every issue. Same with telling or not telling others you have a certain condition. Here are some questions to ask that may shed light on when to share personal information with others:

- Are you playing a sport with others that may be affected by your condition?
- What would you prefer to know if you were dating someone with your condition?
- Decide if this dating relationship may be long-term, which could make a difference in what you divulge.
- Will knowing change the way someone views you?
- Are you ready to answer someone else's questions about your condition?
- How does your genetic condition, if you have one, influence your relationships or sex life?[d]

Bullying

Any teens who contend with a different physical or mental condition deal with enough in their everyday life. You don't need the stress of being bullied because of these differences. Bullying causes stress, embarrassment, depression, and anxiety—not anything that helps you stay healthy. Excessive teasing affects sleep, focus, and eating, sometimes causing flare-ups of your condition. Time to stop bullies in their tracks. Here are some suggestions:

- Take care of yourself and your health. That's your first priority. If you need the bathroom more, need to sit out a game in gym, need to eat a special diet, do it. Don't let anyone say you can't or make fun of you for helping yourself. *You have done nothing wrong. It's your right to attend classes and other community activities without fear of intimidation.*

- Keep calm. Bullies like to rattle their prey. It makes them feel powerful. Walk away if you can. Try joking to defuse what is being said about you. Perhaps ask why the bully is picking on you. The response may surprise you—and the bully.

- Educate those around you. Bullying is often based on misinformation. Knowledge is power, something that reduces unwarranted fear. Explain your condition. Offer to present to the class. *Reinforce that you are never contagious, the biggest misunderstanding.*

- Build a support group. Try to travel with a friend. Bullies prefer to get their prey alone. *There is safety and support in numbers.*

- Get help if you can't handle the teasing or bullying or you fear for your physical well-being. Tell teachers or administrators. Devise a plan to alert your teacher if someone makes fun of you. Teachers should never allow teasing in class. *If the school remains unsupportive, involve your parents.*

- Keep a detailed journal of what happens to you. The journal is one way to release your feelings. Writing also verifies your experiences, should you need to contact a school administrator, lawyer, or police.

- Make sure the school promotes a culture of acceptance. Ask that your teacher and school administration prepare and distribute a clear antibullying policy.

- Reach out. Organize your class to hold a fund-raiser or other event to increase awareness of individual differences.

- Talk with a professional—counselor, doctor, psychologist—if teasing makes you depressed. Any extreme sadness that lasts more than a couple weeks is a sign you may need help.

- *Never believe what bullies say about you. You do not deserve their treatment.*[e]

In the end, sharing health information is your decision. Try to balance that decision with how important the relationship is, how important others knowing about you is for your own safety, and whether you believe sharing is a way to reduce prejudice against teens who are different.

"Yup, I tell about having melanoma," Kody said. "They're like surprised. But no one treats me differently."[5]

Be an Antibullying Advocate

Check your own behavior. You may believe you never bully or seriously tease anyone. But any time you call out someone about any differences, no matter what they are, you are a bully. When you support someone who is different, that contributes to a positive environment for everyone.

"Other kids treat me nicely," said Sam, who has Down syndrome. "But some kids say bad words—and curse, too. Kids at school. I just don't like it. Teasing is so mean. People shouldn't pick on anyone. I don't like bullying."[f]

- Whenever someone else crosses the line between joke and bullying, try to change the negative environment. Allowing bullying to continue in your presence can be just as hurtful as bullying.

- Personalize the situation. Explain to the bully you once teased friends, then talked with them about how they felt. They were upset. Let teasers know they just insulted a friend.

- Engage the bully. Sometimes, teens throw out labels without understanding what they mean and how they insult the other person. Name-calling is never cool.

- Share accurate information about the condition. Ask, if someone was part of this group, would he or she find the offending comments funny or hurtful?

- Try to use humor to deflate situations. Guilt and insulting responses only shut down offenders.

- Speak up. At times, you may need to just tell someone not to talk like that around you.

- Model positive interactions yourself. If you take pride in yourself and those around you, others will pick up your kind vibes.[g]

Sean

You really realize who your true friends are. When you start using a walker in high school, you start to understand who's there to catch you, provide assistance, and be your friend throughout this situation. I didn't get much teasing, but it's easy to understand who your true friends are.

True friends would still give me a call. I used to drive but got into an accident that wasn't officially my fault [brakes locked up]. I stopped driving. Once I stopped driving, having friends pick you up from the house, you see the true friends who call to ask: "You need a ride, whatever." Or the ones who say: "I just can't drive that far."

MS did affect dating because walking with a walker isn't that attractive to a girl. I've really been able to kind of get out of that shell thinking that all women see me as an old man walking with my walker. Now I understood the fact that MS may be able to affect me in many ways, but I'm still me, Sean.[h]

Life outside Your Condition

Hospitalizations. Food limitations. Lagging energy. These issues may make a social life more difficult. You might find you need to work harder to carve out time to locate other teens who value you for being you. But you can still develop friends, even dating friends.

Hobbies and Interests

You probably have some activities you like to do more than others. Most teens do. Pursuing them helps balance your life.

"I like swimming, basketball, and soccer," Sam said. "I like comics, school, and summer camp. I'm in a drama group. We made two movies, one where teens wrote the story. I had to try out. Everyone who has Down syndrome gets in."[6]

Sometimes, your condition means altering what you love to do. You may need to rest more during activity. Or you may need to find another way to do the same thing.

"Before I was diagnosed with MS I used to play drums. I love my drum set," Sean said. "Unfortunately through years when I lost function with my left foot, I

Finding something you enjoy doing boosts confidence and reduces stress.

slowly stopped playing because I couldn't hit the left pedal and high hat. When that happened I picked up hand drums. They are good for hand function and getting out feelings."[7]

Camps

Most conditions discussed in this book have associations that advocate for teens who have the specific condition (see the Resources section at the close of each chapter). These umbrella organizations either sponsor or have links to camps for kids and teens with the illness, condition, or syndrome they support. Take advantage of these camps. They offer a chance to have fun and be yourself minus the worry about being sick or feeling different.

You enjoy the benefits of staying away from home. You can participate in activities any other camper enjoys. You experience the same relationships as other teens who camp. But you are relieved of worrying about medications, diet, or treatments. Camp medical teams carry that burden for you. Camp counselors know how to help you if you have an attack or require special adaptations and support. Another bonus of camp is hanging around other teens who know what you experience. Whatever your health differences, they share a similar journey.

When you are looking for a summer job, think about being a counselor at one of these camps. Who can help younger campers better than someone who lives with their issues?

"I love Camp Oasis," Carly said. "It's a camp for kids with Crohn's and colitis. I started going a year after getting diagnosed [eighth grade]. I just returned from my second year as a counselor. It's quite a journey and experience watching campers go through this change."[8]

Traveling with Certain Conditions

Being away from home can be stressful when you have a chronic condition. But you don't have to avoid evenings or weekends out or vacations and sleepover camps because you feel safer in your planned environment, one with medications and a nearby bathroom or whatever you need. Here are some activities to consider before leaving home.

- Pack enough medication to last your trip and longer, if there is a chance transportation can be delayed. Leave the entire supply in a labeled container in your suitcase. Count smaller doses that are lighter and fit into a pill box for the day. You might also ask your doctor for copies of your prescriptions, in case you get delayed or lose your medicines.

- Keep a list of medications and special directions concerning your health to help someone else help you, should you become incapacitated.

- Identify where bathrooms are located.

- Stick with any diet you eat. Being away from home isn't the time to experiment.

- Call ahead whenever possible, whether it is to a restaurant or hotel. If you need to know, ask about foods you can eat, a refrigerator for your medicines, accessibility, should you use a wheelchair or need guardrails, and so on.

- Ask your doctor for a physician recommendation if you are traveling to a different state—just in case.

> ### Michael
>
> MS encircles you with this malaise that makes you not want to get up and not want to go because you are so exhausted. Basketball has been cool for me because I love it, so I go anyway. Once I get out and stretch I can run. As I exercise I improve. If you don't exercise, you will feel worse. If you do work out, you will feel better. Stretch out and go for a walk. Do as much as you can. Do what you want to do physically, and you will feel better.[i]

You and Your Siblings

Many children and young adults admit that having a sibling who is different, whatever the difference, is a mixed blessing. On the positive side, the experience made them more sensitive and patient. These siblings learn to appreciate the gifts they possess and to accept other people's differences.

They also admit that they faced many emotional challenges not experienced in other families. Having a condition, such as Down syndrome, or an illness, such as Crohn's, can alter the kind of relationships brothers and sisters have. Sibling rivalry and jealousy are common reactions to feeling left out when doctor and therapy visits keep parents busy and unavailable to the typical sibling. Some siblings find it difficult to compete with a brother or sister who often feels sick, is slower mentally, or requires constant medical attention. They may find that adjusting to having a sibling with a chronic condition takes longer than parents would prefer.

Some teens may resent the attention a sibling with a chronic condition requires. They may feel neglected themselves yet be burdened with care of a sibling, especially one who may behave in an unusual way. Siblings may become more self-conscious or embarrassed about having a brother or sister who looks and acts differently, no matter what the reason. At a time when teens try to fit in, they feel saddled with a person who may talk or act oddly or unexpectedly writhe in pain. No matter what their feelings about the sibling relationship, they still may become upset overhearing taunts of names like "dummy" or "retard" directed at them or their sibling.

Being the "normal" or "healthy" child brings its own problems. Some siblings feel pressure to be extra agreeable so parents never have to worry about them. Other siblings act out, pick fights, or purposefully get bad grades to get attention. Emotions can be jumbled as typical siblings feel angry, embarrassed for their sibling, and guilty for not being like him or her.

Talk with your parents. Find out the real story about why your sibling is different. Some of your reactions may come from misinformation. You may think your sibling has worse problems than is the case. Your parents may have kept secrets about your sibling to protect you. Explaining the situation may provide a welcome relief for you all.

If asking parents proves difficult for you, try a school counselor or trusted teacher. Several programs recognize the support siblings need when one family member is different. Some are offered through organizations that deal with the specific condition. Others are listed in Resources.

Managing Stress: Mind over Illness

Chronic illness can be stressful and exhausting. You wait for your next flare-up. You need to be vigilant with foods you eat. You need to be on constant alert to keep your body working in a healthy fashion. Or you are bullied because of how you look. All this stress can get depressing at times. Time to learn to chill—and take care of your body and mind.

Those around you may keep telling you to reduce stress. You will be happier; you will be healthier, they say. But managing stress can be easier said than done.

The good news is there are ways to help yourself keep up your spirits. Different techniques work for different teens. Your job is to find which activities allow you to reduce stress and remain stress-free.

Take Deep Breaths

Relaxing often involves something as simple as thinking differently. Basically, you want to take your mind off your cares. The easiest method to relax involves slow, deep breathing. When you concentrate on rhythmic breathing, your mind refocuses and muscles relax. Worry lessens. Your relaxed muscles create a sense of well-being.

Exercise Regularly

The idea is to keep moving in any way you can. If your condition slows you down, then so be it. Move slower but move. Regular exercise reduces aches and pain. Keeping limber increases your ability to bounce back after an episode of your condition.

Since range-of-motion exercises reduce joint-related discomfort, ask your doctor to recommend that you see a physical therapist. The therapist can help you learn exercises that will help keep you flexible and within a good weight range. If you

Playing unscheduled games with friends is fun and adds movement to your day.

don't want to exercise in a formal way, walk a little farther or place something you use regularly in a place that will require you to stretch or move more than usual. Perform arm exercises with weights or soup cans, if you don't feel like walking or completing leg exercises. Your grandparent is right. If you don't move it, you lose it.

Feel the Beat

In addition to deep breathing, music refocuses the mind and encourages relaxing. For teens who cannot stay still enough to relax, music gives their movements purpose. Music can provide alternatives to a worried mind that refuses to allow sleeping. A good night's sleep alone can heal and reduce stress. Peaceful sounds, such as ocean waves or harp music, lessen muscle tension and slow blood flow and breathing—all helpful for reducing stress. Some teens find the white noise of a fan or filtering machine helpful when trying to sleep at night.

Meditate

Meditation is another method for relaxing. You can take classes or practice exercises at home. Check with your library for DVDs with meditation tips. Some teens who meditate focus on a single word or object as a means of achieving a

Join a parent for regular meditation sessions.

relaxed state. As your mind refocuses, it lets go of distracting—and stressful—thoughts. Many teens find meditation calms their body and mind, thereby reducing stress and relaxing tense muscles.

Visualize Stress Away

Another relaxing technique similar to meditation is visualization. With visualization, you create a mental picture of health, rather than focusing on a single word or object. You can visualize yourself exercising, playing sports, swimming at the beach, spending long hours at a museum, anything that may be difficult for you to accomplish.

Picturing yourself in a healthy state reinforces the message that your body can be strong and heal itself. This image changes how you view yourself and your chronic condition. In turn, positive thinking produces a positive impact on how your immune system responds to illness. Books and workshops help teens learn how to visualize healthy pictures.

Relax Your Muscles

Some teens find stress relief from a process called progressive muscle relaxation. It's a long name for an easy exercise. The idea is to consciously relax one muscle

> ### Michelle L.
>
> Have someone to talk about your health. In the hospital, I had a friend who had leukemia [Michelle had melanoma]. We could talk to each other about things that parents might not understand. Great to have someone to talk you through it or to talk to when I was scared or didn't want to go through another treatment cycle. It was great to have him there. I did not join a specific group, but I had friends and nurses in the hospital to help me out.[j]

group in your body at a time. You lay in bed or sit in a comfy chair. Then you tense one part of your body, notice the tension, then let the tension go. You can begin with your fingers and toes and move inward, even to your eyes and tongue. Or you can start with internal organs and work outward to extremities. Progressive relaxation gets your day started peacefully. The technique also helps your body relax enough to sleep.

Time for Talking Therapy

When stress becomes too much, and you cannot reduce it on your own, it's time to talk with someone. Keep lines of communication open with your parents. If that won't work, consider talking with a trusted friend or other relative who's a good listener. Think about confiding in someone responsive from your medical team or a religious leader. Talking relieves stress. Otherwise, it builds, like Sean and Michael mentioned, and you find functioning even more difficult than dealing with your condition.

If these options do not work for you, see a professional. Find someone at your local hospital or social service organization. Contact the local organization for your condition, and ask if there is a counselor who can meet with you. Or ask if there are teen support groups you can join or mentors you can connect with who understand your situation. You don't have to experience stress alone.

The Future

New research into causes, treatments, and medications. Updated laws. Novel options for support. There is still more to discover about each condition in this book. But there is much to bring hope.

Scientists are investigating a new test using a tiny drop of blood. Supposedly, the inexpensive test can identify "nearly every virus a person has ever been exposed to."[9] Researchers claim, if perfected, the test could also check for the body's immune response to these viruses. The results could further study into how the immune system affects chronic diseases and cancers.

Other studies are still looking into the healing effects of marijuana. Already reports point to medical marijuana helping teens with multiple sclerosis, sickle cell anemia, and other pain-related diseases. Some doctors offer marijuana to teens involved in chemotherapy, as it reduces nausea and discomfort for some patients.

What do these innovations and research mean for you? They mean hope that someday your symptoms may ease or go away. Keep up with your condition, follow what's new, and see if anything can improve your situation, whatever it is. And remember: your condition is not all of you.

"I learned a lot about myself, those around me, and my ability to adapt to change," Dan said. "I've learned how to enjoy life, love another person, participate in activities . . . and feel comfortable in my own skin. All of that nonsense [with Crohn's] also gave me some much-needed perspective on what really is important in life—health, family, smiling, and giving."[10]

Resources

Organizations

Condition Identification

MedicAlert Foundation
2323 Colorado Avenue
Turlock, CA 95382
888-633-4298
www.medicalert.org
Organization that sells a variety of wearable items that inform others you have a specific medical issue that they should understand when assisting you, should you be unable to communicate.

Antibullying

Born This Way Foundation
bornthiswayfoundation.org

Group founded by singer Lady Gaga and her mother, Cynthia Germanotta, to encourage acceptance of individual differences. The organization maintains a website and various activities supported by the Berkman Center at Harvard University.

Kids Health
www.kidshealth.org/teens
Site that includes a range of topics related to growing healthy teens, including bullying, homework tips, and public speaking anxiety.

National Bullying Prevention Center
Pacer Teen against Bullying
8161 Normandale Boulevard
Bloomington, MN 55437
800-537-2237
www.pacer.org/bullying
Site for teens against bullying that offers resources, personal stories, and action plans to prevent and stop bullying.

Southern Poverty Law Center
400 Washington Avenue
Montgomery, AL 36104
334-956-8200
www.splcenter.org
National advocacy and legal organization that battles discrimination and bullying. The group produces free classroom materials (videos, *Teaching Tolerance* magazine, newsletters) and offers legal assistance when other avenues fail.

StopBullying.gov
www.stopbullying.gov
Federally run website managed by the U.S. Department of Health and Human Services to provide advice about bullies and how to stop them, bullying research, and information about cyberbullying.

We Stop Hate
www.westophate.org
Emily-Anne Rigal created this project to end the cycle of bullying and becoming a bully. The nonprofit maintains a strong web presence dedicated to building confidence and stopping bullying. Lady Gaga, Meryl Streep, other celebrities, and several corporations lend their support.

Financial Assistance and Insurance

Benefits.gov
www.benefits.gov
Site that takes you to all government programs that might apply to lessen your financial burdens.

Care Connect USA
careconnectusa.org
Financial assistance hotline for families that has compiled a free list of financial relief for health care issues.
Hill-Burton Free and Reduced Cost Health Care
www.hrsa.gov/health care/affordable/hillburton
Program established in 2003 as a result of legislation that requires health care institutions to provide services to patients unable to pay for services if the facility received government payments. One problem is the benefits only apply to the health care facilities listed online.

NeedyMeds
www.needymeds.org
Nonprofit organization that seeks to help people who cannot afford medicine or health care costs.

Patient Advocate Foundation Co-Pay Relief Program
421 Butterfarm Road
Hampton, VA 23666
866-512-3861
www.copays.org
Group that provides direct financial support to insured patients, including Medicare Part D beneficiaries. But patients must qualify financially and medically to be eligible for pharmaceutical copay assistance.

Patient Access Network Foundation
202-661-8074
www.panfoundation.org
Program that helps the underinsured access health care necessary to carry on everyday activities.

Patient Services, Inc.
PO Box 5930
Midlothian, VA 23112

800-366-7741

www.patientservicesinc.org

Nonprofit that helps patients living with specific chronic illnesses locate health insurance in all fifty states, subsidizes the cost of health insurance, provides medicine and treatment copays, and helps advocate for Social Security Disability, if needed.

RxAssist

www.rxassist.org

Program run by pharmaceutical companies that offers a database of patient assistance programs, free medications to patients who cannot afford them, and practical tools and news for how health-care professionals and patients can locate appropriate information.

U.S. Department of Health and Human Services

200 Independence Avenue SW

Washington, DC 20201

877-696-6775

www.hhs.gov

Government program that offers information about paying for medical care for low-income families. Click on "Families and Children."

Having Fun

Definitely check resources at the back of each chapter to find camps, meetups, and social gatherings devoted to helping teens with specific conditions have fun away from home.

Serious Fun Children's Network

203-562-1203

www.seriousfunnetwork.org

Global community of independently managed and financed programs and camps for seriously ill kids and teens.

Double "H" Hole in the Woods Ranch

97 Hidden Valley Road

Lake Luzerno, NY 12846

One of the Serious Fun places, this camp provides specialized year-round programs and support for teens and their families. The program was cofounded by Charles Wood and actor Paul Newman, who manufactured food products to gain proceeds that fund the camp.

New Directions for Young Adults
3275 West Hillsboro Boulevard
Deerfield Beach, FL 33442
877-763-5102
www.ndfya.com
A nonprofit organization that offers local, national, and international travel vacation and holiday programs for young adults ages eighteen to thirty who experience educational or psychological challenges.

Housing during Treatment

Hospitality Homes
PO Box 15265
Boston, MA 92215
888-595-4678
www.hosp.org
Boston-based program that provides temporary housing in volunteer host homes and other donated accommodations. There are others like it nationwide. Check whether there is a hospitality home network in your city. In some areas hospitality homes formed alliances with Ronald McDonald Houses (www.rmhc.org), a network of local programs that provide free housing so families can stay close to their teens receiving hospital care.

National Association of Hospital Hospitality Houses
Housing Hospitality Network, Inc.
PO Box 1439
Gresham, OR 97030
800-542-9730
www.hhnetwork.org
National network of two hundred nonprofit groups that offer free or low-cost housing to teens receiving medical care away from home and their families.

Sibling Assistance

Sibling Information Network
A.J. Pappanikou Center
263 Farmington Avenue, MC6222
Storrs, CT 06030
www.uconnucedd.org
National clearinghouse for information related to helping brothers and sisters of siblings with disabilities and illnesses.

Sibling Support Project
6512 23rd Avenue NW, Suite 322
Seattle, WA 98117
206-297-6368
siblingsupport.org
Amazing national project devoted to concerns of brothers and sisters of teens with special health and developmental needs. The project hosts more than four hundred Sibshops, which are local support activities for siblings of different ages, in most states and beyond, and provides online communities for siblings, including SibNet, SibTeen, and Sib20, and offers workshops, training, and publications.

Medical-Related Transportation

Air Charity Network Transportation
4620 Haygood Road, Suite 1
Virginia Beach, VA 23455
877-621-7177
aircharitynetwork.org
Group that coordinates a network of volunteer pilots who shuttle patients in need to special health-care facilities and camps for clinical trials, chemotherapy, or other repeat treatment.

Miracle Flights for Kids
2764 North Green Valley Parkway, Suite 115
Green Valley, NV 89014-2120
800–359–1711
www.miracleflights.org
Group that offers free flights to specialized medical treatment for teens struggling with severe illness.

National Patient Center Travel HELPLINE
4620 Haygood Road, Suite 1
Virginia Beach, VA 23455
800-296-1217
www.patienttravel.org
Center that provides information about long-distance medical air transportation (airline tickets, escorts, volunteer pilots, long-distance ground travel) to ensure that financial need does not interfere with quality medical care due to distance.

Transportation Security Administration/TSA Cares

www.tsa.govtravel/special-procedures or www.tsa.gov/contact/contact-center

866-289-9673 (contact center)

Helpline that assists travelers with disabilities and medical conditions get through security screening. The TSA suggests calling seventy-two hours before you travel to discover what to expect during screening and how to best navigate the nation's complicated air travel systems.

Glossary

Americans with Disabilities Act (ADA): federal law that requires schools to provide alternatives to accommodate students with different disabilities, including gluten-free diets or different testing situations

amino acids: naturally occurring compounds that comprise all proteins in plants and animals

amniocentesis: diagnostic test for women between weeks fourteen and eighteen of pregnancy to study an amniotic fluid sample for presence of an extra chromosome in the twenty-first pair

anemia: condition that results from lack of red blood cells, or hemoglobin, which makes teens tired from lack of iron

antibodies: substances in the body that fight disease in reaction to invading bacteria

assay: clotting factor test

autoimmune reaction: conditions that result from error in how antibodies work, causing them to attack healthy tissue in addition to the invading bacteria or virus

basal cells: cells deep in the epidermis that contain other cells that control pigment, or color, of the skin

behavior therapy: treatment options that help teens with Tourette syndrome learn to manage their tics in different situations by practicing alternative actions

benign growth: cluster of cells on the body that is free of cancer

biopsy: medical test that requires cutting or scraping of body tissue or cells to study for presence or degree of disease

bone marrow: part of bone that produces red blood cells

bone marrow transplant: when bone marrow of one person is replaced with bone marrow from a matching healthy donor, such as with sickle cell disease

Brushfield spots: white specks on the outer rim of iris of each eye in people with DS

cannabis: plant that patients with chronic disease claim eases pain and stress when ingested or smoked; also called marijuana

capsule endoscopy: medical examination that involves swallowing a capsule with a camera that sends images of the gastrointestinal tract to a computer worn on the belt to be analyzed for disease

cataracts: cloudy film that grows over part of the eye and blurs vision but can be surgically removed

chemotherapy: use of drugs through cream, injection, or pills to rid the body of cancer cells

chorionic villus sampling: diagnostic test of the unborn fetus that involves a needle inserted into the sac holding the fetus to determine genetic problems

clotting: process of sticky blood cells rushing to an injury and stopping the flow of blood

clotting factors: proteins that work together to help blood platelets seal a wound

colon: large intestine

colonoscopy: test whereby the doctor inserts a flexible tube with a camera into the colon to examine for clusters of inflamed cells that help identify intestinal disease

colostomy: surgery that relieves symptoms of extreme colon damage that involves making an opening in the abdominal wall to permit feces to exit into a bag outside the body

complex tics: tics that involve several muscle groups that cause patterns of movement

compulsions: actions taken repeatedly to satisfy urges to resolve certain obsessive thoughts

computerized tomography (CT): body scans that use X-ray machinery to look into and outside different parts and systems of the body, such as the bowel

coprolalia: vocal tic that causes cursing or saying socially inappropriate words or phrases for a specific culture

copropaxia: tics that involve making offensive gestures

cryosurgery: procedure to remove skin cancer cells that relies on liquid nitrogen applied directly to the skin, which freezes off cancer cells rather than cutting them as with traditional surgery

demyelination: process of damaging the protective covering of nerve cells

dermatologist: skin doctor

dermis: thicker middle layer of the skin that gives it strength and elasticity

disability: inability to perform behaviors because of a problem with the body, mind, or emotions

disease: condition with known causes and definite symptoms that signal what it is

echolalia: tics that provoke a person to repeat the last sound, word, or phrase uttered by someone else

echopraxia: tics involving imitating actions of others

endoscopy: medical examination that involves inserting a tube-like instrument called an endoscope into a body organ or canal to look for the source of illness

epicanthal folds: folds of skin that cover the inner corners of both eyes in babies born with Down syndrome

epidermis: outer layer of the skin containing protein that makes skin tough and durable

evoked potential test: test that measures how quickly and accurately the nervous system responds, which can help identify problems from multiple sclerosis

factor VIII: protein produced from a gene in the X chromosome that is lacking in teens with hemophilia A

factor IX: a protein produced from an X chromosome gene that is lacking in teens with hemophilia B

fecal occult blood test: test for red blood cell levels in a stool sample that may indicate the possibility of anemia

fetus: cells of developing unborn human inside a pregnant woman

flexible sigmoidoscopy: procedure that involves winding a lighted tube into the body, much like a colonoscopy, but it only goes into the last section of the colon, or sigmoid

gastrointestinal (GI) tract: pathway from the mouth to the anus that food and liquid take

genes: basic message centers within the body that determine varied characteristics, such as hair and skin color and the type of hemoglobin in blood

habit reversal: therapy plan that helps teens with Tourette syndrome become aware of their tics and situations that promote ticking and alternative responses to prevent the tic

hematologist: medical professional who identifies, tests, and helps manage blood conditions

hematology: study of blood

hemoglobin: iron-containing substance in red blood cells that carries oxygen throughout the body and creates the red color

hemoglobin electrophoresis: common blood test for sickle cell anemia that measures blood oxygen levels in hemoglobin

human genetics: study of how genes influence how the body operates

hydroxyurea: medication that reduces chest and joint pain and the number of hospital trips for pain from sickle cell disease

ileostomy: surgical procedure that involves making a hole in the small intestine, or ileum, to permit feces to exit into a bag outside the body

ileum: small intestine

inflammatory bowel disease: group of chronic conditions that involve inflammation of the digestive tract

liquid biopsy: blood test for melanoma being tested to replace the biopsy that requires cutting or scraping a sample of body cells or tissue

lymph nodes/system: drainage system of vessels, glands, and ducts that allows body fluids from tissues to travel throughout the bloodstream and back into the bloodstream; part of the immune system that fights infection and cancer

magnetic resonance imaging (MRI): painless photographic scanner that sends pictures of the body to a computer that translates magnetic information into slices of the brain, spinal cord, and other body parts; an important tool for diagnosing multiple sclerosis

meditation: relaxation exercise that involves focusing on a single word or object as a means of achieving a relaxed state

melanoma: skin cancer that can be serious, depending upon which stage is diagnosed

melanoma in situ: skin cancer that involves the top layer of skin only

Mohs surgery: process a trained surgeon uses to remove and test one tissue layer at a time until all skin cells look cancer-free

motor tics: sudden uncontrollable movements that can arise from any muscle of the body

myelin: fatty coating encasing nerves that protects them as they relay messages

nervous system: brain, spinal cord, and network of nerve cells that tell the body what to do

neurologist: medical doctor who specializes in problems with the nervous system

neurons: cells that comprise the nervous system

obsessions: thoughts that compel teens to repeat an action so often to satisfy an urge that normal daily activities are disrupted

obsessive-compulsive disorder (OCD): condition whereby teens become trapped in a pattern of repetitive thoughts and behavior that may seem senseless and distressing but are difficult to overcome

ophthalmologist: medical doctor who specializes in everything related to the eye

orphan diseases: term that indicates how little the medical community knows about a specific condition or its origins

pediatric melanoma: skin cancer that arises between birth and nineteen years of age

percutaneous umbilical blood sampling: test to examine blood from the umbilical cord connecting the fetus to the sac that surrounds it inside the mother to look for presence of an extra chromosome

peristalsis: wavelike movement of muscles around organs of the gastrointestinal tract that allows food and liquid to break down, nourish, and pass through the body

phenylalanine (phe): amino acid necessary for overall normal growth and development of infants and children

phenylalanine hydroxylase (PAH): liver enzyme that results in normal balance of phe but causes PKU when the gene that produces it is faulty

phenylketonuria (PKU): rare inherited condition that causes buildup of the amino acid phenylalanine in the body; babies are born with PKU and remain on a phenylalanine-free diet for their entire lives to prevent major health problems

photodynamic surgery: procedure for removing skin cancer cells using a drug with a special light source

physical therapist: trained professional who can match stretching exercises and relaxation techniques to relieve specific aches and pains

platelets: sticky blood cell particles involved in the clotting process to stop bleeding

pores: tiny openings at the surface of the skin

progressive muscle relaxation: stress-relieving exercise that involves consciously relaxing one muscle group in the body at a time

red blood cells: cells that contain hemoglobin and circulate throughout the body carrying oxygen

remission: time without symptoms between episodes of disease

seizures: abnormal electrical discharges in an injured or scarred part of the brain

sickle cell anemia: inherited disorder of red blood cells that includes abnormally (sickle) shaped hemoglobin that blocks blood flow and distribution of oxygen throughout the body

sickle cell trait: inheritance of one gene from a single parent that contains sickle hemoglobin, which makes someone a carrier, rather than a victim of, full-blown sickle cell disease

simple tics: individual repeated movements of one muscle or body part, such as shoulder shrugging

sleep apnea: sleeping problem that involves repeated episodes when a person stops breathing while asleep

sprue: form of celiac disease that refuses to allow intestines to absorb nutrients for the body

squamous cells: flat cells that comprise the outer layer of the skin

strep: disease-causing bacteria that may play a role in increasing abnormal behaviors in obsessive-compulsive disorder

stroke: brain injury caused by either an interruption of blood supply to the brain or blood leakage from the vessel walls

subcutaneous layer: undermost deep layer of the skin that contains fat cells that protect the skin and inner tissue from shock

syndrome: disorder with a combination of symptoms

tics: involuntary movements and vocalizations that characterize Tourette syndrome

tumor: abnormal growth of tissue cells that reproduce in an uncontrolled manner

visualization: stress-relieving exercise whereby someone creates a mental picture of health

vocal tics: sudden uncontrollable movements that erupt from muscles controlling speech, thereby causing sounds and words to emerge

Notes

Chapter 1

1. Frederick Mish, ed., *Merriam-Webster Collegiate Dictionary*, 11th ed., Springfield, Mass.: Merriam-Webster, Inc., 2003, p. 221.
2. Jerrold Leikin, *American Medical Association, Complete Medical Encyclopedia*, Chicago/New York: American Medical Association/ Random House Reference, 2003, p. 365.
3. Marlene Targ Brill, *Tourette Syndrome*, Minneapolis: Twentieth Century Books, 2013, p. 42; also, Dan Vergano, "10 Years after Genome Project, How Did We Do?" *USA Today*, Money, Section B, February 22, 2011.

a. Cole, "Cole (15 Years Old)," *That Darn Tic: A Newsletter by and for Kids with Tourette Syndrome*, Tourette Syndrome Association, no. 41 (Winter 2012), tourette.org/Publications/ChildrensNewsletter/darntic_winter2012.pdf (accessed February 23, 2015).
b. Denise Grady, "Every Virus a Person Has Had Can Be Seen in a Drop of Blood, Researchers Find," *New York Times*, June 5, 2015, A14.
c. Michelle Laraia, interview with author, April 17, 2015.
d. Molly Lamick, interview with author, May 13, 2015.
e. NORD, "I Am Stephanie—National Organization for Rare Disorders," www.rarediagdisease.org/patients-and-families/patient-stories/stephanie-foster, p. 1 (accessed September 7, 2014). NORD alternates online personal stories, and this one was taken down after I accessed it in 2014.

Chapter 2

1. The University of Chicago Celiac Disease Center, "Symptoms," www.celiacdisease.net, p. 1 (accessed February 5, 2015).
2. PubMed Health, "Celiac Disease," A.D.A.M. Medical Encyclopedia [Internet]. Atlanta, GA: A.D.A.M., 2013, p. 1. www.ncbi.nlm.nih.gov/pubmedhealth/PMH0001280 (accessed February 5, 2015).
3. PubMed Health, "Celiac Disease," p. 2.
4. The University of Chicago Celiac Disease Center, "Celiac Disease Facts and Figures," www.celiacdisease.net, p. 2 (accessed February 5, 2015).
5. The University of Chicago Celiac Disease Center, "Celiac Disease Facts and Figures," p. 1.
6. The University of Chicago Celiac Disease Center, "What Is the Prevalence for Others in My Family to Have Celiac Disease since I've Been Diagnosed with It?" www.celiacdisease.net (accessed February 5, 2015).
7. Jane Brody, "A Common, but Elusive, Diagnosis," *New York Times*, September 30, 2014, D5.

8. National Institutes of Health, Rare Diseases and Disorders, "Human Microbiome Project," www.commonfund.nih.gov/hmp/index (accessed June 15, 2015).

9. Jane Brody, "CDF Medical Advisory Board Member Dr. Joseph Murray Quoted in The New York Times Article about Celiac Disease," *New York Times*, September 29, 2014; posted on the *New York Times* website by Jane Brody; downloaded from celiac.org/blog/2014/09/29/cdf-medical-advisory-board-member-dr-joseph-murray-quoted, February 6, 2015.

10. The University of Chicago Celiac Disease Center, "What Common Nutrient Deficiencies Might Add Adult Experience Prior to Diagnosis?" www.celiacdisease.net (accessed February 5, 2015).

11. National Organization for Rare Disorders, "Celiac Disease," rarediseases.info.nih.gov/gard/11998/celiac-disease/resources/1 , p. 2 (accessed February 23, 2015).

12. Celiac Disease Foundation, "Poorly Responsive Celiac Disease," celiac.org/celiac-disease/poorly-responsive-celiac-disease (accessed February 5, 2015).

13. Visually, "America's Universities Receive Poor Grades on the Subject of Gluten-Free," visual.ly/americas-universities-receive-poor-grades-subject-gluten-free (accessed February 5, 2015).

14. Billy Buhring, interview with author, June 10, 2015.

15. Billy, interview.

16. Molly Lamick, interview with author, May 13, 2015.

17. Michelle R., interview with author, April 7, 2015.

a. Michelle R., interview with author, April 7, 2015.

b. Molly Lamick, interview with author, May 13, 2015.

c. Billy Buhring, interview with author, June 10, 2015.

d. Rachel Brill, interview with author, March 2, 2015.

e. Molly, interview.

f. Michelle R., interview.

g. Rachel, interview.

h. Billy, interview.

i. Michelle R., interview.

j. Molly, interview.

Chapter 3

1. Mike McCready, "Watch: Mike McCready of Pearl Jam talks Crohn's disease," Q13 Fox interview, September 3, 2014, q13fox.com/2014/09/03/watch-mike-mccready-of-pearl-jam-talks-crohns-disease/ (accessed September 14, 2015).

2. Dan Weber, interview with author, August 31, 2015.

3. Crohn's and Colitis Foundation of America, "What Is Crohn's Disease/Causes of Crohn's," www.ccfa.org/what-are-crohns-and-colitis/what-is-crohns-disease, p. 2 (accessed February 12, 2015).

4. Mayo Clinic Staff, "Crohn's Disease: Definition," Mayo Foundation for Medical Education and Research, www.mayoclinic.org/diseases-conditions/crohns-disease/basics/definition/CON-20032061, p. 2 (accessed February 12, 2015).

5. Ashley, "Ashley's Advice," Crohn's Disease Web Site, www.angelfire.com/ga/crohns/tips.html (accessed August 10, 2015).

6. Carly Festenstein, interview with author, August 28, 2001.
7. Mayo Clinic Staff, "Crohn's Disease," p. 2.
8. Erik, "Erik's Comments," Crohn's Disease Web Site, www.angelfire.com/ga/crohns/stories.html (accessed August 10, 2015).
9. Carly, interview.
10. Crohn's and Colitis Foundation of America, "Crohn's Treatment Options," www.ccfa.org/what-are-crohns-and-colitis/what-is-crohns-disease/crohns-treatment-options.htmlp. 2 (accessed February 12, 2015).
11. Crohn's and Colitis Foundation of America, "Crohn's Treatment Options," p. 2.
12. Crohn's and Colitis Foundation of America, "A New Life with IBD," pp. 17–18, www.ccfa.org/resources/a-new-life-with-ibd.html (accessed February 12, 2015).
13. Erik, "Erik's Comments."
14. Erik, "Erik's Comments."

a. Carly Festenstein, interview with author, August 28, 2001.
b. Dan Weber, interview with author, August 31, 2015.
c. Crohn's and Colitis Foundation of America, "What Is Crohn's Disease/Causes of Crohn's," www.ccfa.org/what-are-crohns-and-colitis/what-is-crohns-disease, p. 2 (accessed February 12, 2015).
d. Bernard Aserkoff, MD, "The Scoop on Poop," WebMD, www.webmd.com/women/features/digestive-problems (accessed August 7, 2015).
e. "Jocelyn's Comments," Crohn's Disease Web Site, www.angelfire.com/ga/crohns/stories.html (accessed August 10, 2015).
f. Alan, "Alan's Tips/Advice," Crohn's Disease Web Site, www.angelfire.com/ga/crohns/tip.html (accessed August 10, 2015).
g. Carly, interview.
h. National Institutes of Health, "Treatment for Irritable Bowel Syndrome," National Institute of Diabetes and Digestive and Kidney Diseases, www.niddk.nih.gov/health-information/health-topics/digestive-diseases/irritable-bowel-syndrome/Pages/treatment.aspx, pp. 4–5 (accessed July 12, 2015).
i. Crohn's and Colitis Foundation of America, *Diet, Nutrition, and Inflammatory Bowel Disease*, www.ccfa.org/assets/pdfs/diet-nutrition-2013.pdf, p. 1 (accessed February 12, 2015).
j. Carly, interview.
k. Dan, interview.

Chapter 4

1. Leah Jensen, "Madeline Stuart, Teen Model with Down Syndrome, Lands Two More Campaigns," *Daily Signal*, dailysignal.com/2015/07/15/madeline-stuart-teen-model-with-down-syndrome-lands-two-more-campaigns/ (accessed July 15, 2015).
2. Adrian Drower, interview with author, August 10, 2015.
3. Sam Radinsky, interview with author, July 7, 2015.
4. Marlene Targ Brill, *Keys to Parenting a Child with Down Syndrome*, Hauppauge, NY: Barron's Educational Series, 1993; National Down Syndrome Society, "Down Syndrome Facts," www.ndss.org/Down-Syndrome/Down-Syndrome-Facts (accessed September 3, 2015); Centers

for Disease Control and Prevention, "Facts about Down Syndrome," www.cdc.gov/ncbddd/birthdefects/DownSyndrome.html (accessed November 19, 2015).

5. Adrian, interview.

6. National Down Syndrome Society, "Obstructive Sleep Apnea and Down Syndrome," www.ndss.org/Resources/Health-Care/Associated-Conditions/Obstructive-Sleep-Apnea—Down-Syndrome (accessed November 19, 2015).

7. National Institutes of Health Eunice Kennedy Shriver National Institute of Child Health and Human Development, "What Conditions or Disorders Are Commonly Associated with Down Syndrome?" www.nichd.nih.gov/health/topics/down/conditioninfo/Pages/associated.aspx (accessed November 19, 2015).

8. Sietske Heyn, PhD, "News and Views: Down Syndrome and Epilepsy," Stanford Medicine Down Syndrome Research Center (accessed November 15, 2015).

9. Brill, *Keys to Parenting*, p. 65.

10. Adrian, interview.

11. National Down Syndrome Society, "Down Syndrome Facts," www.ndss.org/Down-Syndrome/Down-Syndrome-Facts/ (accessed September 3, 2015).

12. P. M. Dunn, "Dr. Langdon Down (1828–1896) and 'Mongolism,'" *Archives of Disease in Childhood* 66, no. 7 (July 1991, Special): 827–828.

13. O Conor Ward, "Down Syndrome Research and Practice," *Great Britain: Down Syndrome Educational Trust* 6, no. 1 (1999): 21.

14. Ann Garcia, National Association for Down Syndrome Family Support Coordinator, interview with author, August 28, 2015.

15. Renata Lindeman, "Down Syndrome Screening Isn't about Public Health. It's about Eliminating a Group of People," *Washington Post*, June 16, 2015, www.washingtonpost.com/posteverything/wp/2015/06/16/down-syndrome-screening-isnt-about-public-health-its-about-eliminating-a-group-of-people/ (accessed July 1, 2015).

16. Cynthia Magriel Wetzler, "Meeting the Challenges of Down Syndrome," *New York Times*, August, 24, 1997, www.nytimes.com/1997/08/24/nyregion/meeting-the-challenge-of-down-syndrome.html (assessed September 9, 2015).

17. Sam, interview.

18. Sam, interview.

19. Anne Sewel, "Spain's Down Syndrome Councillor Wants to Be an Honest Politician," *Politics Valladolid*, August 1, 2013, www.digitaljournal.com/article/355671 (accessed September 2, 2015).

20. Wetzler, "Meeting the Challenges of Down Syndrome."

---

a. Centers for Disease Control, "Facts about Down Syndrome," www.cdc.gov/ncbddd/birthdefects/downsyndrome.html, pp. 1–2 (accessed June 24, 2015).

b. Mayo Clinic Staff, "Down Syndrome," Mayo Foundation for Medical Education and Research, www.mayoclinic.org/diseases-conditions/down-syndrome/basics/risk-factors/con-20020948 (accessed September 8, 2015).

c. Mayo Clinic Staff, "Down Syndrome."

d. Cavan Sieczkowski, "John Franklin Stephens, Special Olympics Athlete, Pens Open Letter to Ann Coulter over 'Retard' Remark," *Huffington Post*, October 24, 2012, www.huffingtonpost.com/2012/10/24/ann-coluter-retard-john-franklin-stephens-special-olympics-open-letter_n_2008538.html (accessed September 9, 2015).

e. Julie Zellinger, "When Is It OK to Use the R-Word?" *Identities Mic*, April 15, 2015, mic.com/articles/115540/when-it-is-ok-to-use-the-r-word (accessed September 9, 2015).

Chapter 5

1. "Meet Jamie," Real People: Real Stories, www.yourtrueid.com/realStories_blog_jamie.html (accessed July 16, 2015). If the site does not show Jamie's story it is because the webmaster rotates biographies.
2. Living with Hemophilia, "About Hemophilia," www.livingwithhemophilia.ca/about (accessed February 11, 2015).
3. National Hemophilia Foundation, "Hemophilia A," www.hemophilia.org/Bleeding-Disorders/Types-of-Bleeding-Disorders/Hemophilia-A (accessed February 11, 2015).
4. "Meet Trevor," Real People: Real Stories, www.yourtrueid.com/real-stories/trevor.html (accessed July 16, 2015).
5. "Meet Jamie."
6. National Hemophilia Foundation, "History of Bleeding Disorders," www.hemophilia.org/Bleeding-Disorders/History-of-Bleeding-Disorders (accessed July 7, 2015).
7. Shelby Smoak, *Bleeder*, East Lansing: Michigan State University Press, 2013, p. 1.
8. Suzanne Nielsen, MD (last reviewer), "Hemophilia," Connecticut Children's Medical Center, www.connecticutchildrens.org/healthinfo/teens/diseases-and-conditions/blood-disorders, p. 1 (accessed February 11, 2015).
9. National Hemophilia Foundation, "Hemophilia A: Genetics," www.hemophilia.org/Bleeding-Disorders/Types-of-Bleeding-Disorders/Hemophilia-A (accessed February 11, 2015).
10. "Meet Trevor."
11. "Meet Trevor."
12. Living with Hemophilia, "Treating Hemophilia," www.livingwithhemophilia.ca/managing/treating.php, p. 2 (accessed February 11, 2015).

---

a. Shelby Smoak, *Bleeder*, East Lansing: Michigan State University Press, 2013, p. 1.
b. Marlene Targ Brill, *Extraordinary Young People*, New York: Children's Press, 1996, pp. 156–158.
c. National Heart, Lung, and Blood Institution, "What Are the Signs and Symptoms of Hemophilia?" National Institutes of Health, www.nhlbi.nih.gov/health/health-topics/topics/hemophilia/signs (accessed February 11, 2015).
d. Smoak, *Bleeder*, p. 1.
e. "Meet Craig," Real People: Real Stories, www.yourtrueid.com/realStories_blog_craig.html (accessed July 16, 2015). If the site does not show Craig's story it is because the webmaster rotates biographies.
f. The Missing Factor, "Famous People with Hemophilia," missingfactor.weebly.com/famous-people-with-hemophilia.html; also in Admin, "Famous Hemophiliacs," U.S. College Search, March 9, 2011, www.uscollegesearch.org/blog/medical-assisting-resource/medical-assisting-info/famous-hemophiliacs (both accessed February 11, 2015).

Chapter 6

1. Skin Cancer Foundation, "Skin Cancer Facts," p. 1, www.skincancer.org/skin-cancer-information/skin-cancer-facts (accessed February 19, 2015). Also in J. K. Robinson, "Sun Exposure, Sun Protection, and Vitamin D," *JAMA*, no. 294 (2005): 43–54; R. S. Stern, "Prevalence of a History of Skin Cancer in 2007: Results of an Incidence-Based Model," *Archives*

of Dermatology 146, no, 3 (2010): 279–282; and G. P. Guy and S. R. Machlin, "Prevalence and Costs of Skin Cancer Treatment in the U.S. 2002–2006 and 2007–2011," *American Journal of Preventive Medicine* 104 (2014): e69–e74. DOI: dx.doi.org/10.1016/j.amepre.2014.08.036.

2. MD Anderson Cancer Center, "Pediatric Melanoma Facts," University of Texas, https://www.mdanderson.org/patient-and-cancer-information/cancer-information/cancer-types/childhood-melanoma/index.html (accessed November 23, 2015).

3. Skin Cancer Foundation, "Skin Cancer Facts," p. 2; also from American Cancer Society, "Cancer Facts & Figures," 2015, http://www.cancer.org/acs/groups/content/@editorial/documents/document/acspc-044552.pdf; and A. Bleyer and M. O'Leary, eds., *Cancer Epidemiology in Older Adolescents and Young Adults 15 to 29 Years of Age, Including SEER Incidence and Survival: 1975–2000*, Bethesda, MD: National Cancer Institute, 2006.

4. David Cornfield Melanoma Fund, "Dear 16-Year-Old Me," www.youtube.com/watch?v=_4jgUcxMezM (accessed June 4, 2015).

5. H. M. Gloster and K. Neal, "Skin Cancer in Skin of Color," *Journal of American Dermatology* 55 (2006): 741–760.

6. Jerrold Leikin and Martin Lipsky, ed., *The American Medical Association Complete Medical Encyclopedia*, New York: Random House Reference, 2003, p. 1127.

7. F. El Ghissassi et al., "Special Report: Policy. A Review of Human Carcinogens—Part D: Radiation," *Lancet* 10, no. 8 (2009): 751–752. Also in Skin Care Foundation, "Skin Cancer Facts," p. 4.

8. Centers for Disease Control and Prevention, "Indoor Tanning Is Not Safe," www.cdc.gov/cancer/skin/basic_info/indoor_tanning.htm, last checked November 4, 2014. Also in Skin Care Foundation, "Skin Cancer Facts," p. 4.

9. National Cancer Institute, *What You Need to Know about Melanoma and Other Skin Cancers*, Washington, DC, National Institutes of Health, 2010, pubs.cancer.gov/ncipl/detai .aspx?prodid=p196, pp. 21, 36

10. National Cancer Institute, "Biological Therapies for Cancer," www.cancer.gov/about-cancer/treatment/types/immunotherapy/bio-therapies-fact-sheet (accessed November 23, 2015).

11. National Cancer Institute, *What You Need to Know about Melanoma*, p. 36.

12. Jennifer Jolly, "Wearable Sunburn Prevention," *New York Times*, June 16, 2015, D6.

13. Michelle Laraia, interview with author, April 17, 2015.

---

a. Kody Beach, interview with author, May 8, 2015.

b. Natalie, quoted in "Teen Tanners: The New Faces of Melanoma," Skin Cancer Foundation, p. 1, www.skincancer.org/true-stories/teen-tanners (accessed February 19, 2015).

c. National Cancer Institute, *What You Need to Know about Melanoma and Other Skin Cancers*, Washington, DC, National Institutes of Health, 2010, www.cancer.gov/Publications/patient -education/wyntk-skin-cancer, p. 13.

d. Chelsea, quoted in "Teen Tanners," pp. 2–3.

e. National Cancer Institute, *What You Need to Know about Melanoma*, p. 20.

f. Kate, quoted in "Teen Tanners," p. 2.

g. Bo Laraia, interview with author, April 17, 2015.

h. Kody Beach, interview with author, May 8, 2015.

i. Kate, quoted in "Teen Tanners," p. 2.

j. Bo, interview.

k. Ken Burns, "Story of Cancer," PBS documentary, April 1, 2015.

l. Associated Press, "New Test Could Spare Patients from Biopsies," *New York Times*, May 12, 2015, p. A16.
m. Claudia Dreifus, "Arming the Immune System against Cancer," *New York Times*, May 2, 2015, p. D2.
n. George Johnson, "Turning Nature against Cancer," *New York Times*, May 29, 2015, p. D3.
o. Vitamin B study, *CBS Evening News*, 6:00 p.m. CST, May 14, 2015.

Chapter 7

1. National MS Society, "Estimating the Prevalence of MS," www.nationalmssociety.org/About-the-Society/MS-Prevalence (accessed July 27, 2015).
2. National MS Society, "Estimating the Prevalence of MS."
3. National MS Society, "Estimating the Prevalence of MS."
4. National MS Society, "Initiative on Gender Differences in MS," www.nationalmssociety.org/Research/Research-We-Fund/Past-Research-Efforts#section-1 (accessed July 27, 2015).
5. National MS Society, "Who Gets MS? (Epidemiology)," www.nationalmssociety.org/What-is-MS/Who-Gets-MS (accessed July 27, 2015).
6. National MS Society, "Genetics," p. 2, www.nationalmssociety.org/For-Professionals/Clinical-Care/About-MS/Interaction-of-Genetics-and-the-Environment/Genetics (accessed July 27, 2015).
7. National MS Society, "Evoked Potential; EP," www.nationalmssociety.org/Symptoms-Diagnosis/Diagnosing-Tools/Evoked-Potentials (accessed July 27, 2015).
8. Suzi Shulman, interview with author, July 6, 2007.
9. National MS Society, "Treating MS?" www.nationalmssociety.org/Treating-MS (accessed July 27, 2015).
10. Sean Giblin, interview with author, March 30, 2015.
11. National MS Society, "MS symptoms," p. 2, www.nationalmssociety.org/Symptoms-Diagnosis/MS-Symptoms (accessed July 27, 2015).

a. Sean Giblin, interview with author, March 30, 2015.
b. Michael Goodman, interview with author, July 6, 2007.
c. National MS Society, "MS Symptoms."
d. Suzi Shulman, interview with author, July 6, 2007.
e. Sean, interview.
f. Suzi, interview.
g. Sean, interview.

Chapter 8

1. Olivia Cummings, interview with author, June 3, 2015.
2. National PKU Alliance, "About PKU," www.npkua.org/Education/AboutPKU.aspx, pp. 2–3 (accessed April 16, 2015).
3. Siegried Centerwall and Willard Centerwall, "The Discovery of Phenylketonuria: The Story of a Young Couple, Two Retarded Children, and a Scientist," *Pediatrics* 105,

no. 1 (January 2000): 89–103, pediatrics.aappublications.org/content/105/1/89?variant= abstract&sso=1&sso_redirect_count=1&nfstatus=401&nftoken=00000000-0000-0000-0000 -000000000000&nfstatusdescription=ERROR%3a+No+local+token (accessed February 16, 2015).

4. Diane Paul, "Appendix 5: The History of Newborn Phenylketonuria Screening in the U.S.," National Human Genome Research Institute, Final Report of the Task Force on Genetic Testing, pp. 3–4, www.cchfreedom.org/pdf/CCHCpkuReportInBrief092408FINAL.pdf (accessed June 29, 2015).

5. Virginia Schuett, ed., "Celebrating 75 Years Since the Discovery of PLU," *National PKU News* 21, no. 2 (Fall 2009), pkunews.org/about/History_of_PKU.pdf, (accessed June 29, 2015).

6. National PKU Alliance, "About PKU," p. 3.

7. National PKU Alliance, "About PKU," pp. 3–4 (accessed April 16, 2015).

8. National PKU Alliance, "About PKU," pp. 3–4 (accessed April 16, 2015).

9. Leah Kanihan, interview with author, April 7, 2015.

10. Kristi Eichorst, "Teens Living with PKU," *National PKU News*, p. 3, www.pkunews.org/adults/teens/htm (accessed February 16, 2015).

11. Quoted in "Teens Living with PKU," pp. 6–7.

12. Matthew Roberts, interview with author, April 14, 2015.

a. "Teens Living with PKU," *National PKU News*, p. 10, www.pkunews.org/adults/teens/htm (accessed February 16, 2015).

b. Leah Kanihan, interview with author, April 7, 2015.

c. Mayo Clinic, "Phenylketonuria (PKU) Definition—Diseases and Conditions," www .mayoclinic.org/diseases-conditions/phenylketonuria/basics/definition/con-20026275 (accessed February 17, 2015).

d. Olivia Cummings, interview with author, June 3, 2015.

e. Leah, interview.

f. Robin Roberts, interview with author, April 10, 2015.

g. Matthew Roberts, interview with author, April 14, 2015.

h. Leah, interview.

i. Olivia, interview.

j. Leah, interview.

k. Brittany, quoted in "Teens Living with PKU," p. 5.

l. Larry, quoted in "Teens Living with PKU," p. 2.

m. Olivia, interview.

n. Leah, interview.

o. Olivia, interview.

p. Leah, interview.

Chapter 9

1. Angie Crouch and Heather Navarro, "Feels Like Someone Is Punching You:' Sufferers Living with Disease Speak Out for National Sickle Cell Awareness Month," NBC4 Southern California News, September 23, 2015, www.nbclosangeles.com/news/local/sickle-cell-month

-awareness-disease-september-Feels-like-someone-is-punching-you-Children-Living-With -Disease-Speak-Out-for-National-Sickle-Cell-Awareness-Month-328957261.html (accessed September 24, 2015).

2. William Winer, "A Brief History of Sickle Cell Disease," www.sicklecell.howard.edu/A BriefHistoryofSickleCellDisease.htm (accessed September 23, 2015).
3. Food and Drug Administration, "FDA Helps Tackle Sickle Cell Disease," www.fda.gov/ ForConsumers/ConsumerUpdates/ucm418232.htm (accessed August 18, 2015).
4. UIC Sickle Cell Center, "About Sickle Cell Disease," hospital.uillinois.edu/primary-and -specialty-care/sickle-cell/about-sickle-cell-disease (accessed August 18, 2015).
5. St. Jude Children's Research Hospital, *Taking Control: Teens with Sickle Cell Disease*, Memphhis, TN: St. Jude's Children's Research Hospital, 2012, p. 7.
6. St. Jude Children's Research Hospital, *Taking Control*, p. 11.
7. St. Jude Children's Research Hospital, *Taking Control*, p. 26.

a. Allan Platt, James Eckman, and Lewis Hsu, *Hope and Destiny: The Patient and Parent's Guide to Sickle Cell Disease*, revised 3rd ed., Indianapolis: Hilton Publishing, 2011, p. 143.
b. Geno Atkins, "Real Stories from People Living with Sickle Cell Disease: Geno Atkins' Story," CDC—Sickle Cell Disease, www.cdc.gov/ncbddd/sicklecell/stories.html (accessed February 16, 2015).
c. AJ Green, "Real Stories from People Living with Sickle Cell Disease: The Green Family Story," CDC—Sickle Cell Disease, www.cdc.gov/ncbdd/sicklecell/stories/html, pp. 1–2 (accessed February 16, 2015).

Chapter 10

1. Lillian, "Lillian (15 Years Old)," *That Darn Tic: A Newsletter by and for Kids with Tourette Syndrome*, Tourette Syndrome Association, no. 49 (Winter 2014), p. 2, tourette.org/Publications/ChildrensNewsletter/darntic-winter2013_14.pdf (accessed February 23, 2015).
2. Oliver Sacks, *An Anthropologist on Mars* (New York: Knopf, 1995), p. 97; also in Marlene Targ Brill, *Tourette Syndrome* (Minneapolis: Twenty-First Century Books, 2002), pp. 25–26.
3. University of Calgary, "Tourette Syndrome and ADHD Frequently Occur Together," ScienceDaily, April 20, 2009, New Jersey Center for Tourette Syndrome & Associated Disorders, www.sciencedaily.com/releases/2009/04/090415102134.htm; New Jersey Center for Tourette Syndrome & Associated Disorders, "20 Facts about Tourette Syndrome You May or May Not Know," *TS Parents Online* (blog), www.njcts.org/tsparents/20-facts-about-tourette -syndrome-you-may-or-may-not-know (both accessed March 15, 2015).
4. Marlene Targ Brill, *OCD in the Classroom*, New Haven, CT: The Obsessive-Compulsive Foundation, 2004.
5. Brill, *Tourette Syndrome*, pp. 29–30.
6. Andy, interview with author, April 8, 2002
7. Mark, interview with author, May 14, 2002.
8. Jeremy, interview with author, March 15, 2002.
9. Jeremy's father, interview with author, March 15, 2002, for Brill, *Tourette Syndrome*, p. 35.
10. D. Martino, G. Defazio, and G. Giovanni, "The PANDAS Subgroup of Tic Disorders and Childhood-Onset Obsessive-Compulsive Disorder," *Journal of Psychosomatic Research* 67, no.

6 (December 2009): 547–557. doi: 10.1016/j.jpsychores.2009.07.004 (accessed November 29, 2015).

11. National Institute of Neurological Disorders and Stroke, "How Is TS Treated?" www.ninds.nih.gov/disorders/Tourette/detail_tourette.htm (accessed March 19, 2015).

12. Centers for Disease Control and Prevention, "Treatments," www.cdc.gov/ncbddd/tourette/treatments.html (accessed March 19, 2015).

13. Lysso, "Lysso (12 Years Old)," *That Darn Tic: A Newsletter by and for Kids with Tourette Syndrome*, Tourette Syndrome Association, no. 41 (Winter 2012), p. 3, tourette.org/Publications/ChildrensNewsletter/darntic_winter2012.pdf (accessed February 23, 2015).

a. Ryan, interview with author, 2002.

b. Lillian, "Lillian (15 Years Old)," *That Darn Tic: A Newsletter by and for Kids with Tourette Syndrome*, Tourette Syndrome Association, no. 49 (Winter 2014), p. 2, tourette.org/Publications/ChildrensNewsletter/darntic-winter2013_14.pdf (accessed February 23, 2015).

c. Sandy, interview with author, June 22, 2002.

d. Jeremy, interview with author, March 15, 2002.

e. Cindy, interview with author, June 3, 2002.

f. American Psychiatric Association, "*DSM-5* Diagnostic Criteria for Tourette Disorder," Tourette Canada, www.tourettesyndrome.ca/showthread.php?7200-DSM-5-Diagnostic-Criteria-For-Tourette-Disorder (accessed March 3, 2015).

g. Sandy, interview.

h. Andy, interview with author, April 8, 2002.

i. Jeremy, interview.

j. Dennis, "Dennis (17 Years Old)," *That Darn Tic: A Newsletter by and for Kids with Tourette Syndrome*, Tourette Syndrome Association, no. 41 (Winter 2012), p. 3, tourette.org/Publications/ChildrensNewsletter/darntic_winter2012.pdf (accessed February 23, 2015).

k. Dennis, "Dennis (17 Years Old)," p. 3.

Chapter 11

1. Bo Laraia, interview with author, April 17, 2015.

2. Department of Justice, "2010 ADA Regulations," ada.gov/2010_regs.htm (accessed August 28, 2015).

3. Carly Festenstein, interview with author, August 28, 2015.

4. Crohn's and Colitis Foundation of America, "Preparing for College, Work, Etc." www.ibdetermined.org/ibd-information, p. 3 (accessed February 12, 2015).

5. Kody Beach, interview with author, May 8, 2015.

6. Sam Radinsky, interview with author, July 7, 2015.

7. Sean Giblin, interview with author, March 30, 2015.

8. Carly Festenstein, interview with author, August 28, 2015.

9. Denise Grady, "Every Virus a Person Has Had Can Be Seen in a Drop of Blood, Researchers Find," *New York Times*, June 5, 2015, A14.

10. Dan Weber, interview with author, August 31, 2015.

a. Cancer Financial Assistance Coalition, "Reading Room: Tips for Taking Control of Your Finances," www.cancerfac.org/reading/sources.php (accessed August 24, 2015).

b. Michelle Laraia, interview with author, April 17, 2015.

c. Kody Beach, interview with author, May 8, 2015.

d. Living with Hemophilia, "Young Adults: 16–25 Years of Age," www.livingwithhemophilia .ca/adults-teens/16-25.php (accessed February 11, 2015).

e. Marlene Targ Brill, *Speech and Language Challenges: The Ultimate Teen Guide*, Lanham, MD: Rowman & Littlefield, p. 54.

f. Sam Radinsky, interview with author, July 7, 2015.

g. Robin Smith, "Can I Handle It?" *Tuesday's Child Magazine*, March/April 1998.

h. Sean Giblin, interview with author, March 30, 2015.

i. Michael Goodman, interview with author, July 6, 2007.

j. Michelle L., interview.

Index

About the Author

Marlene Targ Brill is an award-winning author of more than seventy books for readers of all ages—babies through adults. She loves writing about quirky topics, such as *Tooth Tales from around the World*, a 1998 Children's Choice and 2013 Illinois Reads selection, and *Shoes through the Ages*. But she especially enjoys the detective work involved in researching facts for nonfiction books about history, people's lives, and health care.

Ever since her years teaching special education, she has tried to advocate for individual differences of all children and teens with specific mental and physical conditions. One way to advocate beyond teaching is to share factual information that dispels myths and misinformation. This focus compels her to write about many health-care topics, including autism, Down syndrome, Tourette syndrome, diabetes, and multiple sclerosis. Marlene covered many of these topics in individual books in addition to chapters in this book. She discusses different health-care issues in her other Rowman & Littlefield book, *Speech and Language Challenges: The Ultimate Teen Guide*.

To learn more about Marlene, her books, and her presentations, check out her website: www.marlenetargbrill.com.